edited by
Dr. Robert Stanley Oden

2nd edition

D0520958

A SOCIAL POLITICAL
HISTORY OF THE
RIVERS OF
STRUGGLE
AND
RESISTANCE

UNDERREPRESENTED
IN THE UNITED STATES

cognella® ACADEMIC PUBLISHING

Bassim Hamadeh, CEO and Publisher
Kassie Graves, Director of Acquisitions
Jamie Giganti, Senior Managing Editor
Miguel Macias, Senior Graphic Designer
Carrie Montoya, Acquisitions Editor
Natalie Lakosil, Senior Licensing Manager
Allie Kiekhofer and Kaela Martin, Associate Editors
Kat Ragudos, Interior Designer

Cover images: Copyright in the Public Domain
            Copyright © 2013 iStockphoto LP/Willard

Printed in the United States of America

ISBN: 978-1-5165-1066-5 (pbk) / 978-1-5165-1067-2 (br)

IN MEMORY OF

My daughter, Dr. Tatia Malika Oden French

and her daughter, Zorah Allie Mae Oden French

CONTENTS

ACKNOWLEDGMENTS

Upon publication of this anthology, I want to acknowledge the many people who have helped me throughout my journey as an academic and an activist. First and foremost, I want to thank my parents, Allie Mae and Clyde Oden Sr., who were inspirational lifelines for my personal achievement and my love of life. To my brothers, Rev. Dr. Clyde Oden, whose steadfast dignity and faith provide with me constant sustenance, and Douglas Oden, Esq., whose constant prodding and positive support for my endeavors have been vital in my success: I thank you immeasurably for your support. Additionally, I want to thank members of my family, especially my sons, Marcus and Kofi, and their wives and children, for being there for me, as well as my other close relatives and friends who also celebrate this publication.

This academic endeavor would not have occurred unless some perceptive, progressive-minded individuals had opened some gates for me. I want to deeply thank my mentor and great friend, Dr. Hardy Frye, Sociology Professor Emeritus, U. C. Santa Cruz, for his friendship and guidance throughout my graduate study and beyond. I will never forget all he has given. And to my other great professors and friends at U.C. Santa Cruz, too many to name here, a thank you for assisting me throughout my Ph.D. work to help get me to the starting line, which ultimately led to producing this anthology. I also want to greatly thank former chair of the CSUS Department of Government, Dr. Mignon "Mimi" Gregg, for her confidence in me and for her guidance. As well, to all my colleagues in the Government Department, a thanks for the opportunity to teach the course on which this anthology is based, "The Politics of the Underrepresented." I want also to thank the professors who taught this course before me; most especially, the late Mayor of Sacramento, Joe Serna, whose untimely death due to cancer in 1999 was a great loss to us all. Additionally, my writing and my academic career would not be where it is today without the support and kindness of Dr. Wendy Martyna, whose editorial assistance over the years has been greatly appreciated. I also want to thank my dear friend, Ms. Regina Wander, for assisting in editing this introduction and for her continual support of my academic success.

Finally, I want to thank the staff at Cognella Publishers and University Readers, for their outstanding efforts and cooperation in assembling this anthology. I particularly want to thank Brent Hannify, Production Assistant, and Amy Wiltbank, Graphics Designer, for their technical assistance. I want to give a special thanks to Melissa Accornero, Acquisitions Editor, who discovered my course curriculum and presented me the valuable opportunity to produce this anthology.

And lastly, this anthology is in memory of my late daughter Tatia Malika Oden French and my late granddaughter Zorah Allie Mae. Tatia's life who both inspire me every day to fight for social change and justice with all of my heart and soul.

FOREWORD

BY JOSEPH A. PALERMO

In this work, Professor Stan Oden has brought together a unique set of readings designed to deepen students' understanding of the ongoing struggles of workers, women, and ethnic minorities in the United States. He has produced a collection of inspiring articles that chronicle, with first-hand accounts and scholarly interpretations, the conflicts, events, and ideas that have been central to shaping 20th Century American history and the ongoing challenge to live up to the ideals enshrined in the nation's founding documents. Professor Oden's emphasis in these writings is on the struggles people of color have faced in overcoming the barriers to inclusion in American society. He has culled readings relating to Native Americans, Latinos, and African Americans, as well as women and working-class whites, who fought for decades to secure their basic rights or simply to form their own independent organizations and associations.

Professor Oden draws upon his expertise in the fields of sociology and government, as well as his extensive experience as a civil rights activist and community organizer, to create this important collection. He spent many years at the forefront of movements for social justice, particularly during the 1960s and 1970s, and this distinctive experience is reflected in his choice of these essays. The overarching theme of these articles demonstrates Professor Oden's firsthand knowledge of the nexus between thought and action and the key role social movements have played as a vital engine of progressive historical change. Like the authors he has chosen to fill these pages, he understands that armchair musings are not enough but must be matched by the hard work of thousands of individuals coming together with shared goals and sometimes a shared identity to move society forward.

Professor Oden is cognizant of the forms that inequality and oppression can take having been active his entire life in the struggle for African-American equality and empowerment. He also recognizes that no social group can go it alone, and only through building coalitions and through solidaristic social networks can progress be made. The works contained herein reflect Professor Oden's intellectual understanding of the central issues that have confronted (and will continue to confront) multi-ethnic and multi-racial America. He also recognizes the vital role played by those who have successfully combined their scholarship with their activism, such as Howard Zinn, Cornell West, Huey Newton, Ida B. Wells, and W.E.B. DuBois, among others. This remarkable compilation will expose young people to the ideas and actions from America's rich tradition of social activism, and encourage them to participate in moving the ball forward in the pursuit of social justice.

This anthology promises to be a superb addition to any college course on American history, ethnic studies, or social movements. Students will come away with a deeper knowledge and understanding of the past struggles around ethnicity and gender. Most importantly, they will have a better idea about how the sacrifices of past activists have breathed new life into American democracy throughout the 20th Century and inspire them to take action themselves.

Joseph A. Palermo is a Professor of American History at California State University, Sacramento. He has written three books: In His Own Right: The Political Odyssey of Senator Robert F. Kennedy *(Columbia University Press, 2001);* Robert F. Kennedy and the Death of American Idealism *(Pearson Longman, 2008); and* The Eighties *(Pearson, 2013), and he is a frequent contributor to* The Huffington Post.

EDITOR'S INTRODUCTION

In 2011, when the first edition of *Rivers of Struggle and Resistance* was published (actually written in 2010), President Barack Obama was in the middle of his first term of office. As the first African American president, Mr. Obama was eclipsing political territory deemed unthinkable by most Americans in the historical trajectory of race relations in the United States. Even at that time, President Obama was experiencing exceptional headwinds from conservative and ultraconservative Republicans and from commentators on almost any initiative that he put forth. It was during this time that he was battling the deepest economic recession since the Great Depression of 1929. Despite the relentless opposition from congressional Republicans, Senate leader Mitch McConnell proclaimed that it was his goal to make President Obama "a one-term president." This statement became the oppositional mantra that fueled the Republican congressional majority to quash any presidential initiative. The salient fact is that on the night of President Obama's 2009 inauguration, leading Republicans met to plot out the opposition to Obama's presidency. This fact was dismissed by the mainstream media as "business as usual." However, had Obama been a white president, the immediate dismissal of his presidency would not have been the top priority of the oppositional party in the midst of a deep recession. Shortly after that meeting, the country witnessed the rise of the Tea Party—a corporate-derived grassroots movement of mostly white conservatives and self-described libertarians—which fueled the reactionary racial voices and engendered racially inspired images of President Obama as a black Hitler, as well as heinous portrayals of the president as a monkey. Those images hark back to the 1870s, the Reconstruction era, when opposition to Southern black legislators after the passage of the 15th Amendment granting black males the vote, that white Southern journalists and ex-Confederates portrayed black politicians dressed in suits with either monkey or gorilla faces.

Despite the rise of the Tea Party and the constant haranguing by conservative radio and television talk show hosts and FOX News, President Obama very impressively won a second presidential term in office, defeating Republican Mitt Romney in 2012 by 51.1 percent to 47.2 percent and carrying 332 electoral votes to Romney's 206 votes. Obama's triumph was a remarkable achievement, as his two presidential victories changed the electoral landscape in the twenty-first century, indicating the strength of the "Obama coalition" in 2012 comprising 93 percent African Americans, 71 percent of Latinos, and 73 percent of Asian Americans. In addition, Obama captured the all-important millennial vote (ages eighteen to twenty-nine) by 60 percent to 37 percent. He also carried women by 55 percent to 44 percent for Romney. Despite President Obama's historic presidential victories, his political legacy is being threatened by nationalistic expressions of white working-class voters who have endorsed the campaign of billionaire Donald Trump.

This second edition is published in the midst of the era of Trumpism. The sudden emergence of New York business mogul Donald Trump as the Republican nominee for the president of the United States has concretized the conservative forces that have conspired to halt the Obama presidency in its tracks during his second term. Trump introduced himself in 2008 by falsely claiming that President Obama was not born in the United States and thus not eligible to be president. This extreme attack on the legitimacy of the Obama presidency became the basis for Trump's presidential run in 2016. To many, Trump represents the racial resentment and feelings of conservative white people, as well as those individuals who sense a loss of white privilege over the past eight years of Obama's presidency and beyond. It is within this racialized and misogynistic moment that Trump has opposed Muslims entering the United States (due to the San Bernardino terror attack on December 2, 2015) as well as Mexicans, who he claims are rapists and drug dealers being sent by the Mexican government to cross over the border illegally. Additionally, Trump's continued attack on women's right to have an abortion and historic negative comments about women is the political environment in which this second edition is being presented. It is more important than ever for individuals to read this anthology to seek historic understanding of the challenges, strategies, and solutions that underrepresented individuals have endured to seek racial, sexual, and economic equality in the United States.

The selections in this anthology will weave a journey through the rivers of struggle and resistance that have enabled the United States to elect a black president in 2008 and again in 2012. This journey did not result in one person being elected president, but represented a historic moment for those who have fought for freedom and racial equality in this country. The historic journey by Native Americans, African Americans, Latinos, Asian Americans, and gay, lesbian, bisexual, and transgendered communities, the disabled, and others resisting oppression has been recorded and studied by a legion of social scientists and historians. The purpose of this anthology is to highlight readings from distinguished activists, thinkers, and revolutionaries who represent the voices, aspirations, anguish, and creativity of underrepresented groups in the United States. These selections are shaped by the course I teach at California State University–Sacramento entitled The Politics of the Underrepresented. This book represents the historic trajectory of the slow, Sisyphus-like movement of social change and transformation. Like the slow-moving Mississippi River, it is fed by tributaries, which adds to the flow of the river. Social and political tributaries that represent the movement of racial and social progress in the United States are represented on the book cover as: the abolition of slavery; women's liberation; racial terror; and revolution. These themes and others outlined in this anthology provide a mosaic of African American struggle, multicultural histories of immigration, genocide, and imperial conquest by the US government. Past and present oppression still plagues this country, even after the successful legal and political battle for same-sex marriage.

This anthology is divided into five chapters, each providing context and details of political, economic, and social battles that express the conditions in which the underrepresented existed in the United States. Chapter One, "Racial and Historical Beginnings," provides a framework to understand the meanings of race in the formation of this country and how racial meanings frame the inhuman conditions for Native Americans, African people, and poor whites. In *The Color of Politics* (1997), Michael Goldfield provides in his introductory chapter a historical analysis of race theories and the impact of American exceptionalism as it relates to race and class in the United States. Goldfield's selection opens the discussion of the primacy of race and the practice of racism as determining factors to assess life's chances in America. The second selection in Chapter One includes two chapters from Howard Zinn's seminal book, *The People's History of the United States: 1492 to the Present* (1980). The chapters "A Kind of Revolution" and "Long as Grass Grows and Water Runs" illustrate the contradictions of principles on which this country was supposedly founded in terms of the enduring practice of slavery and the destruction of native peoples—all in the name of God, freedom, liberty, and justice for all. Zinn poignantly describes how Native Americans, Africans, women, and men without property were all left out of the Constitution. The details of these travesties and the destructive role of Andrew Jackson are indicative of how the United States was formed.

In Chapter Two, "Multicultural Emergence" presents selections of the history of the struggles of the Mexican people conquered by an imperialistic US government. Mario Barrera, from his chapter in *Race and Class in the Southwest* (1979), analyzes the resulting loss of land through the machinations of gringos determined to capture the West. In her chapter from *Asian Americans: An Interpretive History* (1991), Sucheng Chan speaks to the unimaginable battles of survival for Chinese immigrants who were seeking fortune and comfort in the West and how they were exploited and terrorized—and then excluded from entering the United States. The final selection in this chapter, "The Making of Radical Reconstruction" by Eric Foner from *A Short History of Reconstruction, 1863–1877* (1990), details the political battle in Congress to obtain political and economic rights for the newly freed black slaves.

"The Century of the Color Line" in Chapter Three presents the problem of the color line and how African Americans could navigate that line that were the primary missions of two distinguished African Americans, Booker T. Washington and Dr. W.E.B Du Bois. Their approaches and attitudes on how blacks should proceed in the early 1900s provide a sharp contrast in the selections from Booker T. Washington's *Up From Slavery* (1912). Some individuals at the time felt that in "The Atlanta Exposition Address," which is a chapter in his book, the speech provided impetus to the Southern white supremacists to continue their exploitation and lynching of African Americans. In the selection by Du Bois from his classic *The Souls of Black Folk* (1961), in "Of Booker T. Washington and Others," Washington's accommodationist ideas and practices were challenged and were beginning to shape the strategic choices for African Americans in seeking both economic equality and social justice. The final two selections in this chapter present the brutality of racial terror inflicted by racist whites in the form of lynchings and white invasions of black neighborhoods. Ida B. Wells-Barnett, who wrote and acted against the causes, motivation, and consequences for these terroristic acts, is memorialized by Patricia Hill Collins in *On Lynchings* as an important woman of her time who understood the social structural patterns that produced this violence against African Americans. In her own words, Wells-Barnett describes in "The Black and White of It" the sexual motivation of white women implicating the true nature of relationships between white women and black men leading many white men in the South to destroy the black man through intimidation and serial lynchings. In "Invasion," the final selection by James S. Hirsch from *Riot and Remembrance: America's Worst Race Riot and Its Legacy* (2002), Hirsch meticulously describes the white invasion of black Greenwood in Tulsa, Oklahoma, in May-June 1921 and the wholesale slaughter of black residents by white Tulsans and the state police in a racial terror frenzy based on white fears of black control of their women and territory. This writing of racial terror is one of the most riveting examples of horror that African Americans were faced with in the United States in the early twentieth century.

"Black Political Awakening in America" in Chapter Four represents the organized resistance that African Americans created between the post–World War I period and the civil rights era of the 1960s. Theodore G. Vincent's chapter "The New Negro: Garveyites and Others" in *Black Power and the Garvey Movement* (1971) lays out Marcus Garvey's vision of self-help and racial pride and the New Negro movement of the Harlem Renaissance of the 1920s, which created a black identity forming the basis of the emergence of a black political movement. In the final selection in Chapter Four, from *Modern Black Nationalism: From Marcus Garvey to Louis Farrakhan* (1997), William Van Deburg presents several essays and programs that delineate the development of black nationalism. He traces this development from the doxology of the Nation of Islam in "The Making of Devil" by the Honorable Elijah Muhammad in *Message to the Blackman in America* to the most famous Nation of Islam leader, Malcolm X, who left the Nation of Islam in 1964 after a suspension and split from the racial philosophies of the Nation of Islam. In the manifesto "From Basic Unity Program Organization of Afro-American Unity" by Malcolm X, this document creates a new black liberation pathway forged through combining the concepts of cultural nationalism that expresses an Afrocentric appreciation of black culture and a politically self-determining framework to include the right to self-defense by any means necessary.

In the final chapter of this anthology, "Human Rights and Peoples' Liberation in the U.S.," Malcolm X's ideology of self-determination and self-defense was conceived and practiced by the Black Panther Party. The origins of this dynamic and controversial organization led by Dr. Huey P. Newton and Bobby Seale is detailed in the foreword of *The Black Panthers Speak* (1995), written by Clayborne Carson, who writes about the significance and the impact of the Black Panther Party to the overall black liberation movement and the government's attacks against the organization. The selection from *The Huey Newton Reader* (2002), edited by David Hilliard and Donald Weise, is Newton's "Patrolling," which gives readers an "on-the-streets" viewpoint about the confrontations with local police forces and the conditions facing the fledgling Black Panther Party organization during 1967.

The next selection amplifies the quest for human rights exemplified by the award-winning work of Randy Shilts in *And the Band Played On* (1987). "Glory Days" is a chapter from the book where he trumpets the origins of a politicized gay and lesbian movement and the tragedies of the AIDS epidemic. This movement evolved out of the political organizing and subsequent assassination of Board of Supervisor Harvey Milk, whose death enraged the San Francisco gay community. This tragic event spurred on greater political successes by the gay community, only to have this community struck down by the AIDS epidemic in the 1980s.

The last selection of this concluding chapter is an inspirational and thoughtful essay by Cornel West, "Learning to Talk About Race." It takes this anthology back to where it began, analyzing and understanding the impact of race in US society. West deconstructs the meaning of race in the aftermath of the Rodney King rebellion of 1992. In a way only he can do, West challenges the conventional presumptions of race that could only see the blackness of the Rodney King rebellion and misses the human suffering that ellipses many ethnicities. West points to a consumptive society that devalues human dignity and also instrumental in creating the conditions for change in the 1960s.

In conclusion, this anthology is a culmination of my academic approach to students and individuals, where I teach about the true nature of oppression in the United States and about the indomitable strength that individuals and groups have had to continually exhibit down the rivers of struggle and resistance. It is to those unheralded and unknown warriors of social justice that this book is dedicated. Power to the People!

CHAPTER ONE

RACIAL AND HISTORICAL BEGINNINGS

THE COLOR OF POLITICS

MICHAEL GOLDFIELD

One thing people, I want everybody to know You gonna find some Jim Crow everyplace you go.

I'm gonna tell you people something that you don't know It's a lotta Jim Crow in a moving-picture show.

I'm gonna sing this verse—I ain't gonna sing no More, Please get together—break up this old Jim Crow.

—Jim Crow by Leadbelly

This is the United States of America, the U.S.A., the land of the free and the home of the brave, the land of equality and opportunity for all. Yet, race consciousness and racism pervade every fiber of our social existence. It is, as Studs Terkel notes, "the American obsession" (Terkel 1992). One sees and hears it everywhere. There is hardly a contemporary political issue that is not imbued with racial overtones: welfare reform, drugs, crime, punishment, and the death penalty, immigration, and of course, affirmative action—these being only some of the most obvious.

Long before I attempted to engage in research or writing about the subject, I was, like most Americans, experiencing, reacting to, and thinking about it. Although I did not know it at the time, I attended my first two grades in a segregated grammar school in Maryland, a border state whose separate restaurants, hotels, and general social space only barely qualified it at the time as Up South. During the 1960s, when I was active in the civil rights movement, we would stop—in integrated groups—at the still-segregated eating places in Maryland along Route 40 on our way to Washington, D.C., passing by the apartment complex where my family and I used to live. When my family moved to New Jersey in the early 1950s, I belonged to a racially integrated Boy Scout troop with a Native American scoutmaster, a janitor at the local high school whose Leni-Lenape heritage made him a fount of wisdom on our many hikes and outings. Our assistant scoutmaster was a southern-born white truck driver whose frequent vulgarity, racist and anti-Semitic remarks were combined with a generosity to all of us. Our troop was filled both with conviviality and bouts of racial tension, as when we whites would be chased home by our Black fellow scouts. The shadow of the plantation, however, still reached deep into North Jersey during the 1950s. This became clear in 1956 when Plainfield High School's former All-State football star and national high school multiple track record-holder Milt Campbell, an African-American, won the gold medal in the decathalon at the Olympics in Melbourne, Australia. The city fathers quite naturally planned an elaborate homecoming celebration. It was discovered that the Park Hotel, Plainfield's finest, was racially segregated. This being the North, not Mississippi, segregation in this small venue quickly gave way to civic pride as the whole area shared in the triumph of one of its native sons. White gentile housing covenants and country club exclusions, no less job and education discrimination, of course, remained intact.

While I was growing up, white racism was continually on display. As a child in the 1950s, I used to listen to Jewish adults (a group rightfully considered more liberal and tolerant than most other whites), many of whom, like my own family, had lost relatives in Nazi concentration camps. They would often denounce Naziism and anti-Semitism as racism but, in the next breath, make racist remarks about Blacks, or *schwartze,* as they called them. Although I had no political consciousness at the time, the hypocrisy of my *lantsman* repulsed me greatly. In the early 1960s, I worked in a machine shop, earning money for college. The workplace was all white, most of the workers were from Eastern Europe; many had never met, no less had extensive contact with, African-Americans. Yet, the vehemence with which they repeated the most bigoted of stereotypes and my inability to sway them with facts or rational argument troubled me.

The civil rights movement of the 1960s, of course, brought many changes in the old Jim Crow. Yet, racial issues and racial cleavages are more pivotal to national political campaigns today than they were in the decades immediately before the 1960s. The centrality of these racial issues in current politics and the deep emotions that they stir sometimes appear baffling, even irrational. Yet, their dominance, even in defiance of elementary facts or logic, is undeniable. Let us briefly rehearse some highlights.

The economy has been uneven; wages and family incomes are not growing for the vast majority of the population; college education and housing for first-time buyers are being priced out of reach. Although there are strong complaints about taxes and government spending, the objects are peculiar. The extraordinary peacetime military buildup under Presidents Carter, Reagan, and Bush hardly stirs emotions, although many view it as unnecessary. Yet, the several decades-long expansion of social welfare programs is a political issue for which the drums beat loudly. But it is not just any social welfare program.

The biggest focus is on Aid to Families with Dependent Children (AFDC), whose real benefits contracted greatly in the decades prior to 1995 (some estimate that the level had fallen back to the 1967 level) and make up barely 1 percent of the total federal budget. The stereotyped, stigmatized face of the welfare mother in political imagery is young and African-American (see Piven 1996:61–67).

The stagnating and reorganized domestic economy has led to downsizing and layoffs of people previously thought secure. With some notable exceptions, job opportunities for young people have diminished, especially for those with low education. Resentment, however, is not directed strongly at those who are managing the economy, at those who are reaping enormous profits and benefits, or at the system as a whole, but at affirmative action, at nonwhite foreign (especially Asian and Mexican) competition, and at immigrants. As I will argue later, this is nothing if not irrational. Affirmative action is one of those programs that is much talked about but has had little effect in all but a small number of venues. As Louisiana Governor Edwin Edwards stated in his 1991 gubernatorial campaign against former Ku Klux Klan leader David Duke, "I don't think there are 500 people in Louisiana that have either been adversely affected or benefited from affirmative action. But everyone who doesn't have a job or whose son cannot get into law school believes it's because of affirmative action" (quoted in Moore 1992:54). If affirmative action is so limited in its scope, why are so many white people so worked up about it?

Immigration also has strong racial tones. In most states, there are hardly any immigrants to speak of. In several states (California, Texas, Florida, and New York) the number of immigrants is indeed large, especially in urban areas. Yet, studies about the degree to which immigrants contribute to the economies of these states, in contrast to the degree to which they use tax-supported services (including schools, welfare, and health facilities), are inconclusive. There is also little evidence that areas of immigrant concentrations have seen either lower wages in general or greater degrees of decline in the incomes of lesser educated white males (to cite the group most often mentioned) than areas with few immigrants. What is behind the intensity of emotion many white people feel against Asian and Latino immigrants?

Most U.S. inhabitants are rightly concerned about rampant crime and the deterioration of the nation's cities. But a focus on providing jobs and rebuilding urban areas seldom gets a hearing. Few are interested in looking at the reasons why Canadian cities (nearer to many residents of the Northeast, upper Midwest, and Northwest than most of our own country's cities) are cleaner, freer of crime, and generally more livable. What gets support are more prisons and increased punishment, hardly a cost-effective method. The United States, with the highest percentage of prisoners of any country in the world, now spends over $25,000 a year per prisoner, according to conservative estimates. Prisons are now one of our fastest-growing industries, are an incredible expense, and are arguably an inefficient use of money. Were it not for the racial agenda of those who propose harsher punishments and more prisons, many Americans would accept the old homespun wisdom that "an ounce of prevention is worth a pound of cure" (see, e.g., Freeman 1994 and Shapiro 1995 for useful summaries).

Since the 1960s, we have seen the shameless and unfortunately too often successful use of racist rhetoric in political campaigns across the country. It is clear that the appeals to the baser and more uncharitable feelings of many whites are no less bigoted because they have appeared in coded or indirect form: George

Wallace's and Richard Nixon's opposition to "forced" busing; Ronald Reagan's tales of wealthy Black "welfare queens" who neither worked nor paid taxes; his championing of the "Lost Cause" in Philadelphia, Mississippi, the town where three civil rights workers were murdered in 1964; and perhaps the most racially incendiary of all, George Bush's use of African-American rapist Willie Horton to influence white voters in his 1988 campaign. Such demagoguery, of course, was successful. On the fringes, not so far from this mainstream, is Pat Buchanan, who, like David Duke, is often explicitly racist and anti-Semitic and has had leaders of Nazi and white supremacist organizations on his staff, including the white supremacist and Nazi Larry Pratt as his campaign cochair, all the while claiming to be against racial discrimination and not himself personally racist (see *New York Times,* February 16, 17, and 23, 1996).

Democrats, too, use a brand of racial appeals to white voters, more nuanced because they attempt to maintain African-American voting support while giving bigotted signals to whites. Jimmy Carter first won the Georgia governorship by successfully wooing Wallace supporters in his state, long before he emphasized his belief in "ethnic purity" during his winning 1976 presidential campaign. Bill Clinton's snubbing of Jesse Jackson and his calculated attack on hip-hop singer Sister Souljah at a Rainbow Coalition meeting during the 1992 campaign gave the same assurances to whites.

The increased importance of race in national politics since the successes of the civil rights movement is paradoxical. During the 1930s and 1940s, traditional liberals and industrial unionists believed that conservatism had unwarranted support from poor and working-class whites in the South because the race question diverted them from pursuing their real interests. V. O. Key, for example, argued:

> In fact, apart from the restraint imposed by that [the race] question, the South ought, by all the rules of political behavior, to be radical. A poor, agrarian area … it offers fertile ground for political agitation. The overshadowing of the race question, in which the big farmers have the most immediate stake, blots up a latent radicalism by converting discontent into aggression against the Negro. (Key 1984: 44).

In the late 1940s, Key and others believed that the gaining of the franchise and civil rights for southern Blacks would lead to a diminishing importance of racial issues. White southerners would act like northern working-class whites, becoming more left-wing and solidaristic with blacks. With the successes of the civil rights movement, a new day seemed to have arrived. In 1964, northern senators and congressmen of both parties were nearly unanimous in their support of the Civil Rights Act; only southern Democrats opposed it in significant numbers. Instead of the class-based realignment predicted by many, however, the politics of the North and the nation as a whole since the late 1960s has become more like that of the old South. Not that race was not always there, but it is now more successfully used in defense of conservative politics in the country as a whole. How do we explain this seeming anomaly?

The really important question for us, however, is, not why politicians exploit racial prejudices and fears, but why such tactics work. Why are whites, especially lower-class, traditionally working-class whites so easily taken in by those who seem to offer little to solve their deepest problems? What is behind not merely the racial animosity but the moral righteousness that often accompanies it? Are they being snookered, are their prejudices that important to them, or is there something more? The answer to this question, I will argue, is both important and complex. We must dig deeper than merely looking at present racial attitudes. Although the current racialized politics has its own unique characteristics, in its main contours it is not new; it is also the product of a long process of American social and political development. A clear understanding of the role of race in the contemporary United States requires an analysis of the role that race has played historically. A large part of this book is devoted to such an analysis.

Before proceeding in this endeavor, however, I beg the indulgence of the reader. I propose to sharpen our focus by initially looking at two sets of questions and a range of answers that have been given to them. First, what is race, and what is the root cause of racism? How permanent and immutable is it (can it be changed, and if so, how?), and why has it been the vehicle for so much divisiveness and conflict? Second, how central has race been to our social, political, and economic life? Exactly what role has it played in American political development? What is distinctive, special, or exceptional about the United States, and what if anything does race have to do with it? So let us take our first cut at these questions.

THEORIES OF RACE

Theories of race, racial inequality, and racism may be distinguished for our purposes by two related criteria: (1) what they propose as the causes of racial inequality and racial discrimination and (2) how immutable they consider racial differences and conflicts to be.

Throughout the nineteenth century and up to the 1920s, biological theories of racial superiority, inferiority, and hierarchy were dominant in this country and elsewhere. These theories posited that certain races (as well as males) were biologically superior in intelligence and other important characteristics. If this theory were true, racial and gender differences would be permanent; inequalities would be based on inherent differences in capacities; equal opportunity for all and selection of people for education and employment based on merit (rather than discrimination) would produce dominant positions for white males and subordinate positions for non-whites and females. By the 1930s, however, biological theories of human racial and gender differences in intelligence were largely discredited among serious scholars and intellectuals. Certain key studies that supposedly proved the biological inferiority of women, African-Americans, and other non-white males turned out to be fraudulent, based on fake data (e.g., Paul Broca's famous experiments on brain sizes). Others had omitted unfavorable data, made unwarranted assumptions, or made elementary, yet decisive, mistakes in logic or scientific method. Recent theories of white male biological intellectual superiority and African-American inferiority, including the much publicized *Bell Curve,* by Richard Herrnstein and Charles Murray (1994), are similarly flawed, although their serious discussion today suggests that a sizable number of people are still influenced by sheer quackery. The bottom line on these questions seems to be that expressed forcefully by Richard Lewontin and others in the early 1970s: So-called racial and ethnic groups throughout the world have a common gene pool, and the variation within groups is far larger than that among groups. Recent anthropological studies only seem to confirm what we know from genetics. All Homo sapiens may have a common origin that is far too recent for there to have been any significant evolutionary differences between differing groups of people.[1]

Although biological theories of racial differences are taken seriously only by the most extreme of racists, they do little to explain the hostility of dominant groups to subordinate groups. Suppose prehistoric peoples or life on other planets were found that really did have lesser or greater mental capacities. For what reason might we feel antagonisms toward them or they toward us? What if future research were to reveal differences in the brain structures of men and women, giving each different capacities in one area or another that were, so to speak, hardwired rather than environmental. None of this would obviate treating people as equals, giving all persons equality of opportunity, even if the end result were, for example, more women psychiatrists and more male mathematicians. Thus, the discriminatory attitudes held by those who still cling to biological theories of race are quite inconsistent with their premises.

Another older theory suggests that racial antagonism is based on deep-seated psychological needs, perhaps instincts. All groups allegedly feel allegiance to their own kinship networks and broader communities and have deep antagonisms to outsiders. Although this theory does not posit any racial hierarchy, it does suggest that racial and ethnic antagonisms are intractable, incapable of change, that it is a waste of time to try. Such theories, although they may have had some partial validity in the precapitalist epoch, are too narrowly based to accord with present-day facts. Immigrant groups do become assimilated. Over time, ethnic groups and nationalities have merged, absorbed each other, and diminished or lost their former antagonisms or, conversely, have gone from peaceful relations to deadly conflict. (For a fascinating discussion of the broader development of solidarity and altruism in both animals and humans and their possible biological basis, see de Waal 1996.)

A more prominent view, until recently the most common among both conservative and liberal intellectuals, is that racism is a set of individual attitudes, or prejudices, based on ignorance or bad taste. Conservative free market economists, in a position elaborated most fully by Gary Becker in his *The Economics of Discrimination* (1971), argue that employer preferences for white rather than non-white employees are irrational in that they diminish the employer's potential profits. A rational, profit-maximizing employer would hire the cheapest, most qualified workers, regardless of their color or racial identity. The solution to racial discrimination (on the presumption that reducing it in the workplace would go a long way to reducing it in society in general) is a freer market (which would financially punish employers with racist tastes) and education. Similarly, certain liberal theorists, perhaps epitomized by Gunnar Myrdal in his *An American Dilemma* (1964), attribute racial discrimination to ignorance and a certain type of provincialism, especially among lower-class whites. The heritage of slavery and the backwardness, isolation, and low levels of education in the South until recently made this region the most racially prejudiced. The changing of discriminatory laws and rising education levels would reduce and eventually eliminate racial discrimination. Both the liberal and the conservative versions of this theory—that racism is basically a problem of individual attitudes rooted in ignorance and narrow-mindedness—are highly optimistic about the degree to which racism would be (one almost wants to say "automatically") eliminated by the normal workings of social development and enlightened leadership. It is, of course, clear that ignorance, prejudice, and bad taste play some role in the history and practice of racial dominance, that individual experiences, education, and insights have at times changed individuals dramatically from racists to anti-racists. Nevertheless, these theories, in either their liberal or their conservative versions, are insufficient as general theories because they tend to minimize the deep historical roots of racist practices, the degree to which these practices are embedded in modern institutions, and the interests that support them. (For an incisive critique of these views, see Cornel West 1987:75–78).

A commonly argued, more nuanced contemporary view is that which Theodore Allen calls the "psycho-cultural approach" (Allen 1975:19; 1994, 4) and George Fredrickson refers to as "liberal pessimism" (Fredrickson 1996). Although race prejudice by groups may not be natural or instinctual, it is nevertheless allegedly rooted in deep-seated psychological needs for cultural identity; although racism may be a set of attitudes, it is inexorably transmitted. Hence, white racism and racial slavery in the United States were the somewhat inevitable consequences of centuries of British and European racist culture and the search by displaced Europeans for a new colonial identity in the Americas. Racist attitudes by whites are in this view deep-seated indeed, incapable of changing in significant ways on a permanent basis. Among historians, Carl Degler and Winthrop Jordan are representative of this approach.[2] Likewise, Derrick Bell, Herbert Hill, and Andrew Hacker, among more recent authors, while being strong defenders of the rights of Blacks in contemporary U.S. society, are extremely pessimistic about whether whites in general will ever change. All these authors believe that racial identities are primary and fundamental; they are rather dismissive of arguments that white racism may be changeable or that other interests may be dominant at times. Each of these scholars has done important research, some of which, in my opinion, casts doubt on their central thesis.

A more sophisticated version of the psycho-cultural view, quite influential, especially in the field of cultural studies, is that of Michael Omi and Howard Winant (Omi and Winant 1986; Winant 1994). Rather than representing a stable feature of Anglo-American identity formation, race in the United States for them is an unstable "decentered," complex of social meanings over which dominant and subordinate racial groups continually struggle (Omi and Winant 1986:68). Unlike the liberal pessimist view, Omi and "Winant's theory of racial formation sees the possibility of large-scale transformation of racial identities by both dominant and subordinate groups. They also persuasively extend their theory of racial formation in the United States to include a number of non-white groups. They argue that different types of racial oppression are based on a "unique form of despotism and degradation" (Omi and Winant 1986:1). Native Americans faced genocide; African-Americans were enslaved; Mexicans were colonized; Asian-Americans were excluded. And one should add that women, even of the dominant groups, were considered private property of men and restricted to the private sphere. Like some of the best analyses of race in the cultural studies field, Omi and Winant's work shows a sensitivity to the ubiquitousness of racial systems of oppression and their social dimensions. In comparison with the liberal pessimists, Omi and Winant stress racial oppression's fluidity. The weakness of this approach as a total theory, however, is its limited analysis of the causes and roots of racial formations and how these systems actually change. Their unwillingness to look at economic factors and social class leads Omi and Winant to give no priority to different types of struggles. Linguistic and cultural criticism may be just as important as broad social struggles. No one group or segment of society is more important than another in transforming racial identities. Their stance also leaves them unable to analyze which groups may actually benefit materially from systems of racial hierarchy and, thus, who might have strong economic and social interests in preserving the racial status quo. Their theoretical weakness in this regard is also suggested by their ambiguous relationship to the Marxist tradition and the crude attempts to distance themselves from it.[3]

The most sophisticated and penetrating analysis of racial identity formation is that of David Roediger, many of whose insights are being appropriated in recent cultural analyses of race. Like Barbara Fields and Theodore Allen, Roediger argues persuasively that race, though central and important, is a social construction in a way that social class is not. He gives many intriguing examples. One of the most stunning is that Ghanaians—who regarded Africans as Black and people of mixed race as white in the 1960s—who had heard Malcolm X speak in Ghana in the early 1960s, described him as a *white man* with astonishing ideas (Roediger 1994:4). Roediger's project is to analyze why white working-class racial identity was formed in the United States, how this identity was shaped from causes inside the working class as well as from outside, and how the identification as whites has held back white workers from understanding their class interests. With a set of more Marxist concerns than Omi and Winant and a determined use of the class-based insights of Du Bois, Roediger is sensitive to a whole series of causal issues that they miss. He states that one cannot understant racism without understanding its class and economic context (Roediger 1986:8). He is also optimistic that certain types of class struggles in which antiracism is prominent will help lead white workers to abandon their identity as whites for one as workers. He often gives intriguing and highly nuanced analyses of the contradictory historical cases of interracial unity among labor organizations (including the Knights of Labor, the National Labor Union, and the Industrial Workers of the World). However, despite his schematic statements about the importance of external contexts, Roediger is primarily concerned with the psychological and cultural roots of white working-class identity. He limits his investigations to one historical period—circa 1800 to 1865—that he sees as critical, leaving little room for the immense changes in the systems of racial domination that have taken place since then. Without a more complete analysis, it is never clear how these processes and products relate to the socio-economic context in which Roediger claims they are rooted.

While attempting to incorporate the best insights from the cultural and attitudinal analyses of race and racism into a broader perspective, I will argue that these theories are not fully informative without a clear analysis of the class and economic roots of racial formation and systems of racial oppression. As with cultural and psychological theories, there is also a wide array of socio-economic analyses. One approach, for example, argues that racial discrimination and white racial identity originate among white workers who benefit materially by the exclusion of their nonwhite competitors in the labor market.[4] If this theory were accurate, racism would be highly intractable and not likely to be changed because it would be in both the immediate and the long-term interests of most white workers. Yet, although the material benefits of racial exclusion may be quite real in certain venues for white workers (as in some elite and tightly controlled skilled trades such as printing pressmen, electricians, and plumbers and even occasionally, if less frequently, for lower-skilled workers such as New York City's Irish longshoremen during the 1850s), for most white workers, especially those with the more typical, limited ability to control the labor market in their occupations and industry, the opposite has most often been the case. As Reich (1981) argues pursuasively, in job situations where discrimination is most intense and racial income differentials have been most extreme (e.g., historically in Mississippi), white workers have often been among the least well paid in the nation. In those parts of the country and those industries where interracial unions have narrowed racial income differentials (e.g., in the automobile industry in the North), white workers have been among the best paid in the United States. Thus, a weakening of racial discrimination at the workplace is often in the immediate interests as well as the long-term interests not only of African-American workers but of white workers as well. So although white workers' defense of racial privileges in hiring, job placement, and promotion is an important part of the racial system in this country, by itself it is insufficient to explain patterns of racial discrimination as a whole. Further, most patterns of racial discrimination in the workplace in hiring, placement, and promotion have been set by employers, not by white employees, who in general have had little leverage to influence these patterns. One must look, therefore, to more powerful, society-wide interests to explain the class and economic bases for racial domination and subordination.

A view that looks to employers, rather than white workers, as the source of racial discrimination and animosity is the divide-and-conquer approach. In this analysis, racism is instilled by employers who attempt to forestall solidaristic, class-based organization on the part of their own employees and workers in general. This view has been argued by Marxists (e.g., Roemer 1979), but it has also been a common one among liberal unionists. It was the argument put forward by racially and economically liberal Alabama Governor "Big Jim" Folsom during the late 1940s and the 1950s. He claimed that "race was a phony issue, a ploy used by the rich and powerful to divide poor people and blind them to their common interests." (Carter, 1995:73). (See also Sims 1985:161–188 for a more detailed account of Folsom's racial views.) Clearly, racially divisive tactics by employers have been an important part of the system of race and class relations in this country, but the theory leaves many forms of racial discrimination unexplained. It also fails to elucidate why the tactic has at times been so successful and how it relates to broader socio-economic questions.

Much criticism by recent analysts has been made of so-called class-reductionist positions. This classification, however, is quite broad and is difficult to analyze as one position. Virtually all analysts who attempt to distinguish themselves from this label include a whole variety of differing views, all of which stress class. It is, however, crucial to make more finegrained (although not necessarily very subtle) distinctions. At one extreme is the position argued by the early Socialist Party (SP) in this country. The SP policy ranged from the benign neglect of Eugene Debs, who said, "We have nothing special to offer the Negro and we cannot make separate appeals to all races," to the undisguised white chauvinism of Wisconsin Congressman and SP leader Victor Berger (Spero and Harris 1968:405). Racial discrimination supposedly would automatically disappear when the class system of capitalism was overthrown. This position not only provided an excuse not to deal with central issues of racial discrimination but was also at times a cover for racist behavior and statements. On the other hand, some theories that emphasize the class roots of racial identity and racial discrimination in this country have argued for its centrality in understanding virtually every aspect of social and political life in this country. I will comment on some of these various positions in my later discussions.

One highly sophisticated socio-economic approach is that of Stanley Greenberg, who argues that the racial systems of discrimination in the United States, as well as in South Africa, did not originate in the modern workplace nor in individual attitudes, psychology, or culture; rather, they were originally rooted in the economic needs and desires of large agricultural producers to have highly exploited and controlled Black labor forces. The social and political structures and the racial identities that were required to sustain such a system were by necessity codified and extended to the societies as a whole. The agricultural interests were supported by other economic elites whose interests were parallel to or at least not incompatible with those of the agriculturalists. The existence of racial oppression and racial attitudes among whites stem from this dominating racial system. Both the difficulty of overcoming racist attitudes among whites and the problems faced by racially solidaristic labor movements must be explained within this context. Changing the systems of racial domination and subordination ultimately requires the challenging and overthrowing of those economic interests that gain the most (Greenberg 1980). If one can identify those social and economic interests that benefit from the systems of racial domination and how they support it, one's strategy for eliminating racism can be more highly focused.

As I mentioned before, certain analysts have stressed that a clear understanding of the system(s) of racial domination in this country must account for the varieties of subjugation faced by non-white peoples in the United States. Much of this domination is, of course, related to economic interests, including the expulsion of Native Americans from their historical lands, often justified by crude racist views; the seizure and subjugation of former Mexican territories also has a clear economic basis. A full understanding of race and race relations in this country surely requires that the situations of all non-white peoples be taken into account. As we begin to move more dramatically to an increasingly multi-racial (rather than biracial) society, this point becomes even more important. Yet, racial discrimination and domination of other non-white peoples in the United States can only be understood in the context of the historical enslavement and oppression faced by Black people in this country, which has played a central and continuing role in the country's development from the very beginning. For this reason, while trying to examine the full range of racial dominance and subordination in the United States, my account will center on the system of domination of Blacks. Why this remains central can be fully explained only by a detailed socio-economic analysis.

Much of what has been raised as central by psychological, cultural, and socio-economic theories of race and racial discrimination must be taken into account in any full theory. The racist attitudes of whites, the creation of racial identities, the resilience of culture and its ability to structure interpretive questions of stable worldviews and traditional patterns of economic and social relations, the immediate interests of workers and employers, and a number of other features need be analyzed. Yet, in the end, I hope to demonstrate that these must be tied to deep-seated socio-economic factors whose analysis is necessary to fully understand not only the creation of racial identities and systems of racial oppression but ultimately how such subordination will eventually be overcome. This will be one of the continuing threads of this book on which I will elaborate.

RACE AND AMERICAN POLITICAL DEVELOPMENT

It is, of course, important to understand the roots of racial oppression and the tractability of racial attitudes and structures of domination. Whatever the underlying causes of racial divisions, racial domination, and racial subordination, however, it is at least as important to know how central these phenomena have been throughout American political history. Is the present focus on race in American politics new, or does it have a long history; are the roots of the present racial politics largely current, or are they at least partially based in the past? It is instructive to look at different views about the role race has played. In short, what is distinctive or exceptional about the United States, and what if anything does race have to do with it?

One perspective on American political development focuses on the actions, statements, and ideas of elites and government bodies—sometimes referred to by its critics as "elite-history." American history for some is a struggle among leaders over the role and policies of the U.S. government: the constitutional debates, the role of the Supreme Court, secession by the Confederacy, whether to go to war, how to solve the Great Depression. Elite history has many variants, both methodologically and across the political spectrum. Methodologically, perhaps the most extreme position sees the ideas of political elites and the working out of these ideas in ideological conflicts among these elites as the key factor in American political development. This position is displayed in its most one-dimensional form in the work of Gordon Wood on the American Revolution and the formation of the Republic. For Wood, race is hardly a factor, if at all. A more nuanced version of this methodological stance is found in the works of Bernard Bailyn, who discusses race and racial slavery but clearly regards these issues as secondary. For others such as Charles and Mary Beard, governmental policies reflect, not ideas, but the conflict and resolution of battles between powerful economic elites. Economic interests, not ideas, are the motor forces of history. More recent adherents to this methodological orientation are the corporate liberal historians, represented by James Weinstein, who regard the economic interests of elites as responsible for virtually all government policies, including even those liberal reforms, such as unemployment insurance and the National Labor Relations Act, that others have attributed to the pressure on the government from popular movements. For all these views, race and racial discrimination are secondary issues in American political history. At most, they are merely regional problems of the South, historically the most backward and supposedly least important section of the country.

The political views expressed in elite histories vary widely. Corporate liberal theorists place themselves on the left. There is also a highly conservative version of elite history, in some cases largely establishment history, often bordering on national chauvinism. Such an approach tends to exaggerate certain of our unique qualities as a nation, to glorify our traditions out of all reasonable proportions, especially in comparison with those of other lands, and to omit many of our outstanding defects. At the extreme end, one has not only the deification of the colonialists and Founding Fathers but also a claim that our culture, politics, and society are God-given and superior to all others. Such accounts can only be made plausible by vastly exaggerating the degree of consensus that has existed historically in our society, minimizing the number of individuals and groups that America has not served well, and omitting those aspects of American society that do not compare favorably with features in other developed capitalist countries.

Perhaps the most prominent historian in this genre is Daniel Boorstin, extolled by Newt Gingrich and other conservatives. Boorstin's work is characterized by one fellow historian as "strident Conservativism, boosterism, and unabashed patriotic celebration" and by the somewhat conservative Bernard Bailyn as an "apologia." Not only are sympathetic discussions of Native Americans, women, Blacks, labor, radicals, and dissidents of all sorts missing, but any people or groups slightly outside the mainstream, including Tom Paine and the Quakers, are dismissed as irrelevant.[5] Race is, of course, not very important at all in this conservative account.

The challenges to elite history have come from several quarters. One such view sees social and economic development as central to political development. This approach is, quite naturally, taken by a number of Marxist writers, many of whom regard race as central. Various works by W. E. B. Du Bois, Oliver Cox, Herbert Aptheker, Philip Foner, and Eric Williams fall into this category. There are also those who look to the centrality of economic factors, including Gabriel Kolko and William Appleman Williams, for whom race hardly plays a major role.

The current most popular challenge to traditional elite history today, however, comes from those practitioners of the "new social history" who argue that a full picture must describe the lives and activities of ordinary people. History must be studied, not from the top down, but from the bottom up. The new social history includes detailed narratives of social movements, particularly those by the lower classes, and rich discussions of the plight and accomplishments of Native Americans, African-Americans, Latinos, Asian-Americans, women, and the labor movement. Also contained are fascinating discussions of family and community life, embracing much that was at one time considered outside the purview of historians. The new social history thus presents a more inclusive—and, one might add, more accurate—view of the American experience. Among those who may be considered part of this approach, there is a large variance in the attention given to race. Gary Nash, one of the most eminent of the new social historians, goes to great lengths to examine the importance of people of color in early American history. For others, including Sean Wilentz (whose account of early nineteenth–century New York City white working men has been widely criticized for its blindness to questions of race), race and racial hierarchy hardly come into play at all.

Recently, there has been a public battle over general conceptions of American history taking place between defenders of conservative elite history and advocates of the new social history (battle is perhaps a misnomer in that this chapter of the cultural wars has mostly involved conservatives attacking and crushing their opponents). The struggle emerged into public view over the 1995 publication of the National Standards for United States History by the National Center for History in the Schools at the University of California at Los Angeles. Although nominally independent, the report was funded by both the National

Endowment for the Humanities and the U.S. Department of Education and has been viewed by both critics and proponents as an integral part of the program of Goals 2000: Educate America Act, which was passed by Congress in 1994. The standards reflect a certain amount of the themes of the new history mentioned above, although the National Standards are rather circumspect in this respect. Further, the recommended supplemental sources cover all the traditional materials, including *The World's Greatest Speeches;* a biographical encyclopedia of great Americans, material on the U.S. constitutional debates, including the *Federalist* papers—contrary to the implications of Lynne Cheney in her widely reprinted and circulated piece, "The End of History" (Wall *Street Journal,* October 20, 1994); and a large array of other standard and important materials.

Conservatives have attacked the National Standards outline as an orgy of political correctness, trashing America, giving a history of victimization, rather than accomplishments, "loaded up with crude anti-Western and anti-American propaganda" (Leo 1994). Yet, when one gets behind the rhetoric and examines the detailed criticisms, it is surprising how little is there. There is supposedly too much discussion of "pre-literate" Native Americans and Africans and not enough of Anglo-white males (who still, incidentally, make up the bulk of the discussion and references). Lynne Cheney decries the dropping of the picture and mention of Robert E. Lee—many of his current champions seem to lose sight of the fact that he was the military leader of the war to defend African-American slavery—and the failure to emphasize leading congressional figures, including Henry Clay and Daniel Webster.[6] The recommended supplementary readings, of course, include ample material along these lines. The right-wing Republican Family Research Council attacks the National Standards for not underscoring the landing on the Moon "as *the* most significant event of our time" and for neglecting "to mention that the United States won the space race," finding it "hard to overstate the magnitude of the failure." (Gary Bauer, N.D.: Family Research Council circular) On the basis of these and other alleged historical atrocities, the U.S. Senate on January 18, 1995, voted its disapproval of the standards by 99 to 1.

The disjunction between what Garry Wills describes as the "storm of vituperation" from conservatives about political correctness and the new McCarthyism, and the nitpicking nature of the actual criticisms forces one to only one conclusion: Many conservatives do not seem interested in obtaining an accurate, inclusive picture of the American past nor in having historians engage in serious investigations; rather, they want the "reinforcement of old myths" and the celebration of the type of life and values they mythologize as having existed in the 1950s (Wills 1995). On one level, of course, the conservative attack can be rightfully written off as an attempt to stifle critical discussion (the search for truth that Lynne Cheney supposedly cherishes) and to glorify business leaders and other, even more dubious establishment figures.

Yet, the story as often told in the new social history is also wanting in important respects. Virtually all the conflicts of importance in their accounts seem to take place between people on the top (i.e., various elites in control of society) and those on the bottom. The virtuous, democratic masses, the many, versus the corrupt, self-aggrandising, undemocratic, greedy few. Many accounts, of course, rescue from historical oblivion important struggles of ordinary people. In the process, however, the most prominent accounts tend to stress the nobility of the participants, especially of white working-class people, and the solidarity between them and non-white, oppressed peoples. They thus give an overly romantic view of the racial and ethnic comity that has existed throughout American history and of American political development in general, leaving us little in the way of explanation of why these supposedly unified and inclusive social movements failed at all. The sometimes violent conflicts between various groups, the exclusionary attitudes of some at times, and the fact that these groups were often unable to sustain unified struggles, are downplayed. Why were the ruling groups able to dominate so thoroughly in the United States? Why were the struggles of people at the bottom so much less successful in the United States than in other developed capitalist countries? These questions are difficult to address in the context of much of the new historical writing. This issue appears in particularly problematic form in the fascinating, highly informative, ultimately unsatisfactory monument to the new social history, the two-volume work *Who Built America*. In the end, this romanticized view of American political development, although it is an important corrective to some of the more traditional views, ends up downplaying the role of race, racial identities, racial discrimination, and racial conflict.

Thus, in a somewhat perverse way, the conservative critics do have a point. The "consensus" seen throughout American history by certain historians is not pure fantasy, although they almost certainly have its contours wrong. The dominance and ideological hegemony of the ruling classes in the United States is a phenomenon that is central to American political development. This hegemony must be understood, not dismissed. I wish, therefore, to proceed neither by denying it, as do many current social historians, nor by uncritically glorifying it, as do the establishment historians.

In order to get an initial grasp on the uniquely long-term, exceptional history of ruling-class hegemony in the United States, let us return to the more traditional views and see what we can learn from them in conjunction with the insights from the new social history. It is interesting and a sign of the times (as well as amusing) that House Speaker and former history professor Newt Gingrich (in his course "Renewing American Civilization") explicitly presents us with a caricature of the consensus view of American political development. In his class, Gingrich raises the issue of American exceptionalism, claiming that it is the defining concept around which to understand the history and present of our society. He mistakenly states that this concept was coined and elaborated by Everett Carli Ladd, a contemporary conservative political scientist. He also mistakenly takes the notion to mean that scholars have used the term to mean that this country was both unique and superior to others. Nevertheless, the notion of American exceptionalism provides us with a convenient starting place to deepen our discussion of race and U.S. political development.[7]

American Exceptionalism

An enormous, long-standing literature, popular as well as academic, has developed over the last century and a half that purports to discover and explain the nature, essence, or mainspring of American politics.[8] Much of this extensive body of writing focuses on what is peculiar or exceptional about the United States in comparison with other economically developed capitalist countries, (viz., Japan, Australia,

New Zealand, Canada, Britain, and those in Western Europe. The topic itself is usually referred to as American exceptionalism.

The main focus of the American exceptionalism literature historically has been to answer the question of why the United States has no substantial, independent working-class party.[9] In times when social movements and labor organizations are strong and radicalism is influential, much of the emphasis has been on those factors that kept the movements from being more radical, their organizations from becoming more permanent, and a stable third political party from emerging.[10]

In those times, however, as in the present, when social protest is at a low ebb or is fragmented, when labor organizations have become less radical or have been weakened, a whole new thrust in the analysis of American exceptionalism often emerges. The study of American politics and political development either ignores social movements, labor organization, and radicalism or at most views them as marginal sideshows (or curiosities) to the main drama of American politics. Not only mass mobilizations but also class and racial divisions are conveniently ignored in such times. The 1950s and early 1960s, shaped by Cold War imperatives, the crushing of dissent, and the destruction of radicalism in the labor movement, ushered in an intellectual climate in which society was viewed as homogenized (and generally seen through white blinders). Class conflict had supposedly ended, labor was at most a pluralist interest group, consensus reigned, and America was on its way to becoming a happy, middle-class society (see Boorstin 1958; Bell 1960; Kerr et al. 1960).

In the 1980s, with conservative, probusiness Republican administrations in Washington, with Democrats seeking ways to recapture the seemingly conservative white vote in the South and the apparently racially antagonistic urban white Catholic working-class vote in the North, with organized labor declining in strength, class politics and class analysis hardly seemed appropriate to many people. Social movements and even race were also downplayed. One expression of this orientation perhaps is the fashionable view that the state and the main arena of politics are largely autonomous from social forces (for a critique of this perspective, see Goldfield 1989b). Another indicator is that various views from the 1950s (most prominent of which is Louis Hartz's (Hartz 1955), which stresses the individualism of American culture) have become popular again, along with an uncritical nostalgia for that decade. This trend has continued into the 1990s unabated, if anything in ever cruder form, finding expression in the popular writings of Lynne Cheney, Newt Gingrich, and Rush Limbaugh.

What Is Distinctive About America?

THE WEAKNESS OF U.S. LABOR

Still, the central starting point of the more substantive American exceptionalism literature has been the organizational and political weakness of American labor. Ours is the only economically developed capitalist country with no major working-class party, no labor, social-democrat, socialist, or communist party. All other comparable countries have or have had such parties. Further, and not unrelated (since working-class parties are often to a significant extent based on the trade unions), is the general weakness and recent decline of trade unions in the United States. The percentage of the civilian labor force in trade unions in 1997 was less than 15 percent. This figure is far lower than that in other developed countries. Canada has 37 percent, Germany and the United Kingdom have about 40 percent, while Sweden and the Netherlands have over 90 percent. Japan, the second-lowest country, has approximately 25 percent.[11]

From the last peak of approximately 35 percent union membership in 1953 to the present, union density (the percentage of union members in the labor force) has declined continuously. No other developed country has had such a continuous decline in the post–World War II period. Attempts to find an explanation for these trends in the relative affluence of our society or in changes in the industrial or occupational structure are clearly misplaced because all other developed countries have undergone similar transformations and development (see Goldfield 1989a for a more detailed discussion of this question).

Despite the recent weakening of trade unions and the lessening political influence of labor parties in many European countries, the historical weakness of labor in the United States and the lack of political influence of working-class organizations are relatively unique features of U.S. society and cry out for an explanation.[12] The weakness of U.S. labor has also had a tremendous impact on virtually all aspects of society, especially those that most people regard as troublesome.

THE RESULTS OF WEAK WORKING-CLASS ORGANIZATION

Comparative scholars have often focused their attentions on some of the unique or exceptional deficiencies of the United States compared with other developed countries. Despite our existence, still, as perhaps the most affluent country in the world, of all the developed capitalist countries in Asia, Europe, and North America, we have the highest crime and murder rates, the largest percentage of prisoners, the highest concentrations of poverty, and the most problem-infested cities. In some instances, the severity of these conditions approaches that in the most economically impoverished lands. Some of these problems are recent; some are quite old. Many can be traced, at least indirectly, to the weakness of working-class organization.

Our voting turnout is the lowest of any developed country and has been declining throughout the century. The percentage of eligible voters who voted in the 1992 presidential election was 55.2 percent, the highest since 1972, when an independent (John Anderson) garnered a substantial percentage of the vote (*Congressional Quarterly* 1995:80); in 1996 the figure was 49% (*New York Times* November 7, 1996). Other developed countries have much higher turnout rates, including West Germany with over 90 percent and Sweden with slightly less. Canada, at the low end comparatively, has had a 75 to 80 percent turnout rate in the post–World War II period.[13] Even more disturbing than the low turnout rates is the class skew of voting. Turnout rates have consistently been far lower in this country among poor and working people than among the more affluent. One set of figures, for example, places turnout for people with incomes of less than $15,000 per year at less than 14 percent in 1990, 11 percent in 1992, and 7.4 percent in 1994—astounding numbers for a country with democratic pretenses (*New York Times,* August 11, 1996). And since 1989, the number of people living below this poverty-level figure has increased substantially. This class skew is not evident in other developed countries. Walter Dean Burnham has concluded that we have "an essentially oligarchical electoral universe" (Burnham 1982:142), and E. E. Schattschneider in 1960 spoke of this as a "crisis in democracy," (Schattschneider 1960:109). Some have even suggested that this makes us hardly an electorally democratic country. There have been many attempts to explain what virtually all thoughtful commentators have recognized as a serious problem. Some have pointed to the many obstacles in this country that have been placed in the way of those attempting to register, especially those of the lower classes. Of far more importance, although not unrelated to the roadblocks to registration, is the lack of major electoral alternatives for the bulk of the population, especially the lack of a major working-class party.[14] This defect in American political life—a defect, of course, unless one is antidemocratic and elitist—is also exceptional among developed countries.

Our social welfare benefits are less extensive in this country than those in other developed capitalist countries. As we all know, this country has resisted a national health plan long after other comparable states have adopted one. As a consequence, we have less coverage and higher per capita medical costs than any other land. This country has less government expenditures per capita (even with a large military) than other developed countries, with less coverage rates for pensions, sickness insurance, and unemployment. Only Japan vies with us in some categories at the bottom. (See Goldfield 1989a:27–32 for an extended discussion. For more recent figures and discussion, see Stephens 1994; Huber, Ray, and Stephens 1994; Huber and Stephens 1992; Garrett and Lange 1991; P. Baldwin 1990; Esping-Anderson 1990; Janoski and Hicks, 1994; and Mishel and Bernstein 1994). Although labor movements are not the only political forces in developed capitalist countries that have striven for extensive social welfare coverage, they are by far the most powerful and influential. The weakness of labor organization is not unrelated to the weakness of social benefits in the United States.

In a recent book, Seymour Martin Lipset presents a long list of other characteristics that he sees as endemic to U.S. society, some tied to those things that many regard as positive. The emphasis on individual rights and the divided nature of national governmental institutions make ours a highly litigious society. We have many times the number of lawyers per capita and almost five times the tort costs as a percentage of gross national product (GNP)—an incredible 2.4 percent—as any other country (Lipset, 1996:50). Lipset even argues that the higher rates of teenage pregnancy and divorce in this country are a product of our historical culture and values. And these statistics are not to be explained by the existence of the African-American poor. Although the rates for Blacks are proportionately higher than those for whites, the rate of teenage pregnancy for whites is twice that of the closest European country, and divorce rates in the United States have only a modest class and racial skew (Lipset 1996:50). Finding the supposed roots of American exceptionalism has been a long-standing quest for many students of U.S. political and social life. The attempts at explanation have been both diverse and numerous, dating back well into the nineteenth century.

THEORIES OF AMERICAN EXCEPTIONALISM

For over a century, the United States has been one of the most economically developed capitalist countries in the world; from the 1920s until recently, it has been the most developed. Marx's original account of capitalist development, at least insofar as it appears in schematic form in the *Communist Manifesto,* suggests that working-class movements will be most developed, most fully organized, with broader class conscious, and perhaps more radical in the most developed countries. Most late nineteenth- and early twentieth-century non-Marxist commentators had similar expectations. Yet, Marxists and others, too, have long noted that working-class politics in the United States has been decidedly less advanced along this path.[15] All have noted the absense here of a labor, social democratic, socialist, or communist party with significant electoral and organizational support. Unlike all other developed capitalist countries, the United States of America has no substantial, independent working-class party. The key question, then, is why working-class politics in the United States is so undeveloped. Attempts to explain this apparently unique feature of U.S. society have been manifold for over a century. Analysts have ranged across the political spectrum, from Marxists (including Marx, Engels, Lenin, and Trotsky), who have tried to explain the conjunctural reasons for what they have seen as the historical, temporary retardation of the American working-class movement, to more conservative commentators who have argued that the United States is, not merely exceptional, but a permanent, enduring proof to the falsity of Marxist prognosis (Bell 1960; Kerr et al. 1960). Among a sampling of explanations for this American exceptionalism are the following:

1. Alexis de Tocqueville and Werner Sombart have identified the supposedly more democratic, egalitarian features of U.S. society as the reason for the absense of developed working-class politics.
2. Others, e.g., Stephen Thernstrom, have pointed to alleged higher rates of social mobility.
3. Geographic mobility, the uprooting of the poorest members of the working-class population, has also been cited as a key factor. The transient character of the worst-off parts of the population precluded the formation of stable working-class communities, the basis in many other countries for enduring labor politics (Karabel 1979).
4. Louis Hartz, in his *The Liberal Tradition in America* (1955) argues for the importance of a nonfeudal past in this country and the acceptance by the general population of a strong belief in Lockean individualism. These factors are sometimes said to be reflected in the frontier images and the Horatio Alger myth.
5. Conservatives, including Professor Gingrich, sometimes point to the highly religious character of large percentages of the populace. Seymour Martin Lipset argues that the historically large number and size of dissenting Protestant sects has played a significant contributing role.

6. Some assert that workers have historically had higher wages here. Or in the words of Sombart, in the United States, "All Socialist Utopias came to nothing on roast beef and apple pie" (Sombart 1976:106).

7. The historian Frederick Jackson Turner and his followers have pointed to the existence of a frontier in the western United States as a "safety valve" for nineteenth century working-class frustration and discontent.

8. Political scientist Theodore Lowi has stressed the federal structure of U.S. politics as the main obstacle to the formation of an influential working-class party (Lowi 1984).

9. Others have located working-class failures in a lack of solidarity rooted in the historical (white) ethnic diversity of the country.

10. Still others have argued for the centrality of early white manhood suffrage, gained more easily here than in Europe and other countries.

11. The savage repression of working-class radicals by the state and the extreme nature of capitalist opposition to working-class politics and organization are additional reasons given by some analysts.

12. In a global, anti-Marxist argument, Kerr and his associates (1960) claim that sharp class conflict is a feature, not of developed capitalist society, but of emerging pre-industrial society. Thus, the United States may be more advanced than, not behind, comparative countries in the weakness of its labor movement.

13. And the list goes on.[16]

All these theories are, in my view, problematic; some are misleading; the best provide only partial insights. It is not my goal to delve deeply into the various positions on American exceptionalism here.[17] It is worth noting briefly, however, that social mobility studies have shown little difference between the United States and other capitalist countries during the relevant comparable historical periods despite sharp assertions to the contrary by Speaker Gingrich and others (see, e.g., Lipset and Bendix 1964). White manhood suffrage was extremely limited in the pre–Civil War period and in the South after 1900. From the dawn of the twentieth century until the 1960s, disenfranchisement affected poor whites almost as much as it did blacks in the South (see Key 1984). Even at its fullest, however, white male suffrage never touched on the disenfrachisement of nonwhites, women before their enfranchisement in 1920, and noncitizen immigrants. Feudalism was long gone in Europe before working-class movements emerged there. Finally, the frontier (whatever its impact in an earlier time—and I would argue that it is mixed) has long since departed from the U.S. landscape.

Reconceptualization of the Problem

The problem of American exceptionalism must be posed differently. An important argument can be made that politics goes through long periods in which viable political options are relatively constrained. During other shorter, often more volatile periods, the options and possibilities for change are usually much broader. These latter periods are turning points or moments whose outcomes structure and set the limits on politics during subsequent periods. Thus, to understand the more limited, stable periods, it is necessary to examine also the previous critical turning points that shaped them.

Athough not necessarily subscribing to a theory of critical moments, most students of American political development recognize at least three pivotal periods. These include the founding of the Republic, the Civil War, and the depression–New Deal era. Each of these periods, in the eyes of many authors, was an important turning point in U.S. political history. In addition, each left a decided impact on contemporary and later political life. There is less agreement on which other periods are turning points. There are those who argue, however, for the centrality of Andrew Jackson's presidency (e.g., Schlesinger 1950), Reconstruction (e.g., Du Bois 1964), the 1890s (e.g., Goodwyn 1976; Burnham 1986), the Progressive Era (e.g., Skowronek 1988), and also the present. Even the choice of period or periods often depends on what factors are considered important, with emphasis ranging from critical elections (e.g., Sundquist 1983) to sectionalism (e.g., Bensel 1987) and to economic interests (e.g., Beard and Beard 1944).

If one accepts this general perspective about pivotal turning points as reasonable, however, in examining American political development, it will not do to investigate merely the more stable periods when the United States has seemed to many people to be relatively serene and homogeneous. Nor is it adequate to take as a putative norm those periods in which class conflict seemed weak and fragmented. Rather, one must also examine those periods in which the situation was quite different. For as any careful examination of U.S. history will show, and as many of the new labor historians have documented convincingly, contrary to the views of the consensus and elite historians, class struggle and militance have been anything but mild in this country. There have been many times when mass, radical, left-wing, broad-based, occasionally violent working-class upheavals have taken place. These struggles have sometimes had both the breadth and the intensity of those in other countries that led to the establishment of independent working-class political organization there. Later, I will refer to a number of these struggles. And contrary to received wisdom, third parties far to the left of either the Democrats or the Republicans have at various times attained widespread influence in the United States. The Socialist Party, with its hundreds of elected local officials before the First World War, is a case in point. During the 1920s, 1930s, and 1940s, local and state-level labor, radical agrarian, and other third parties were a central fixture of the political landscape. The Minnesota Farmer-Labor Party, Wisconsin's Progressive Party, the American Labor Party of New York City, End-Poverty-In-California (EPIC), the North Dakota Nonpartisan League, the Oklahoma Farmer-Labor Reconstruction League, and hundreds of local labor parties all had substantial influence (Davin and Lynd 1979–1980; Davin 1989). The real question, then, is not why such broad class struggles and the formation of independent working-class political organizations have not taken place (since, of course, they have); rather, the question is why they were so comparatively short-lived, why they were repressed or unsuccessful, why they did not lead to the formation of a more enduring national form of class-based organization. And it is from this perspective that the historical political weakness of the American working class is best examined.[18]

By what criteria can one select the critical periods or turning points in American political development. One criterion is easily agreed to: Each critical turning point must have a decisive impact on the way the country is governed and ruled and on social relations. In addition, I will argue that at each such juncture, social—usually class—conflict was at a high level. I will argue further that questions of race were central to the outcome of the struggles. The resolution of each of these conflicts led to altered social and political relations in general, new arrangements of social control, and a reorganized system of racial domination and subordination. It is important to emphasize that identification and analysis of critical periods of American political development, as well as the configuration of the criteria used to identify these periods, are the central organizing feature and theme of much of this book. In particular, the argument that race was central to each of the critical turning points is the distinguishing—and undoubtedly the most controversial—feature of my analysis. By these criteria, I identify five periods:

The first such critical period was during the colonial era, when the southern colonies turned from indentured servitude of people of all ethnic groups and nationalities as the main source of labor to Black slaves. It was at this time that the colour line was drawn and racial identities, which continue to this day, were established. A system of white supremacy in laws, customs, and social relations was established, developed, and enforced.

The second period was the Revolutionary War/constitutional period, in which the nature of what constituted political freedom and democracy was fixed. The role of slaves and slave owners within the polity was codified; and notions of states' rights, divided government, and property rights were institutionalized. In all these aspects, I will argue, slavery and race were central.

The third great turning point was the Civil War/Reconstruction era, which emancipated the slaves and destroyed the national power of the southern slave-owning class. The war was over slavery and, later, the role of the ex-slaves within the polity. The South formed a new system of labor, based on a changed white supremacy that dominated the country as a whole well into the next century.

The fourth critical movement in American political development was the Populist one, out of which came the System of 1896, which solidified the rule of northern business and the national political dominance of the Republican Party for almost four decades. Political participation for the lower classes, North and South, was restricted. Segregation became more rigid in both the North and the South. An era of conservative rule was established as America's ruling classes took up more fully the "white man's burden" at home and abroad.

The fifth critical period in the United States was the Depression/New Deal era. This period marked the rise of industrial unions, broad social policies at the federal level, and the beginning of the breakup of the old Jim Crow. Politics and social relations, however, were only partially transformed. And the contradictions and legacies, the successes and failures, of the Depression/New Deal era continue to shape the politics of the United States today despite the immense changes in the economy, culture, race and gender relations, and almost everything else.

Each of these periods installed new or modified systems of racial domination and new methods of white domination. The key to understanding and solving the old conundrum of American exceptionalism—the peculiarities of American politics and the political weakness of its working class is the interplay between class and race. Race is the key to unraveling the secret of American exceptionalism, but it is also much more. A focus on exceptionalism only gets us so far. Race has been the central ingredient, not merely in undermining solidarity when broad struggles have erupted, not merely in dividing workers, but also in providing an alternative white male nonclass worldview and structure of identity that have exerted their force during both stable and confrontational times. It has provided the everyday framework in which labor has been utilized, controlled, and exploited by those who have employed it. And race has been behind many of the supposed principles of American government (most notably states' rights) that are regarded as sacred by some people today.

MY hypothesis about the reasons for the inability of U.S. workers to develop sustained forms of class organization and consciousness focuses on white supremacy. I make several claims: First the system of white supremacy has played a central role in all the critical turning points of U.S. politics from colonial times to the present. This, in fact, is the main thesis and continuing thread of this book. Second, the development of the system of white supremacy and the ideology used to justify it originate from and are based in the socio-economic system. Third, the primary function of both the system and the ideology has been on the one hand, to control and exploit African-American (and by extension other nonwhite) labor; on the other hand it has been to control white workers, isolating them from their potential allies among nonwhites. Fourth, I wish to suggest that the system of white supremacy and the ideology of white chauvinism used to justify it have not merely kept African-Americans and other nonwhites oppressed, not only weakened their organizations. The system and the ideology have also been detrimental for white workers in two ways: On the one hand, the system of white supremacy has been a major impediment to the development of a sustained, solidaristic, class-based labor movement; on the other hand, it has often hurt white workers in their immediate economic interests. Fifth, there have been many economic, political, ideological and other institutional supports for the pervasiveness of white supremacist ideology and beliefs. These factors have played a central role in keeping workers from organizing on a class basis. Sixth, even with these latter factors, the failure to recognize the importance of white supremacy and the unwillingness of white workers, white labor leaders, and all too often, white radicals to confront it head on have been a primary factor in keeping workers from organizing on a class basis. Seventh, a number of the highlights of labor struggle, however, when class consciousness and organization seemed to be blooming, have been accompanied by strong commitments to placing the fight against racial discrimination at the top of the political agenda. At key junctures, I will attempt to draw some of the lessons about racial domination in the United States and the possibilities for overcoming it.

Before proceeding with this agenda, however, I must make a small caveat: All broad historical analyses are inevitably fraught with difficulties. It is unlikely that any one investigator might have detailed knowledge, even where possible, of all the periods that she or he discusses. I certainly make no such claim and am painfully aware that in certain areas, I may be skimming along on thin ice. Even less possible, however, is doing justice to the full range of issues, to various nuances and complexities with which a more detailed, limited focus would inevitably deal. Such is especially the case in a book that still bears many of the birthmarks of its origin as a lengthy article, originally based on a conference talk. One could, of course, lace one's analysis with a large number of hedges and qualifications, being noncommittal on various controversial points. My purpose, however, is to present a broad hypothesis, suggesting its wide applicability. Thus, I have deemed it better to attempt to state things sharply, to take positions on a large number of controversial issues, to range over a wide scope, and to err on the side of overstatement rather than to cover my tracks by making things even less clear, realizing that I am skipping merrily through the minefields in which more knowledgeable specialists cautiously tread, hoping not to set off too many unpleasant and potentially embarrassing explosions.[19]

How, one might ask, can such a broad, multifaceted hypothesis be carefully examined? How does one decide whether this hypothesis or one of the other hypotheses is most adequate? Here, of course, I only wish to suggest its plausibility. The proper approach to a fair evaluation, however, similar in certain respects to the method relied on in the physical sciences for confirming and rejecting broad theories and hypotheses, should be based on a comparison of this hypothesis with other plausible candidates, including those theories of race and the approaches to American political development already discussed in this introduction. We would want to know for each theory whether it is able to account for the most important facts and fundamental events of U.S. history. We would also want to assess the degree to which each candidate leads its adherents to gloss over, omit, or distort important aspects of reality. That is, does it do violence to the facts? Finally, in a fair comparison, we want to know how it fares generally in relation to its competitors, which theory makes the most sense of the problems it aims to solve.[20] My burden here will be to give sufficient facts and arguments to suggest the plausibility of each aspect of the hypothesis throughout the course of American political development.[21]

1. Biological differences in receptivity to diseases, genetic proclivities to skin cancer, or even propensities to heart disease are of a different category and are not unusual forms of within-species variations. For a penetrating analysis of the history of intelligence testing, see Stephen J. Gould's *Mismeasure of Man* (1981). For a comprehensive and perhaps exhaustive discussion of the Bell Curve, see *The Bell Curve Debate,* edited by Russell Jacoby and Naomi Glauberman (1995) as well as *Inequality by Design* by Claude S. Fischer et al. (1996). For a wide-ranging discussion of biology and human nature, see Richard Lewontin et al., *Not in Our Genes* (1984); for a classic summary of the relationship between genetics and racial and ethnic groups, see Richard Lewontin, *The Genetic Basis of Evolutionary Change* (1974).

2. For a detailed analysis and brilliant, devastating critique of both Degler and Jordan, see Allen (1994:4–14). For a somewhat surprising, uncritical acceptance of Jordan's argument, see Nash and Weiss (1970:11, 18); and Nash (1990:10–11). Tocqueville seems also to have held this view, as Fredrickson (1971:22) incisively argues.

3. Omi and Winant are often quite favorable, for example, to W. E. B. Du Bois, even as he identified himself as a Marxist, and the Italian Marxist Antonio Gramsci. On the other hand, they attempt to sharply distinguish themselves from a crude form of Marxism that they see as class reductionist

and economic determinist, rarely including more sophisticated versions in their critiques and discussions. One hardly knows what to think when Winant gives a listing of early twentieth-century activists and intellectuals who challenged race as a natural phenomenon (the list includes the Chicago school of sociology and American nationalists, of whom Marcus Garvey was one); the only group that is qualified in a negative way is "a few Marxists (whose perspectives had their own limitations)" (Winant 1994:13).

4. For the most prominent statement of this position, see Bonacich (1972, 1976, 1979, 1980).

5. See Boorstin (1958). For the quotes and discussions of Boorstin, see Novick (1988:327–34); for a trenchant analysis and critique of Boorstin's writings, see Lemisch (1975, passim).

6. The Confederate general most forgotten in accounts of the Civil War is James Longstreet, who after the war became a supporter of Reconstruction and an outspoken champion of rights for African-Americans. When he died in 1903, the Daughters of the Confederacy refused to send flowers to his funeral. To this day, there are no statues of him in the South (Foner 1988:298).

7. Contrary to Speaker Gingrich's assertions in his recent course, the term American exceptionalism actually owes its prominence to a debate within the Communist Party of the United States (CP) and the Communist International (Comintern) during the late 1920s. Jay Lovestone and his associates, who took over the leadership of the CP in 1927, albeit with strong minority opposition, attempted to justify the weakness of their party and its need for a "non-revolutionary" American approach on the basis of the historic strength and adaptability of U.S. capitalism. His opponents in the U.S. party, eventually supported by the Comintern, accused him of a break with Marxism that they labeled American exceptionalism. During the late 1920s, the 1930s, and the 1940s, large numbers of U.S. intellectuals were involved in the radical movement in this country; many eventually became prominent, albeit often relatively conservative, academics. They did, however, provide the transmission belt for this terminology to become absorbed into the mainstream of academic social science literature.

8. For introductions to this literature, see Allen (1968), Laslett and Lipset (1974), and Lipset (1977, 1996).

9. Or, in Werner Sombart's (1976) classic formulation: "Why no socialism in the United States?"

10. The most recent period of insurgency, the 1960s, for example, brought forth a whole new interpretive literature. For works explicitly on American exceptionalism from this genre, see Allen (1968, 1994), Katznelson (1978), Karabel (1979), and Markovits (1987). For works that emphasize class possibilities in American labor history, see the extensive review in Brody (1979). For detailed reviews of recent research on the CP, see Goldfield (1980 and 1985) and Wald (1995).

11. For more detailed discussion of these and other comparisons and a discussion of the special case of France, including the comparability of the figures, see Goldfield (1989a). For the up-to-date comparative figures cited above, I have used unpublished data from the U.S. Department of Labor, Bureau of Labor Statistics, Office of Productivity and Technology, Division of Foreign Labor Statistics.

12. For critiques of the usefulness of the notion of American exceptionalism, see Zolberg (1986) and Wilentz (1984).

13. For comprehensive but slightly outdated comparative figures, see Mackie and Rose (1974); see also the discussions in Burnham (1982).

14. For a definitive discussion of the debates over these issues and a careful analysis see Chapter 4 of Piven and Cloward (1988). For further analyses, see Burnham (1982), Teixiera (1987, 1992), Conway (1991), Kleppner (1982), and Rosenstone and Hansen (1993).

15. William Z. Foster (1952:33) notes that in the 1850s, Marxists were already concerned about the lack of class consciousness of U.S. workers, especially in contrast with their high degree of trade union militancy.

16. I first became aware of the arguments over American exceptionalism from a pithy and cogent piece by Allen (1968), in which a brief analysis of some of the above explanations is presented (see also Allen 1994). A comprehensive discussion of these and other theories may also be found in Lipset (1977); convenient excerpts for many positions are available in a collection by Laslett and Lipset (1974).

17. Broad critiques may be found in Allen (1968), Lipset (1977), and Katznelson (1981).

18. My understanding of the problem in this fashion relies heavily on Allen's seminal essay (Allen 1968).

19. For my own small part, I can only say that I am working on a much more detailed treatment of many of the themes discussed here for one historical turning point, the 1930s and 1940s.

20. These issues are discussed in the philosophy of science literature, e.g., in Lakatos 1970, especially pp. 132–138, 154–177; Putnam 1978; and R. Miller 1988.

21. I make no claims to complete originality of this hypothesis. A compelling version was put forth eloquently and convincingly over sixty years ago by W. E. B. Du Bois in Black Reconstruction. Since the 1960s, Theodore Allen (in several articles and in one recent and another forthcoming major work), Lerone Bennett, and others have put forward chunks of this hypothesis. Yet, like the attention paid to white supremacy itself, the hypothesis and its supporting arguments

A KIND OF REVOLUTION

HOWARD ZINN

The American victory over the British army was made possible by the existence of an already-armed people. Just about every white male had a gun, and could shoot. The Revolutionary leadership distrusted the mobs of poor. But they knew the Revolution had no appeal to slaves and Indians. They would have to woo the armed white population.

This was not easy. Yes, mechanics and sailors, some others, were incensed against the British. But general enthusiasm for the war was not strong. While much of the white male population went into military service at one time or another during the war, only a small fraction stayed. John Shy, in his study of the Revolutionary army (*A People Numerous and Armed*), says they "grew weary of being bullied by local committees of safety, by corrupt deputy assistant commissaries of supply, and by bands of ragged strangers with guns in their hands calling themselves soldiers of the Revolution." Shy estimates that perhaps a fifth of the population was actively treasonous. John Adams had estimated a third opposed, a third in support, a third neutral.

Alexander Hamilton, an aide of George Washington and an up-and-coming member of the new elite, wrote from his headquarters: "... our countrymen have all the folly of the ass and all the passiveness of the sheep. ... They are determined not to be free. ... If we are saved, France and Spain must save us."

Slavery got in the way in the South. South Carolina, insecure since the slave uprising in Stono in 1739, could hardly fight against the British; her militia had to be used to keep slaves under control.

The men who first joined the colonial militia were generally "hallmarks of respectability or at least of full citizenship" in their communities, Shy says. Excluded from the militia were friendly Indians, free Negroes, white servants, and free white men who had no stable home. But desperation led to the recruiting of the less respectable whites. Massachusetts and Virginia provided for drafting "strollers" (vagrants) into the militia. In fact, the military became a place of promise for the poor, who might rise in rank, acquire some money, change their social status.

Here was the traditional device by which those in charge of any social order mobilize and discipline a recalcitrant population—offering the adventure and rewards of military service to get poor people to fight for a cause they may not see clearly as their own. A wounded American lieutenant at Bunker Hill, interviewed by Peter Oliver, a Tory (who admittedly might have been looking for such a response), told how he had joined the rebel forces:

> I was a Shoemaker, & got my living by my Labor. When this Rebellion came on, I saw some of my Neighbors got into Commission, who were no better than myself. I was very ambitious, & did not like to see those Men above me. I was asked to enlist, as a private Soldier ... I offered to enlist upon having a Lieutenants Commission; which was granted. I imagined my self now in a way of Promotion: if I was killed in Battle, there would be an end of me, but if my Captain was killed, I should rise in Rank, & should still have a Chance to rise higher. These Sir! were the only Motives of my entering into the Service; for as to the Dispute between Great Britain & the Colonies, I know nothing of it. ...

John Shy investigated the subsequent experience of that Bunker Hill lieutenant. He was William Scott, of Peterborough, New Hampshire, and after a year as prisoner of the British he escaped, made his way back to the American army, fought in battles in New York, was captured again by the British, and escaped again by swimming the Hudson River one night with his sword tied around his neck and his watch pinned to his hat. He returned to New Hampshire, recruited a company of his own, including his two eldest sons, and fought in various battles, until his health gave way. He watched his eldest son die of camp fever after six years of service. He had sold his farm in Peterborough for a note that, with inflation, became worthless. After the war, he came to public attention when he rescued eight people from drowning after their boat turned over in New York harbor. He then got a job surveying western lands with the army, but caught a fever and died in 1796.

Scott was one of many Revolutionary fighters, usually of lower military ranks, from poor and obscure backgrounds. Shy's study of the Peterborough contingent shows that the prominent and substantial citizens of the town had served only briefly in the war. Other American towns show the same pattern. As Shy puts it: "Revolutionary America may have been a middle-class society, happier and more prosperous than any other in its time, but it contained a large and growing number of fairly poor people, and many of them did much of the actual fighting and suffering between 1775 and 1783: A very old story."

The military conflict itself, by dominating everything in its time, diminished other issues, made people choose sides in the one contest that was publicly important, forced people onto the side of the Revolution whose interest in Independence was not at all obvious. Ruling elites seem to have learned through the generations—consciously or not—that war makes them more secure against internal trouble.

The force of military preparation had a way of pushing neutral people into line. In Connecticut, for instance, a law was passed requiring military service of all males between sixteen and sixty, omitting certain government officials, ministers, Yale students and faculty, Negroes, Indians, and mulattos. Someone called to duty could provide a substitute or get out of it by paying 5 pounds. When eighteen men failed to show up for military duty they were jailed and, in order to be released, had to pledge to fight in the war. Shy says: "The mechanism of their political conversion was the militia." What looks like the democratization of the military forces in modern times shows up as something different: a way of forcing large numbers of reluctant people to associate themselves with the national cause, and by the end of the process believe in it.

Here, in the war for liberty, was conscription, as usual, cognizant of wealth. With the impressment riots against the British still remembered, impressment of seamen by the American navy was taking place by 1779. A Pennsylvania official said: "We cannot help observing how similar this Conduct is to that of the British Officers during our Subjection to Great Britain and are persuaded it will have the same unhappy effects viz. an estrangement of the Affections of the People from ... Authority ... which by an easy Progression will proceed to open Opposition ... and bloodshed."

Watching the new, tight discipline of Washington's army, a chaplain in Concord, Massachusetts, wrote: "New lords, new laws. The strictest government is taking place and great distinction is made between officers & men. Everyone is made to know his place & keep it, or be immediately tied up, and receive not one but 30 or 40 lashes."

The Americans lost the first battles of the war: Bunker Hill, Brooklyn Heights, Harlem Heights, the Deep South; they won small battles at Trenton and Princeton, and then in a turning point, a big battle at Saratoga, New York, in 1777. Washington's frozen army hung on at Valley Forge, Pennsylvania, while Benjamin Franklin negotiated an alliance with the French monarchy, which was anxious for revenge on England. The war turned to the South, where the British won victory after victory, until the Americans, aided by a large French army, with the French navy blocking off the British from supplies and reinforcements, won the final victory of the war at Yorktown, Virginia, in 1781.

Through all this, the suppressed conflicts between rich and poor among the Americans kept reappearing. In the midst of the war, in Philadelphia, which Eric Foner describes as "a time of immense profits for some colonists and terrible hardships for others," the inflation (prices rose in one month that year by 45 percent) led to agitation and calls for action. One Philadelphia newspaper carried a reminder that in Europe "the People have always done themselves justice when the scarcity of bread has arisen from the avarice of forestallers. They have broken open magazines—appropriated stores to their own use without paying for them—and in some instances have hung up the culprits who created their distress."

In May of 1779, the First Company of Philadelphia Artillery petitioned the Assembly about the troubles of "the midling and poor" and threatened violence against "those who are avariciously intent upon amassing wealth by the destruction of the more virtuous part of the community." That same month, there was a mass meeting, an extralegal gathering, which called for price reductions and initiated an investigation of Robert Morris, a rich Philadelphian who was accused of holding food from the market. In October came the "Fort Wilson riot," in which a militia group marched into the city and to the house of James Wilson, a wealthy lawyer and Revolutionary official who had opposed price controls and the democratic constitution adopted in Pennsylvania in 1776. The militia were driven away by a "silk stocking brigade" of well-off Philadelphia citizens.

It seemed that the majority of white colonists, who had a bit of land, or no property at all, were still better off than slaves or indentured servants or Indians, and could be wooed into the coalition of the Revolution. But when the sacrifices of war became more bitter, the privileges and safety of the rich became harder to accept. About 10 percent of the white population (an estimate of Jackson Main in *The Social Structure of Revolutionary America*), large landholders and merchants, held 1,000 pounds or more in personal property and 1,000 pounds in land, at the least, and these men owned nearly half the wealth of the country and held as slaves one-seventh of the country's people.

The Continental Congress, which governed the colonies through the war, was dominated by rich men, linked together in factions and compacts by business and family connections. These links connected North and South, East and West. For instance, Richard Henry Lee of Virginia was connected with the Adamses of Massachusetts and the Shippens of Pennsylvania. Delegates from middle and southern colonies were connected with Robert Morris of Pennsylvania through commerce and land speculation. Morris was superintendent of finance, and his assistant was Gouverneur Morris.

Morris's plan was to give more assurance to those who had loaned money to the Continental Congress, and gain the support of officers by voting half-pay for life for those who stuck to the end. This ignored the common soldier, who was not getting paid, who was suffering in the cold, dying of sickness, watching the civilian profiteers get rich. On New Year's Day, 1781, the Pennsylvania troops near Morristown, New Jersey, perhaps emboldened by rum, dispersed their officers, killed one captain, wounded others, and were marching, fully armed, with cannon, toward the Continental Congress at Philadelphia.

George Washington handled it cautiously. Informed of these developments by General Anthony Wayne, he told Wayne not to use force. He was worried that the rebellion might spread to his own troops. He suggested Wayne get a list of the soldiers' grievances, and said Congress should not flee Philadelphia, because then the way would be open for the soldiers to be joined by Philadelphia citizens. He sent Knox rushing to New England on his horse to get three months' pay for the soldiers, while he prepared a thousand men to march on the mutineers, as a last resort. A peace was negotiated, in which one-half the men were discharged; the other half got furloughs.

Shortly after this, a smaller mutiny took place in the New Jersey Line, involving two hundred men who defied their officers and started out for the state capital at Trenton. Now Washington was ready. Six hundred men, who themselves had been well fed and clothed, marched on the mutineers and surrounded and disarmed them. Three ringleaders were put on trial immediately, in the field. One was pardoned, and two were shot by firing squads made up of their friends, who wept as they pulled the triggers. It was "an example," Washington said.

Two years later, there was another mutiny in the Pennsylvania line. The war was over and the army had disbanded, but eighty soldiers, demanding their pay, invaded the Continental Congress headquarters in Philadelphia and forced the members to flee across the river to Princeton—"ignominiously turned out of doors," as one historian sorrowfully wrote (John Fiske, *The Critical Period*), "by a handful of drunken mutineers."

What soldiers in the Revolution could do only rarely, rebel against their authorities, civilians could do much more easily. Ronald Hoffman says: "The Revolution plunged the states of Delaware, Maryland, North Carolina, South Carolina, Georgia, and, to a much lesser degree, Virginia into divisive civil conflicts that persisted during the entire period of struggle." The southern lower classes resisted being mobilized for the revolution. They saw themselves under the rule of a political elite, win or lose against the British.

In Maryland, for instance, by the new constitution of 1776, to run for governor one had to own 5,000 pounds of property; to run for state senator, 1,000 pounds. Thus, 90 percent of the population were excluded from holding office. And so, as Hoffman says, "small slave holders, non-slaveholding planters, tenants, renters and casual day laborers posed a serious problem of social control for the Whig elite."

With black slaves 25 percent of the population (and in some counties 50 percent), fear of slave revolts grew. George Washington had turned down the requests of blacks, seeking freedom, to fight in the Revolutionary army. So when the British military commander in Virginia, Lord Dunmore, promised freedom to Virginia slaves who joined his forces, this created consternation. A report from one Maryland county worried about poor whites encouraging slave runaways:

> The insolence of the Negroes in this county is come to such a height, that we are under a necessity of disarming them which we affected on Saturday last. We took about eighty guns, some bayonets, swords, etc. The malicious and imprudent speeches of some among the lower classes of whites have induced them to believe that their freedom depended on the success of the King's troops. We cannot therefore be too vigilant nor too rigorous with those who promote and encourage this disposition in our slaves.

Even more unsettling was white rioting in Maryland against leading families, supporting the Revolution, who were suspected of hoarding needed commodities. The class hatred of some of these disloyal people was expressed by one man who said "it was better for the people to lay down their arms and pay the duties and taxes laid upon them by King and Parliament than to be brought into slavery and to be commanded and ordered about as they were." A wealthy Maryland land-owner, Charles Carroll, took note of the surly mood all around him:

> There is a mean low dirty envy which creeps thro all ranks and cannot suffer a man a superiority of fortune, of merit, or of understanding in fellow citizens—either of these are sure to entail a general ill will and dislike upon the owners.

Despite this, Maryland authorities retained control. They made concessions, taxing land and slaves more heavily, letting debtors pay in paper money. It was a sacrifice by the upper class to maintain power, and it worked.

In the lower South, however, in the Carolinas and Georgia, according to Hoffman, "vast regions were left without the slightest apparition of authority." The general mood was to take no part in a war that seemed to have nothing for them. "Authoritative personages on both sides demanded that common people supply material, reduce consumption, leave their families, and even risk their lives. Forced to make hard decisions, many flailed out in frustration or evaded and defied first one side, then the other. ..."

Washington's military commander in the lower South, Nathanael Greene, dealt with disloyalty by a policy of concessions to some, brutality to others. In a letter to Thomas Jefferson he described a raid by his troops on Loyalists. "They made a dreadful carnage of them, upwards of one hundred were killed and most of the rest cut to pieces. It has had a very happy effect on those disaffected persons of which there were too many in this country." Greene told one of his generals "to strike terror into our enemies and give spirit to our friends." On the other hand, he advised the governor of Georgia "to open a door for the disaffected of your state to come in. ..."

In general, throughout the states, concessions were kept to a minimum. The new constitutions that were drawn up in all states from 1776 to 1780 were not much different from the old ones. Although property qualifications for voting and holding office were lowered in some instances, in Massachusetts they were increased. Only Pennsylvania abolished them totally. The new bills of rights had modifying provisions. North Carolina, providing for religious freedom, added "that nothing herein contained shall be construed to exempt preachers of treasonable or seditious discourses, from legal trial and punishment." Maryland, New York, Georgia, and Massachusetts took similar cautions.

The American Revolution is sometimes said to have brought about the separation of church and state. The northern states made such declarations, but after 1776 they adopted taxes that forced everyone to support Christian teachings. William G. McLaughlin, quoting Supreme Court Justice David Brewer in 1892 that "this is a Christian nation," says of the separation of church and state in the Revolution that it "was neither conceived of nor carried out. ... Far from being left to itself, religion was imbedded into every aspect and institution of American life."

One would look, in examining the Revolution's effect on class relations, at what happened to land confiscated from fleeing Loyalists. It was distributed in such a way as to give a double opportunity to the Revolutionary leaders: to enrich themselves and their friends, and to parcel out some land to small farmers to create a broad base of support for the new government. Indeed, this became characteristic of the new nation: finding itself possessed of enormous wealth, it could create the richest ruling class in history, and still have enough for the middle classes to act as a buffer between the rich and the dispossessed.

The huge landholdings of the Loyalists had been one of the great incentives to Revolution. Lord Fairfax in Virginia had more than 5 million acres encompassing twenty-one counties. Lord Baltimore's income from his Maryland holdings exceeded 30,000 pounds a year. After the Revolution, Lord Fairfax was protected; he was a friend of George Washington. But other Loyalist holders of great estates, especially those who were absentees, had their land confiscated. In New York, the number of freeholding small farmers increased after the Revolution, and there were fewer tenant farmers, who had created so much trouble in the pre-Revolution years.

Although the numbers of independent farmers grew, according to Rowland Berthoff and John Murrin, "the class structure did not change radically." The ruling group went through personnel changes as "the rising merchant families of Boston, New York or Philadelphia ... slipped quite credibly into the social status—and sometimes the very houses of those who failed in business or suffered confiscation and exile for loyalty to the crown."

Edmund Morgan sums up the class nature of the Revolution this way: "The fact that the lower ranks were involved in the contest should not obscure the fact that the contest itself was generally a struggle for office and power between members of an upper class: the new against the established." Looking at the situation after the Revolution, Richard Morris comments: "Everywhere one finds inequality." He finds "the people" of "We the people of the United States" (a phrase coined by the very rich Gouverneur Morris) did not mean Indians or blacks or women or white servants. In fact, there were more indentured servants than ever, and the Revolution "did nothing to end and little to ameliorate white bondage."

Carl Degler says *(Out of Our Past):* "No new social class came to power through the door of the American revolution. The men who engineered the revolt were largely members of the colonial ruling class." George Washington was the richest man in America. John Hancock was a prosperous Boston merchant. Benjamin Franklin was a wealthy printer. And so on.

On the other hand, town mechanics, laborers, and seamen, as well as small farmers, were swept into "the people" by the rhetoric of the Revolution, by the camaraderie of military service, by the distribution of some land. Thus was created a substantial body of support, a national consensus, something that, even with the exclusion of ignored and oppressed people, could be called "America."

Staughton Lynd's close study of Dutchess County, New York, in the Revolutionary period corroborates this. There were tenant risings in 1766 against the huge feudal estates in New York. The Rensselaerwyck holding was a million acres. Tenants, claiming some of this land for themselves, unable to get satisfaction in the courts, turned to violence. In Poughkeepsie, 1,700 armed tenants had closed the courts and broken open the jails. But the uprising was crushed.

During the Revolution, there was a struggle in Dutchess County over the disposition of confiscated Loyalist lands, but it was mainly between different elite groups. One of these, the Poughkeepsie anti-Federalists (opponents of the Constitution), included men on the make, newcomers in land and business. They made promises to the tenants to gain their support, exploiting their grievances to build their own political careers and maintain their own fortunes.

During the Revolution, to mobilize soldiers, the tenants were promised land. A prominent landowner of Dutchess County wrote in 1777 that a promise to make tenants freeholders "would instantly bring you at least six thousand able farmers into the field." But the farmers who enlisted in the Revolution and expected to get something out of it found that, as privates in the army, they received $6.66 a month, while a colonel received $75 a month. They watched local government contractors like Melancton Smith and

Matthew Paterson become rich, while the pay they received in continental currency became worthless with inflation.

All this led tenants to become a threatening force in the midst of the war. Many stopped paying rent. The legislature, worried, passed a bill to confiscate Loyalist land and add four hundred new freeholders to the 1,800 already in the county. This meant a strong new voting bloc for the faction of the rich that would become anti-Federalists in 1788. Once the new landholders were brought into the privileged circle of the Revolution and seemed politically under control, their leaders, Melancton Smith and others, at first opposed to adoption of the Constitution, switched to support, and with New York ratifying, adoption was ensured. The new freeholders found that they had stopped being tenants, but were now mortgagees, paying back loans from banks instead of rent to landlords.

It seems that the rebellion against British rule allowed a certain group of the colonial elite to replace those loyal to England, give some benefits to small landholders, and leave poor white working people and tenant farmers in very much their old situation.

What did the Revolution mean to the Native Americans, the Indians? They had been ignored by the fine words of the Declaration, had not been considered equal, certainly not in choosing those who would govern the American territories in which they lived, nor in being able to pursue happiness as they had pursued it for centuries before the white Europeans arrived. Now, with the British out of the way, the Americans could begin the inexorable process of pushing the Indians off their lands, killing them if they resisted. In short, as Francis Jennings puts it, the white Americans were fighting against British imperial control in the East, and for their own imperialism in the West.

Before the Revolution, the Indians had been subdued by force in Virginia and in New England. Elsewhere, they had worked out modes of coexistence with the colonies. But around 1750, with the colonial population growing fast, the pressure to move westward onto new land set the stage for conflict with the Indians. Land agents from the East began appearing in the Ohio River valley, on the territory of a confederation of tribes called the Covenant Chain, for which the Iroquois were spokesmen. In New York, through intricate swindling, 800,000 acres of Mohawk land were taken, ending the period of Mohawk-New York friendship. Chief Hendrick of the Mohawks is recorded speaking his bitterness to Governor George Clinton and the provincial council of New York in 1753:

> Brother when we came here to relate our Grievances about our Lands, we expected to have something done for us, and we have told you that the Covenant Chain of our Forefathers was like to be broken, and brother you tell us that we shall be redressed at Albany, but we know them so well, we will not trust to them, for they [the Albany merchants] are no people but Devils so ... as soon as we come home we will send up a Belt of Wampum to our Brothers the other 5 Nations to acquaint them the Covenant Chain is broken between you and us. So brother you are not to expect to hear of me any more, and Brother we desire to hear no more of you.

When the British fought the French for North America in the Seven Years' War, the Indians fought on the side of the French. The French were traders but not occupiers of Indian lands, while the British clearly coveted their hunting grounds and living space. Someone reported the conversation of Shingas, chief of the Delaware Indians, with the British General Braddock, who sought his help against the French:

> Shingas asked General Braddock, whether the Indians that were friends to the English might not be permitted to Live and Trade among the English and have Hunting Ground sufficient to Support themselves and Familys. ... On which General Braddock said that No Savage Should Inherit the Land. ... On which Shingas and the other Chiefs answered That if they might not have Liberty to Live on the Land they would not Fight for it. ...

When that war ended in 1763, the French, ignoring their old allies, ceded to the British lands west of the Appalachians. The Indians therefore united to make war on the British western forts; this is called "Pontiac's Conspiracy" by the British, but "a liberation war for independence" in the words used by Francis Jennings. Under orders from British General Jeffrey Amherst, the commander of Fort Pitts gave the attacking Indian chiefs, with whom he was negotiating, blankets from the smallpox hospital. It was a pioneering effort at what is now called biological warfare. An epidemic soon spread among the Indians.

Despite this, and the burning of villages, the British could not destroy the will of the Indians, who continued guerrilla war. A peace was made, with the British agreeing to establish a line at the Appalachians, beyond which settlements would not encroach on Indian territory. This was the Royal Proclamation of 1763, and it angered Americans (the original Virginia charter said its land went westward to the ocean). It helps to explain why most of the Indians fought for England during the Revolution. With their French allies, then their English allies, gone, the Indians faced a new land-coveting nation—alone.

The Americans assumed now that the Indian land was theirs. But the expeditions they sent westward to establish this were overcome—which they recognized in the names they gave these battles: Harmar's Humiliation and St. Clair's Shame. And even when General Anthony Wayne defeated the Indians' western confederation in 1798 at the Battle of Fallen Timbers, he had to recognize their power. In the Treaty of Grenville, it was agreed that in return for certain cessions of land the United States would give up claims to the Indian lands north of the Ohio, east of the Mississippi, and south of the Great Lakes, but that if the Indians decided to sell these lands they would offer them first to the United States.

Jennings, putting the Indian into the center of the American Revolution—after all, it was Indian land that everyone was fighting over—sees the Revolution as a "multiplicity of variously oppressed and exploited peoples who preyed upon each other." With the eastern elite controlling the lands on the seaboard, the poor, seeking land, were forced to go West, there becoming a useful bulwark for the rich because, as Jennings says, "the first target of the Indian's hatchet was the frontiersman's skull."

The situation of black slaves as a result of the American Revolution was more complex. Thousands of blacks fought with the British. Five thousand were with the Revolutionaries, most of them from the North, but there were also free blacks from Virginia and Maryland. The lower South was reluctant to arm blacks. Amid the urgency and chaos of war, thousands took their freedom—leaving on British ships at the end of the war to settle in England, Nova Scotia, the West Indies, or Africa. Many others stayed in America as free blacks, evading their masters.

In the northern states, the combination of blacks in the military, the lack of powerful economic need for slaves, and the rhetoric of Revolution led to the end of slavery—but very slowly. As late as 1810, thirty thousand blacks, one-fourth of the black population of the North, remained slaves. In 1840 there were still a thousand slaves in the North. In the upper South, there were more free Negroes than before, leading to more control legislation. In the lower South, slavery expanded with the growth of rice and cotton plantations.

What the Revolution did was to create space and opportunity for blacks to begin making demands of white society. Sometimes these demands came from the new, small black elites in Baltimore, Philadelphia, Richmond, Savannah, sometimes from articulate and bold slaves. Pointing to the Declaration of Independence, blacks petitioned Congress and the state legislatures to abolish slavery, to give blacks equal rights. In Boston, blacks asked for city money, which whites were getting, to educate their children. In Norfolk, they asked to be allowed to testify in court. Nashville blacks asserted that free Negroes "ought to have the same opportunities of doing well that any Person ... would have." Peter Mathews, a free Negro butcher in Charleston, joined other free black artisans and tradesmen in petitioning the legislature to repeal discriminatory laws against blacks. In 1780, seven blades in Dartmouth, Massachusetts, petitioned the legislature for the right to vote, linking taxation to representation:

> ... we apprehend ourselves to be Aggreeved, in that while we are not allowed the Privilage of freemen of the State having no vote or Influence in the Election of those that Tax us yet many of our Colour (as is well known) have cheerfully Entered the field of Battle in the defense of the Common Cause and that (as we conceive) against a similar Exertion of Power (in Regard to taxation) too well known to need a recital in this place. ...

A black man, Benjamin Banneker, who taught himself mathematics and astronomy, predicted accurately a solar eclipse, and was appointed to plan the new city of Washington, wrote to Thomas Jefferson:

> I suppose it is a truth too well attested to you, to need a proof here, that we are a race of beings, who have long labored under the abuse and censure of the world; that we have long been looked upon with an eye of contempt; and that we have long been considered rather as brutish than human, and scarcely capable of mental endowments. ... I apprehend you will embrace every opportunity to eradicate that train of absurd and false ideas and opinions, which so generally prevails with respect to us; and that your sentiments are concurrent with mine, which are, that one universal Father hath given being to us all; and that he hath not only made us all of one flesh, but that he hath also, without partiality, afforded us all the same sensations and endowed us all with the same facilities. ...

Banneker asked Jefferson "to wean yourselves from those narrow prejudices which you have imbibed."

Jefferson tried his best, as an enlightened, thoughtful individual might. But the structure of American society, the power of the cotton plantation, the slave trade, the politics of unity between northern and southern elites, and the long culture of race prejudice in the colonies, as well as his own weaknesses—that combination of practical need and ideological fixation—kept Jefferson a slaveowner throughout his life.

The inferior position of blacks, the exclusion of Indians from the new society, the establishment of supremacy for the rich and powerful in the new nation—all this was already settled in the colonies by the time of the Revolution. With the English out of the way, it could now be put on paper, solidified, regularized, made legitimate, by the Constitution of the United States, drafted at a convention of Revolutionary leaders in Philadelphia.

To many Americans over the years, the Constitution drawn up in 1787 has seemed a work of genius put together by wise, humane men who created a legal framework for democracy and equality. This view is stated, a bit extravagantly, by the historian George Bancroft, writing in the early nineteenth century:

> The Constitution establishes nothing that interferes with equality and individuality. It knows nothing of differences by descent, or opinions, of favored classes, or legalized religion, or the political power of property. It leaves the individual alongside of the individual. ... As the sea is made up of drops, American society is composed of separate, free, and constantly moving atoms, ever in reciprocal action ... so that the institutions and laws of the country rise out of the masses of individual thought which, like the waters of the ocean, are rolling evermore.

Another view of the Constitution was put forward early in the twentieth century by the historian Charles Beard (arousing anger and indignation, including a denunciatory editorial in the *New York Times*). He wrote in his book *An Economic Interpretation of the Constitution:*

> Inasmuch as the primary object of a government, beyond the mere repression of physical violence, is the making of the rules which determine the property relations of members of society, the dominant classes whose rights are thus to be determined must perforce obtain from the government such rules as are consonant with the larger interests necessary to the continuance of their economic processes, or they must themselves control the organs of government.

In short, Beard said, the rich must, in their own interest, either control the government directly or control the laws by which government operates.

Beard applied this general idea to the Constitution, by studying the economic backgrounds and political ideas of the fifty-five men who gathered in Philadelphia in 1787 to draw up the Constitution. He found that a majority of them were lawyers by profession, that most of them were men of wealth, in land, slaves, manufacturing, or shipping, that half of them had money loaned out at interest, and that forty of the fifty-five held government bonds, according to the records of the Treasury Department.

Thus, Beard found that most of the makers of the Constitution had some direct economic interest in establishing a strong federal government: the manufacturers needed protective tariffs; the moneylenders wanted to stop the use of paper money to pay off debts; the land speculators wanted protection as they invaded Indian lands; slaveowners needed federal security against slave revolts and runaways; bondholders wanted a government able to raise money by nationwide taxation, to pay off those bonds.

Four groups, Beard noted, were not represented in the Constitutional Convention: slaves, indentured servants, women, men without property. And so the Constitution did not reflect the interests of those groups.

He wanted to make it clear that he did not think the Constitution was written merely to benefit the Founding Fathers personally, although one could not ignore the $150,000 fortune of Benjamin Franklin, the connections of Alexander Hamilton to wealthy interests through his father-in-law and brother-in-law, the great slave plantations of James Madison, the enormous landholdings of George Washington. Rather, it was to benefit the groups the Founders represented, the "economic interests they understood and felt in concrete, definite form through their own personal experience."

Not everyone at the Philadelphia Convention fitted Beard's scheme. Elbridge Gerry of Massachusetts was a holder of landed property, and yet he opposed the ratification of the Constitution. Similarly, Luther Martin of Maryland, whose ancestors had obtained large tracts of land in New Jersey, opposed ratification. But, with a few exceptions, Beard found a strong connection between wealth and support of the Constitution.

By 1787 there was not only a positive need for strong central government to protect the large economic interests, but also immediate fear of rebellion by discontented farmers. The chief event causing this fear was an uprising in the summer of 1786 in western Massachusetts, known as Shays' Rebellion.

In the western towns of Massachusetts there was resentment against the legislature in Boston. The new Constitution of 1780 had raised the property qualifications for voting. No one could hold state office without being quite wealthy. Furthermore, the legislature was refusing to issue paper money, as had been done in some other states, like Rhode Island, to make it easier for debt-ridden farmers to pay off their creditors.

Illegal conventions began to assemble in some of the western counties to organize opposition to the legislature. At one of these, a man named Plough Jogger spoke his mind:

> I have been greatly abused, have been obliged to do more than my part in the war; been loaded with class rates, town rates, province rates, Continental rates and all rates … been pulled and hauled by sheriffs, constables and collectors, and had my cattle sold for less than they were worth. …
>
> … The great men are going to get all we have and I think it is time for us to rise and put a stop to it, and have no more courts, nor sheriffs, nor collectors nor lawyers. …

The chairman of that meeting used his gavel to cut short the applause. He and others wanted to redress their grievances, but peacefully, by petition to the General Court (the legislature) in Boston.

However, before the scheduled meeting of the General Court, there were going to be court proceedings in Hampshire County, in the towns of Northampton and Springfield, to seize the cattle of farmers who hadn't paid their debts, to take away their land, now full of grain and ready for harvest. And so, veterans of the Continental army, also aggrieved because they had been treated poorly on discharge—given certificates for future redemption instead of immediate cash—began to organize the farmers into squads and companies. One of these veterans was Luke Day, who arrived the morning of court with a fife-and-drum corps, still angry with the memory of being locked up in debtors' prison in the heat of the previous summer.

The sheriff looked to the local militia to defend the court against these armed farmers. But most of the militia was with Luke Day. The sheriff did manage to gather five hundred men, and the judges put on their black silk robes, waiting for the sheriff to protect their trip to the courthouse. But there at the courthouse steps, Luke Day stood with a petition, asserting the people's constitutional right to protest the unconstitutional acts of the General Court, asking the judges to adjourn until the General Court could act on behalf of the farmers. Standing with Luke Day were fifteen hundred armed farmers. The judges adjourned.

Shortly after, at courthouses in Worcester and Athol, farmers with guns prevented the courts from meeting to take away their property, and the militia were too sympathetic to the farmers, or too outnumbered, to act. In Concord, a fifty-year-old veteran of two wars, Job Shattuck, led a caravan of carts, wagons, horses, and oxen onto the town green, while a message was sent to the judges:

The voice of the People of this county is such that the court shall not enter this courthouse until such time as the People shall have redress of the grievances they labor under at the present.

A county convention then suggested the judges adjourn, which they did.

At Great Barrington, a militia of a thousand faced a square crowded with armed men and boys. But the militia was split in its opinion. When the chief justice suggested the militia divide, those in favor of the court's sitting to go on the right side of the road, and those against on the left, two hundred of the militia went to the right, eight hundred to the left, and the judges adjourned. Then the crowd went to the home of the chief justice, who agreed to sign a pledge that the court would not sit until the Massachusetts General Court met. The crowd went back to the square, broke open the county jail, and set free the debtors. The chief justice, a country doctor, said: "I have never heard anybody point out a better way to have their grievances redressed than the people have taken."

The governor and the political leaders of Massachusetts became alarmed. Samuel Adams, once looked on as a radical leader in Boston, now insisted people act within the law. He said "British emissaries" were stirring up the farmers. People in the town of Greenwich responded: You in Boston have the money, and we don't. And didn't you act illegally yourselves in the Revolution? The insurgents were now being called Regulators. Their emblem was a sprig of hemlock.

The problem went beyond Massachusetts. In Rhode Island, the debtors had taken over the legislature and were issuing paper money. In New Hampshire, several hundred men, in September of 1786, surrounded the legislature in Exeter, asking that taxes be returned and paper money issued; they dispersed only when military action was threatened.

Daniel Shays entered the scene in western Massachusetts. A poor farm hand when the revolution broke out, he joined the Continental army, fought at Lexington, Bunker Hill, and Saratoga, and was wounded in action. In 1780, not being paid, he resigned from the army, went home, and soon found himself in court for nonpayment of debts. He also saw what was happening to others: a sick woman, unable to pay, had her bed taken from under her.

What brought Shays fully into the situation was that on September 19, the Supreme Judicial Court of Massachusetts met in Worcester and indicted eleven leaders of the rebellion, including three of his friends, as "disorderly, riotous and seditious persons" who "unlawfully and by force of arms" prevented "the execution of justice and the laws of the commonwealth." The Supreme Judicial Court planned to meet again in Springfield a week later, and there was talk of Luke Day's being indicted.

Shays organized seven hundred armed farmers, most of them veterans of the war, and led them to Springfield. There they found a general with nine hundred soldiers and a cannon. Shays asked the general for permission to parade, which the general granted, so Shays and his men moved through the square, drums banging and fifes blowing. As they marched, their ranks grew. Some of the militia joined, and reinforcements began coming in from the countryside. The judges postponed hearings for a day, then adjourned the court.

Now the General Court, meeting in Boston, was told by Governor James Bowdoin to "vindicate the insulted dignity of government." The recent rebels against England, secure in office, were calling for law and order. Sam Adams helped draw up a Riot Act, and a resolution suspending habeas corpus, to allow the authorities to keep people in jail without trial. At the same time, the legislature moved to make some concessions to the angry farmers, saying certain old taxes could now be paid in goods instead of money.

This didn't help. In Worcester, 160 insurgents appeared at the courthouse. The sheriff read the Riot Act. The insurgents said they would disperse only if the judges did. The sheriff shouted something about hanging. Someone came up behind him and put a sprig of hemlock in his hat. The judges left.

Confrontations between farmers and militia now multiplied. The winter snows began to interfere with the trips of farmers to the courthouses. When Shays began marching a thousand men into Boston, a blizzard forced them back, and one of his men froze to death.

An army came into the field, led by General Benjamin Lincoln, on money raised by Boston merchants. In an artillery duel, three rebels were killed. One soldier stepped in front of his own artillery piece and lost both arms. The winter grew worse. The rebels were outnumbered and on the run. Shays took refuge in Vermont, and his followers began to surrender. There were a few more deaths in battle, and then sporadic, disorganized, desperate acts of violence against authority: the burning of barns, the slaughter of a general's horses. One government soldier was killed in an eerie night-time collision of two sleighs.

Captured rebels were put on trial in Northampton and six were sentenced to death. A note was left at the door of the high sheriff of Pittsfield:

> I understand that there is a number of my countrymen condemned to die because they fought for justice. I pray have a care that you assist not in the execution of so horrid a crime, for by all that is above, he that condemns and he that executes shall share alike. ... Prepare for death with speed, for your life or mine is short. When the woods are covered with leaves, I shall return and pay you a short visit.

Thirty-three more rebels were put on trial and six more condemned to death. Arguments took place over whether the hangings should go forward. General Lincoln urged mercy and a Commission of Clemency, but Samuel Adams said: "In monarchy the crime of treason may admit of being pardoned or lightly punished, but the man who dares rebel against the laws of a republic ought to suffer death." Several hangings followed; some of the condemned were pardoned. Shays, in Vermont, was pardoned in 1788 and returned to Massachusetts, where he died, poor and obscure, in 1825.

It was Thomas Jefferson, in France as ambassador at the time of Shays' Rebellion, who spoke of such uprisings as healthy for society. In a letter to a friend he wrote: "I hold it that a little rebellion now and then is a good thing. ... It is a medicine necessary for the sound health of government. ... God forbid that we should ever be twenty years without such a rebellion. ... The tree of liberty must be refreshed from time to time with the blood of patriots and tyrants. It is its natural manure."

But Jefferson was far from the scene. The political and economic elite of the country were not so tolerant. They worried that the example might spread. A veteran of Washington's army, General Henry Knox, founded an organization of army veterans, "The Order of the Cincinnati," presumably (as one historian put it) "for the purpose of cherishing the heroic memories of the struggle in which they had taken part," but also, it seemed, to watch out for radicalism in the new country. Knox wrote to Washington in late 1786 about Shays' Rebellion, and in doing so expressed the thoughts of many of the wealthy and powerful leaders of the country:

> The people who are the insurgents have never paid any, or but very little taxes. But they see the weakness of government; they feel at once their own poverty, compared with the opulent, and their own force, and they are determined to make use of the latter, in order to remedy the former. Their creed is "That the property of the United States has been protected from the confiscations of Britain by the joint exertions of all, and therefore ought to be the common property of all. And he that attempts opposition to this creed is an enemy to equity and justice and ought to be swept from off the face of the earth."

Alexander Hamilton, aide to Washington during the war, was one of the most forceful and astute leaders of the new aristocracy. He voiced his political philosophy:

> All communities divide themselves into the few and the many. The first are the rich and well-born, the other the mass of the people. The voice of the people has been said to be the voice of God; and however generally this maxim has been quoted and believed, it is not true in fact. The people are turbulent and changing; they seldom judge or determine right. Give therefore to the first class a distinct permanent share in the government. ... Can a democratic assembly who annually revolve in the mass of the people be supposed steadily to pursue the public good?
> Nothing but a permanent body can check the imprudence of democracy. ...

At the Constitutional Convention, Hamilton suggested a President and Senate chosen for life.

The Convention did not take his suggestion. But neither did it provide for popular elections, except in the case of the House of Representatives, where the qualifications were set by the state legislatures (which required property-holding for voting in almost all the states), and excluded women, Indians, slaves. The Constitution provided for Senators to be elected by the state legislators, for the President to be elected by electors chosen by the state legislators, and for the Supreme Court to be appointed by the President.

The problem of democracy in the post-Revolutionary society was not, however, the Constitutional limitations on voting. It lay deeper, beyond the Constitution, in the division of society into rich and poor.

For if some people had great wealth and great influence; if they had the land, the money, the newspapers, the church, the educational system—how could voting, however broad, cut into such power? There was still another problem: wasn't it the nature of representative government, even when most broadly based, to be conservative, to prevent tumultuous change?

It came time to ratify the Constitution, to submit to a vote in state conventions, with approval of nine of the thirteen required to ratify it. In New York, where debate over ratification was intense, a series of newspaper articles appeared, anonymously, and they tell us much about the nature of the Constitution. These articles, favoring adoption of the Constitution, were written by James Madison, Alexander Hamilton, and John Jay, and came to be known as the *Federalist Papers* (opponents of the Constitution became known as anti-Federalists).

In *Federalist Paper # 10,* James Madison argued that representative government was needed to maintain peace in a society ridden by factional disputes. These disputes came from "the various and unequal distribution of property. Those who hold and those who are without property have ever formed distinct interests in society." The problem, he said, was how to control the factional struggles that came from inequalities in wealth. Minority factions could be controlled, he said, by the principle that decisions would be by vote of the majority.

So the real problem, according to Madison, was a majority faction, and here the solution was offered by the Constitution, to have "an extensive republic," that is, a large nation ranging over thirteen states, for then "it will be more difficult for all who feel it to discover their own strength, and to act in unison with each other. ... The influence of factious leaders may kindle a flame within their particular States, but will be unable to spread a general conflagration through the other States."

Madison's argument can be seen as a sensible argument for having a government which can maintain peace and avoid continuous disorder. But is it the aim of government simply to maintain order, as a referee, between two equally matched fighters? Or is it that government has some special interest in maintaining a certain land of order, a certain distribution of power and wealth, a distribution in which government officials are not neutral referees but participants? In that case, the disorder they might worry about is the disorder of popular rebellion against those monopolizing the society's wealth. This interpretation makes sense when one looks at the economic interests, the social backgrounds, of the makers of the Constitution.

As part of his argument for a large republic to keep the peace, James Madison tells quite clearly, in *Federalist #10,* whose peace he wants to keep: "A rage for paper money, for an abolition of debts, for an equal division of property, or for any other improper or wicked project, will be less apt to pervade the whole body of the Union than a particular member of it."

When economic interest is seen behind the political clauses of the Constitution, then the document becomes not simply the work of wise men trying to establish a decent and orderly society, but the work of certain groups trying to maintain their privileges, while giving just enough rights and liberties to enough of the people to ensure popular support.

In the new government, Madison would belong to one party (the Democrat-Republicans) along with Jefferson and Monroe. Hamilton would belong to the rival party (the Federalists) along with Washington and Adams. But both agreed—one a slaveholder from Virginia, the other a merchant from New York—on the aims of this new government they were establishing. They were anticipating the long-fundamental agreement of the two political parties in the American system. Hamilton wrote elsewhere in the *Federalist Papers* that the new Union would be able "to repress domestic faction and insurrection." He referred directly to Shays' Rebellion: "The tempestuous situation from which Massachusetts has scarcely emerged evinces that dangers of this kind are not merely speculative."

It was either Madison or Hamilton (the authorship of the individual papers is not always known) who in *Federalist Paper #63* argued the necessity of a "well-constructed Senate" as "sometimes necessary as a defence to the people against their own temporary errors and delusions" because "there are particular moments in public affairs when the people, stimulated by some irregular passion, or some illicit advantage, or misled by the artful misrepresentations of interested men, may call for measures which they themselves will afterwards be the most ready to lament and condemn." And: "In these critical moments, how salutary will be the interference of some temperate and respectable body of citizens in order to check the misguided career, and to suspend the blow meditated by the people against themselves, until reason, justice, and truth can regain their authority over the public mind?"

The Constitution was a compromise between slaveholding interests of the South and moneyed interests of the North. For the purpose of uniting the thirteen states into one great market for commerce, the northern delegates wanted laws regulating interstate commerce, and urged that such laws require only a majority of Congress to pass. The South agreed to this, in return for allowing the trade in slaves to continue for twenty years before being outlawed.

Charles Beard warned us that governments—including the government of the United States—are not neutral, that they represent the dominant economic interests, and that their constitutions are intended to serve these interests. One of his critics (Robert E. Brown, *Charles Beard and the Constitution*) raises an interesting point. Granted that the Constitution omitted the phrase "life, liberty and the pursuit of happiness," which appeared in the Declaration of Independence, and substituted "life, liberty, or property"—well, why shouldn't the Constitution protect property? As Brown says about Revolutionary America, "practically everybody was interested in the protection of property" because so many Americans owned property.

However, this is misleading. True, there were many property owners. But some people had much more than others. A few people had great amounts of property; many people had small amounts; others had none. Jackson Main found that one-third of the population in the Revolutionary period were small farmers, while only 3 percent of the population had truly large holdings and could be considered wealthy.

Still, one-third was a considerable number of people who felt they had something at stake in the stability of a new government. This was a larger base of support for government than anywhere in the world at the end of the eighteenth century. In addition, the city mechanics had an important interest in a government which would protect their work from foreign competition. As Staughton Lynd puts it: "How is it that the city workingmen all over America overwhelmingly and enthusiastically supported the United States Constitution?"

This was especially true in New York. When the ninth and tenth states had ratified the Constitution, four thousand New York City mechanics marched with floats and banners to celebrate. Bakers, blacksmiths, brewers, ship joiners and shipwrights, coopers, cartmen and tailors, all marched. What Lynd found was that these mechanics, while opposing elite rule in the colonies, were nationalist. Mechanics comprised perhaps half the New York population. Some were wealthy, some were poor, but all were better off than the ordinary laborer, the apprentice, the journeyman, and their prosperity required a government that would protect them against the British hats and shoes and other goods that were pouring into the colonies after the Revolution. As a result, the mechanics often supported wealthy conservatives at the ballot box.

The Constitution, then, illustrates the complexity of the American system: that it serves the interests of a wealthy elite, but also does enough for small property owners, for middle-income mechanics and farmers, to build a broad base of support. The slightly prosperous people who make up this base of support are buffers against the blacks, the Indians, the very poor whites. They enable the elite to keep control with a minimum of coercion, a maximum of law—all made palatable by the fanfare of patriotism and unity.

The Constitution became even more acceptable to the public at large after the first Congress, responding to criticism, passed a series of amendments known as the Bill of Rights. These amendments seemed to make the new government a guardian of people's liberties: to speak, to publish, to worship, to petition, to assemble, to be tried fairly, to be secure at home against official intrusion. It was, therefore, perfectly designed to build popular backing for the new government. What was not made clear—it was a time when the language of freedom was new and its reality untested—was the shakiness of anyone's liberty when entrusted to a government of the rich and powerful.

Indeed, the same problem existed for the other provisions of the Constitution, like the clause forbidding states to "impair the obligation of contract," or that giving Congress the power to tax the people and to appropriate money. They all sound benign and neutral until one asks: Tax who, for what? Appropriate what, for whom? To protect everyone's contracts seems like an act of fairness, of equal treatment, until one considers that contracts made between rich and poor, between employer and employee, landlord and tenant, creditor and debtor, generally favor the more powerful of the two parties. Thus, to protect these contracts is to put the great power of the government, its laws, courts, sheriffs, police, on the side of the privileged—and to do it not, as in premodern times, as an exercise of brute force against the weak but as a matter of law.

The First Amendment of the Bill of Rights shows that quality of interest hiding behind innocence. Passed in 1791 by Congress, it provided that "Congress shall make no law … abridging the freedom of speech, or of the press. …" Yet, seven years after the First Amendment became part of the Constitution, Congress passed a law very clearly abridging the freedom of speech.

This was the Sedition Act of 1798, passed under John Adams's administration, at a time when Irishmen and Frenchmen in the United States were looked on as dangerous revolutionaries because of the recent French Revolution and the Irish rebellions. The Sedition Act made it a crime to say or write anything "false, scandalous and malicious" against the government, Congress, or the President, with intent to defame them, bring them into disrepute, or excite popular hatreds against them.

This act seemed to directly violate the First Amendment. Yet, it was enforced. Ten Americans were put in prison for utterances against the government, and every member of the Supreme Court in 1798–1800, sitting as an appellate judge, held it constitutional.

There was a legal basis for this, one known to legal experts, but not to the ordinary American, who would read the First Amendment and feel confident that he or she was protected in the exercise of free speech. That basis has been explained by historian Leonard Levy. Levy points out that it was generally understood (not in the population, but in higher circles) that, despite the First Amendment, the British common law of "seditious libel" still ruled in America. This meant that while the government could not exercise "prior restraint"—that is, prevent an utterance or publication in advance—it could legally punish the speaker or writer afterward. Thus, Congress has a convenient legal basis for the laws it has enacted since that time, making certain kinds of speech a crime. And, since punishment after the fact is an excellent deterrent to the exercise of free expression, the claim of "no prior restraint" itself is destroyed. This leaves the First Amendment much less than the stone wall of protection it seems at first glance.

Are the economic provisions in the Constitution enforced just as weakly? We have an instructive example almost immediately in Washington's first administration, when Congress's power to tax and appropriate money was immediately put to use by the Secretary of the Treasury, Alexander Hamilton.

Hamilton, believing that government must ally itself with the richest elements of society to make itself strong, proposed to Congress a series of laws, which it enacted, expressing this philosophy. A Bank of the United States was set up as a partnership between the government and certain banking interests. A tariff was passed to help the manufacturers. It was agreed to pay bondholders—most of the war bonds were now concentrated in a small group of wealthy people'—the full value of their bonds. Tax laws were passed to raise money for this bond redemption.

One of these tax laws was the Whiskey Tax, which especially hurt small farmers who raised grain that they converted into whiskey and then sold. In 1794 the farmers of western Pennsylvania took up arms and rebelled against the collection of this tax. Secretary of the Treasury Hamilton led the troops to put them down. We see then, in the first years of the Constitution, that some of its provisions—even those paraded most flamboyantly (like the First Amendment)—might be treated lightly. Others (like the power to tax) would be powerfully enforced.

Still, the mythology around the Founding Fathers persists. To say, as one historian (Bernard Bailyn) has done recently, that "the destruction of privilege and the creation of a political system that demanded of its leaders the responsible and humane use of power were their highest aspirations" is to ignore what really happened in the America of these Founding Fathers.

Bailyn says:

Everyone knew the basic prescription for a wise and just government. It was so to balance the contending powers in society that no one power could overwhelm the others and, unchecked, destroy the liberties that belonged to all. The problem was how to arrange the institutions of government so that this balance could be achieved.

Were the Founding Fathers wise and just men trying to achieve a good balance? In fact, they did not want a balance, except one which kept things as they were, a balance among the dominant forces at that time. They certainly did not want an equal balance between slaves and masters, propertyless and property holders, Indians and white.

As many as half the people were not even considered by the Founding Fathers as among Bailyn's "contending powers" in society. They were not mentioned in the Declaration of independence, they were absent in the Constitution, they were invisible in the new political democracy. They were the women of early America.

AS LONG AS GRASS GROWS OR WATER RUNS

HOWARD ZINN

I f women, of all the subordinate groups in a society dominated by rich white males, were closest to home (indeed, *in* the home), the most interior, then the Indians were the most foreign, the most exterior. Women, because they were so near and so needed, were dealt with more by patronization than by force. The Indian, not needed—indeed, an obstacle—could be dealt with by sheer force, except that sometimes the language of paternalism preceded the burning of villages.

And so, Indian Removal, as it has been politely called, cleared the land for white occupancy between the Appalachians and the Mississippi, cleared it for cotton in the South and grain in the North, for expansion, immigration, canals, railroads, new cities, and the building of a huge continental empire clear across to the Pacific Ocean. The cost in human life cannot be accurately measured, in suffering not even roughly measured. Most of the history books given to children pass quickly over it.

Statistics tell the story. We find these in Michael Rogin's *Fathers and Children:* In 1790, there were 3,900,000 Americans, and most of them lived within 50 miles of the Atlantic Ocean. By 1830, there were 13 million Americans, and by 1840, 4,500,000 had crossed the Appalachian Mountains into the Mississippi Valley—that huge expanse of land crisscrossed by rivers flowing into the Mississippi from east and west. In 1820, 120,000 Indians lived east of the Mississippi. By 1844, fewer than 30,000 were left. Most of them had been forced to migrate westward. But the word "force" cannot convey what happened.

In the Revolutionary War, almost every important Indian nation fought on the side of the British. The British signed for peace and went home; the Indians were already home, and so they continued fighting the Americans on the frontier, in a set of desperate holding operations. Washington's war-enfeebled militia could not drive them back. After scouting forces were demolished one after the other, he tried to follow a policy of conciliation. His Secretary of War, Henry Knox, said: "The Indians being the prior occupants, possess the right of the soil." His Secretary of State, Thomas Jefferson, said in 1791 that where Indians lived within state boundaries they should not be interfered with, and that the government should remove white settlers who tried to encroach on them.

But as whites continued to move westward, the pressure on the national government increased. By the time Jefferson became President, in 1800, there were 700,000 white settlers west of the mountains. They moved into Ohio, Indiana, Illinois, in the North; into Alabama and Mississippi in the South. These whites outnumbered the Indians about eight to one. Jefferson now committed the federal government to promote future removal of the Creek and the Cherokee from Georgia. Aggressive activity against the Indians mounted in the Indiana Territory under Governor William Henry Harrison.

When Jefferson doubled the size of the nation by purchasing the Louisiana Territory from France in 1803—thus extending the western frontier from the Appalachians across the Mississippi to the Rocky Mountains—he thought the Indians could move there. He proposed to Congress that Indians should be encouraged to settle down on smaller tracts and do farming; also, they should be encouraged to trade with whites, to incur debts, and then to pay off these debts with tracts of land. "... Two measures are deemed expedient. First to encourage them to abandon hunting. ... Secondly, To Multiply trading houses among them ... leading them thus to agriculture, to manufactures, and civilization. ..."

Jefferson's talk of "agriculture ... manufactures ... civilization" is crucial. Indian removal was necessary for the opening of the vast American lands to agriculture, to commerce, to markets, to money, to the development of the modern capitalist economy. Land was indispensable for all this, and after the Revolution, huge sections of land were bought up by rich speculators, including George Washington and Patrick Henry. In North Carolina, rich tracts of land belonging to the Chickasaw Indians were put on sale, although the Chickasaws were among the few Indian tribes fighting on the side of the Revolution, and a treaty had been signed with them guaranteeing their land. John Donelson, a state surveyor, ended up with 20,000 acres of land near what is now Chattanooga. His son-in-law made twenty-two trips out of Nashville in 1795 for land deals. This was Andrew Jackson.

Jackson was a land speculator, merchant, slave trader, and the most aggressive enemy of the Indians in early American history. He became a hero of the War of 1812, which was not (as usually depicted in American textbooks) just a war against England for survival, but a war for the expansion of the new nation, into Florida, into Canada, into Indian territory.

Tecumseh, a Shawnee chief and noted orator, tried to unite the Indians against the white invasion:

The way, and the only way, to check and to stop this evil, is for all the Redmen to unite in claiming a common and equal right in the land, as it was at first and should be yet; for it was never divided, but belongs to all for the use of each. That no part has a right to sell, even to each other, much less to strangers—those who want all and will not do with less.

Angered when fellow Indians were induced to cede a great tract of land to the United States government, Tecumseh organized in 1811 an Indian gathering of five thousand, on the bank of the Tallapoosa River in Alabama, and told them: "Let the white race perish. They seize your land; they corrupt your women, they trample on the ashes of your dead! Back whence they came, upon a trail of blood, they must be driven."

The Creeks, who occupied most of Georgia, Alabama, and Mississippi, were divided among themselves. Some were willing to adopt the civilization of the white man in order to live in peace. Others, insisting on their land and their culture, were called "Red Sticks." The Red Sticks in 1813 massacred 250 people at Fort Miras, whereupon Jackson's troops burned down a Creek village, killing men, women, children. Jackson established the tactic of promising rewards in land and plunder: "… if either party, cherokees, friendly creeks, or whites, takes property of the Red Sticks, the property belongs to those who take it."

Not all his enlisted men were enthusiastic for the fighting. There were mutinies; the men were hungry, their enlistment terms were up, they were tired of fighting and wanted to go home. Jackson wrote to his wife about "the once brave and patriotic volunteers … sunk … to mere whining, complaining, seditioners and mutineers. …" When a seventeen-year-old soldier who had refused to clean up his food, and threatened his officer with a gun, was sentenced to death by a court-martial, Jackson turned down a plea for commutation of sentence and ordered the execution to proceed. He then walked out of earshot of the firing squad.

Jackson became a national hero when in 1814 he fought the Battle of Horseshoe Bend against a thousand Creeks and killed eight hundred of them, with few casualties on his side. His white troops had failed in a frontal attack on the Creeks, but the Cherokees with him, promised governmental friendship if they joined the war, swam the river, came up behind the Creeks, and won the battle for Jackson.

When the war ended, Jackson and friends of his began buying up the seized Creek lands. He got himself appointed treaty commissioner and dictated a treaty which took away half the land of the Creek nation. Rogin says it was "the largest single Indian cession of southern American land." It took land from Creeks who had fought with Jackson as well as those who had fought against him, and when Big Warrior, a chief of the friendly Creeks, protested, Jackson said:

Listen…. The United States would have been justified by the Great Spirit, had they taken all the land of the nation. … Listen—the truth is, the great body of the Creek chiefs and warriors did not respect the power of the United States—They thought we were an insignificant nation—that we would be overpowered by the British. … They were fat with eating beef—they wanted flogging. … We bleed our enemies in such cases to give them their senses.

As Rogin puts it: "Jackson had conquered 'the cream of the Creek country,' and it would guarantee southwestern prosperity. He had supplied the expanding cotton kingdom with a vast and valuable acreage."

Jackson's 1814 treaty with the Creeks started something new and important. It granted Indians individual ownership of land, thus splitting Indian from Indian, breaking up communal landholding, bribing some with land, leaving others out—introducing the competition and conniving that marked the spirit of Western capitalism. It fitted well the old Jeffersonian idea of how to handle the Indians, by bringing them into "civilization."

From 1814 to 1824, in a series of treaties with the southern Indians, whites took over three-fourths of Alabama and Florida, one-third of Tennessee, one-fifth of Georgia and Mississippi, and parts of Kentucky and North Carolina. Jackson played a key role in those treaties, and, according to Rogin, "His friends and relatives received many of the patronage appointments—as Indian agents, traders, treaty commissioners, surveyors and land agents. ..."

Jackson himself described how the treaties were obtained: "... we addressed ourselves feelingly to the predominant and governing passion of all Indian tribes, i.e., their avarice or fear." He encouraged white squatters to move into Indian lands, then told the Indians the government could not remove the whites and so they had better cede the lands or be wiped out. He also, Rogin says, "practiced extensive bribery."

These treaties, these land grabs, laid the basis for the cotton kingdom, the slave plantations. Every time a treaty was signed, pushing the Creeks from one area to the next, promising them security there, whites would move into the new area and the Creeks would feel compelled to sign another treaty, giving up more land in return for security elsewhere.

Jackson's work had brought the white settlements to the border of Florida, owned by Spain. Here were the villages of the Seminole Indians, joined by some Red Stick refugees, and encouraged by British agents in their resistance to the Americans. Settlers moved into Indian lands. Indians attacked. Atrocities took place on both sides. When certain villages refused to surrender people accused of murdering whites, Jackson ordered the villages destroyed.

Another Seminole provocation: escaped black slaves took refuge in Seminole villages. Some Seminoles bought or captured black slaves, but their form of slavery was more like African slavery than cotton plantation slavery. The slaves often lived in their own villages, their children often became free, there was much intermarriage between Indians and blacks, and soon there were mixed Indian-black villages—all of which aroused southern slaveowners who saw this as a lure to their own slaves seeking freedom.

Jackson began raids into Florida, arguing it was a sanctuary for escaped slaves and for marauding Indians. Florida, he said, was essential to the defense of the United States. It was that classic modern preface to a war of conquest. Thus began the Seminole War of 1818, leading to the American acquisition of Florida. It appears on classroom maps politely as "Florida Purchase, 1819"—but it came from Andrew Jackson's military campaign across the Florida border, burning Seminole villages, seizing Spanish forts, until Spain was "persuaded" to sell. He acted, he said, by the "immutable laws of self-defense."

Jackson then became governor of the Florida Territory. He was able now to give good business advice to friends and relatives. To a nephew, he suggested holding on to property in Pensacola. To a friend, a surgeon-general in the army, he suggested buying as many slaves as possible, because the price would soon rise.

Leaving his military post, he also gave advice to officers on how to deal with the high rate of desertion. (Poor whites—even if willing to give their lives at first—may have discovered the rewards of battle going to the rich.) Jackson suggested whipping for the first two attempts, and the third time, execution.

The leading books on the Jacksonian period, written by respected historians (*The Age of Jackson* by Arthur Schlesinger; *The Jacksonian Persuasion* by Marvin Meyers), do not mention Jackson's Indian policy, but there is much talk in them of tariffs, banking, political parties, political rhetoric. If you look through high school textbooks and elementary school textbooks in American history you will find Jackson the frontiersman, soldier, democrat, man of the people—not Jackson the slaveholder, land speculator, executioner of dissident soldiers, exterminator of Indians.

This is not simply hindsight (the word used for thinking back *differently* on the past). After Jackson was elected President in 1828 (following John Quincy Adams, who had followed Monroe, who had followed Madison, who had followed Jefferson), the Indian Removal bill came before Congress and was called, at the time, "the leading measure" of the Jackson administration and "the greatest question that ever came before Congress" except for matters of peace and war. By this time the two political parties were the Democrats and Whigs, who disagreed on banks and tariffs, but not on issues crucial for the white poor, the blacks, the Indians—although some white working people saw Jackson as their hero, because he opposed the rich man's Bank.

Under Jackson, and the man he chose to succeed him, Martin Van Buren, seventy thousand Indians east of the Mississippi were forced westward. In the North, there weren't that many, and the Iroquois Confederation in New York stayed. But the Sac and Fox Indians of Illinois were removed, after the Black Hawk War (in which Abraham Lincoln was an officer, although he was not in combat). When Chief Black Hawk was defeated and captured in 1832, he made a surrender speech:

> I fought hard. But your guns were well aimed. The bullets flew like birds in the air, and whizzed by our ears like the wind through the trees in the winter. My warriors fell around me. … The sun rose dim on us in the morning, and at night it sunk in a dark cloud, and looked like a ball of fire. That was the last sun that shone on Black Hawk. … He is now a prisoner to the white men. … He has done nothing for which an Indian ought to be ashamed. He has fought for his countrymen, the squaws and papooses, against white men, who came year after year, to cheat them and take away their lands. You know the cause of our making war. It is known to all white men. They ought to be ashamed of it. Indians are not deceitful. The white men speak bad of the Indian and look at him spitefully. But the Indian does not tell lies. Indians do not steal.
>
> An Indian who is as bad as the white men could not live in our nation; he would be put to death, and eaten up by the wolves. The white men are bad schoolmasters; they carry false books, and deal in false actions; they smile in the face of the poor Indian to cheat him; they shake them by the hand to gain their confidence, to make them drunk, to deceive them, and

ruin our wives. We told them to leave us alone, and keep away from us; they followed on, and beset our paths, and they coiled themselves among us, like the snake. They poisoned us by their touch. We were not safe. We lived in danger. We were becoming like them, hypocrites and liars, adulterous lazy drones, all talkers and no workers. ...

The white men do not scalp the head; but they do worse—they poison' the heart. ... Farewell, my nation! ... Farewell to Black Hawk.

Black Hawk's bitterness may have come in part from the way he was captured. Without enough support to hold out against the white troops, with his men starving, hunted, pursued across the Mississippi, Black Hawk raised the white flag. The American commander later explained: "As we neared them they raised a white flag and endeavored to decoy us, but we were a little too old for them." The soldiers fired, killing women and children as well as warriors. Black Hawk fled; he was pursued and captured by Sioux in the hire of the army. A government agent told the Sac and Fox Indians: "Our Great Father ... will forbear no longer. He has tried to reclaim them, and they grow worse. He is resolved to sweep them from the face of the earth. ... If they cannot be made good they must be killed."

The removal of the Indians was explained by Lewis Cass—Secretary of War, governor of the Michigan territory, minister to France, presidential candidate:

> A principle of progressive improvement seems almost inherent in human nature. ... We are all striving in the career of life to acquire riches of honor, or power, or some other object, whose possession is to realize the day dreams of our imaginations; and the aggregate of these efforts constitutes the advance of society. But there is little of this in the constitution of our savages.

Cass—pompous, pretentious, honored (Harvard gave him an honorary doctor of laws degree in 1836, at the height of Indian removal)—claimed to be an expert on the Indians. But he demonstrated again and again, in Richard Drinnon's words *(Violence in the American Experience: Winning the West),* a "quite marvelous ignorance of Indian life." As governor of the Michigan Territory, Cass took millions of acres from the Indians by treaty: "We must frequently promote their interest against their inclination."

His article in the *North American Review* in 1830 made the case for Indian Removal. We must not regret, he said, "the progress of civilization and improvement, the triumph of industry and art, by which these regions have been reclaimed, and over which freedom, religion, and science are extending their sway." He wished that all this could have been done with "a smaller sacrifice; that the aboriginal population had accommodated themselves to the inevitable change of their condition. ... But such a wish is vain. A barbarous people, depending for subsistence upon the scanty and precarious supplies furnished by the chase, cannot live in contact with a civilized community."

Drinnon comments on this (writing in 1969): "Here were all the necessary grounds for burning villages and uprooting natives, Cherokee and Seminole, and later Cheyenne, Philippine, and Vietnamese."

If the Indians would only move to new lands across the Mississippi, Cass promised in 1825 at a treaty council with Shawnees and Cherokees, "The United States will never ask for your land there. This I promise you in the name of your great father, the President. That country he assigns to his red people, to be held by them and their children's children forever."

The editor of the *North American Review,* for whom Cass wrote this article, told him that his project "only defers the fate of the Indians. In half a century their condition beyond the Mississippi will be just what it is now on this side. Their extinction is inevitable." As Drinnon notes, Cass did not dispute this, yet published his article as it was.

Everything in the Indian heritage spoke out against leaving their land. A council of Creeks, offered money for their land, said: "We would not receive money for land in which our fathers and friends are buried." An old Choctaw chief said, responding, years before, to President Monroe's talk of removal: "I am sorry I cannot comply with the request of my father. … We wish to remain here, where we have grown up as the herbs of the woods; and do not wish to be transplanted into another soil." A Seminole chief had said to John Quincy Adams: "Here our navel strings were first cut and the blood from them sunk into the earth, and made the country dear to us."

Not all the Indians responded to the white officials' common designation of them as "children" and the President as "father." It was reported that when Tecumseh met with William Henry Harrison, Indian fighter and future President, the interpreter said: "Your father requests you to take a chair." Tecumseh replied: "My father! The sun is my father, and the earth is my mother; I will repose upon her bosom."

As soon as Jackson was elected President, Georgia, Alabama, and Mississippi began to pass laws to extend the states' rule over the Indians in their territory. These laws did away with the tribe as a legal unit, outlawed tribal meetings, took away the chiefs' powers, made the Indians subject to militia duty and state taxes, but denied them the right to vote, to bring suits, or to testify in court. Indian territory was divided up, to be distributed by state lottery. Whites were encouraged to settle on Indian land.

However, federal treaties and federal laws gave Congress, not the states, authority over the tribes. The Indian Trade and Intercourse Act, passed by Congress in 1802, said there could be no land cessions except by treaty with a tribe, and said federal law would operate in Indian territory. Jackson ignored this, and supported state action.

It was a neat illustration of the uses of the federal system: depending on the situation, blame could be put on the states, or on something even more elusive, the mysterious Law before which all men, sympathetic as they were to the Indian, must bow. As Secretary of War John Eaton explained to the Creeks of Alabama (Alabama itself was an Indian name, meaning "Here we may rest"): "It is not your Great Father who does this; but the laws of the Country, which he and every one of his people is bound to regard."

The proper tactic had now been found. The Indians would not be "forced" to go West. But if they chose to stay they would have to abide by state laws, which destroyed their tribal and personal rights and made them subject to endless harassment and invasion by white settlers coveting their land. If they left, however, the federal government would give them financial support and promise them lands beyond the

Mississippi. Jackson's instructions to an army major sent to talk to the Choctaws and Cherokees put it this way:

> Say to my red Choctaw children, and my Chickasaw children to listen—my white children of Mississippi have extended their law over their country. ... Where they now are, say to them, their father cannot prevent them from being subject to the laws of the state of Mississippi. ... The general government will be obliged to sustain the States in the exercise of their right. Say to the chiefs and warriors that I am their friend, that I wish to act as their friend but they must, by removing from the limits of the States of Mississippi and Alabama and by being settled on the lands I offer them, put it in my power to be such—There, beyond the limits of any State, in possession of land of their own, which they shall possess as long as Grass grows or water runs. I am and will protect them and be their friend and father.

That phrase "as long as Grass grows or water runs" was to be recalled with bitterness by generations of Indians. (An Indian GI, veteran of Vietnam, testifying publicly in 1970 not only about the horror of the war but about his own maltreatment as an Indian, repeated that phrase and began to weep.)

As Jackson took office in 1829, gold was discovered in Cherokee territory in Georgia. Thousands of whites invaded, destroyed Indian property, staked out claims. Jackson ordered federal troops to remove them, but also ordered Indians as well as whites to stop mining. Then he removed the troops, the whites returned, and Jackson said he could not interfere with Georgia's authority.

The white invaders seized land and stock, forced Indians to sign leases, beat up Indians who protested, sold alcohol to weaken resistance, killed game which Indians needed for food. But to put all the blame on white mobs, Rogin says, would be to ignore "the essential roles played by planter interests and government policy decisions." Food shortages, whiskey, and military attacks began a process of tribal disintegration. Violence by Indians upon other Indians increased.

Treaties made under pressure and by deception broke up Creek, Choctaw, and Chickasaw tribal lands into individual holdings, making each person a prey to contractors, speculators, and politicians. The Chickasaws sold their land individually at good prices and went west without much suffering. The Creeks and Choctaws remained on their individual plots, but great numbers of them were defrauded by land companies. According to one Georgia bank president, a stockholder in a land company, "Stealing is the order of the day."

Indians complained to Washington, and Lewis Cass replied:

> Our citizens were disposed to buy and the Indians to sell. ... The subsequent disposition which shall be made of these payments seems to be utterly beyond the reach of the Government. ... The improvident habits of the Indian cannot be controlled by regulations. ... If they waste it, as waste it they too often will, it is deeply to be regretted yet still it is only exercising a right conferred upon them by the treaty.

The Creeks, defrauded of their land, short of money and food, refused to go West. Starving Creeks began raiding white farms, while Georgia militia and settlers attacked Indian settlements. Thus began the Second Creek War. One Alabama newspaper sympathetic to the Indians wrote: "The war with the Creeks is all humbug. It is a base and diabolical scheme, devised by interested men, to keep an ignorant race of people from maintaining their just rights, and to deprive them of the small remaining pittance placed under their control."

A Creek man more than a hundred years old, named Speckled Snake, reacted to Andrew Jackson's policy of removal:

> Brothers! I have listened to many talks from our great white father. When he first came over the wide waters, he was but a little man … very little. His legs were cramped by sitting long in his big boat, and he begged for a little land to light his fire on. … But when the white man had warmed himself before the Indians' fire and filled himself with their hominy, he became very large. With a step he bestrode the mountains, and his feet covered the plains and the valleys. His hand grasped the eastern and the western sea, and his head rested on the moon. Then he became our Great Father. He loved his red children, and he said, "Get a little further, lest I tread on thee."
>
> Brothers! I have listened to a great many talks from our great father. But they always began and ended in this—"Get a little further; you are too near me."

Dale Van Every, in his book *The Disinherited,* sums up what removal meant to the Indian:

> In the long record of man's inhumanity exile has wrung moans of anguish from many different peoples. Upon no people could it ever have fallen with a more shattering impact than upon the eastern Indians. The Indian was peculiarly susceptible to every sensory attribute of every natural feature of his surroundings. He lived in the open. He knew every marsh, glade, hill top, rock, spring, creek, as only the hunter can know them. He had never fully grasped the principle establishing private ownership of land as any more rational than private ownership of air but he loved the land with a deeper emotion than could any proprietor. He felt himself as much a part of it as the rocks and trees, the animals and birds. His homeland was holy ground, sanctified for him as the resting place of the bones of his ancestors and the natural shrine of his religion. He conceived its waterfalls and ridges, its clouds and mists, its glens and meadows, to be inhabited by the myriad of spirits with whom he held daily communion. It was from this rain-washed land of forests, streams and lakes, to which he was held by the traditions of his forebears and his own spiritual aspirations, that he was to be

driven to the arid, treeless plains of the far west, a desolate region then universally known as the Great American Desert.

According to Van Every, just before Jackson became President, in the 1820s, after the tumult of the War of 1812 and the Creek War, the southern Indians and the whites had settled down, often very close to one another, and were living in peace in a natural environment which seemed to have enough for all of them. They began to see common problems. Friendships developed. White men were allowed to visit the Indian communities and Indians often were guests in white homes. Frontier figures like Davy Crockett and Sam Houston came out of this setting, and both—unlike Jackson—became lifelong friends of the Indian.

The forces that led to removal did not come, Van Every insists, from the poor white frontiersmen who were neighbors of the Indians. They came from industrialization and commerce, the growth of populations, of railroads and cities, the rise in value of land, and the greed of businessmen. "Party managers and land speculators manipulated the growing excitement. … Press and pulpit whipped up the frenzy." Out of that frenzy the Indians were to end up dead or exiled, the land speculators richer, the politicians more powerful. As for the poor white frontiersman, he played the part of a pawn, pushed into the first violent encounters, but soon dispensable.

There had been three voluntary Cherokee migrations westward, into the beautiful wooded country of Arkansas, but there the Indians found themselves almost immediately surrounded and penetrated by white settlers, hunters, trappers. These West Cherokees now had to move farther west, this time to arid land, land too barren for white settlers. The federal government, signing a treaty with them in 1828, announced the new territory as "a permanent home … which shall under the most solemn guarantee of the United States be and remain theirs forever. …" It was still another lie, and the plight of the western Cherokees became known to the three-fourths of the Cherokees who were still in the East, being pressured by the white man to move on.

With 17,000 Cherokees surrounded by 900,000 whites in Georgia, Alabama, and Tennessee, the Cherokees decided that survival required adaptation to the white man's world. They became farmers, blacksmiths, carpenters, masons, owners of property. A census of 1826 showed 22,000 cattle, 7,600 horses, 46,000 swine, 726 looms, 2,488 spinning wheels, 172 wagons, 2,943 plows, 10 saw mills, 31 grist mills, 62 blacksmith shops, 8 cotton machines, 18 schools.

The Cherokees' language—heavily poetic, metaphorical, beautifully expressive, supplemented by dance, drama, and ritual—had always been a language of voice and gesture. Now their chief, Sequoyah, invented a written language, which thousands learned. The Cherokees' newly established Legislative Council voted money for a printing press, which on February 21, 1828, began publishing a newspaper, the *Cherokee Phoenix,* printed in both English and Sequoyah's Cherokee.

Before this, the Cherokees had, like Indian tribes in general, done without formal government. As Van Every puts it:

The foundation principle of Indian government had always been the rejection of government. The freedom of the individual was regarded by practically all Indians north of Mexico as a canon infinitely more precious than the individual's duty to his community or nation. This anarchistic attitude ruled all behavior, beginning with the smallest social unit, the family. The Indian parent was constitutionally reluctant to discipline his children. Their every exhibition of self-will was accepted as a favorable indication of the development of maturing character. ...

There was an occasional assembling of a council, with a very loose and changing membership, whose decisions were not enforced except by the influence of public opinion. A Moravian minister who lived among them described Indian society:

> Thus has been maintained for ages, without convulsions and without civil discords, this traditional government, of which the world, perhaps, does not offer another example; a government in which there are no positive laws, but only long established habits and customs, no code of jurisprudence, but the experience of former times, no magistrates, but advisers, to whom the people nevertheless, pay a willing and implicit obedience, in which age confers rank, wisdom gives power, and moral goodness secures title to universal respect.

Now, surrounded by white society, all this began to change. The Cherokees even started to emulate the slave society around them: they owned more than a thousand slaves. They were beginning to resemble that civilization the white men spoke about, making what Van Every calls "a stupendous effort" to win the good will of Americans. They even welcomed missionaries and Christianity. None of this made them more desirable than the land they lived on.

Jackson's 1829 message to Congress made his position clear: "I informed the Indians inhabiting parts of Georgia and Alabama that their attempt to establish an independent government would not be countenanced by the Executive of the United States, and advised them to emigrate beyond the Mississippi or submit to the laws of those States." Congress moved quickly to pass a removal bill.

There were defenders of the Indians. Perhaps the most eloquent was Senator Theodore Frelinghuysen of New Jersey, who told the Senate, debating removal:

> We have crowded the tribes upon a few miserable acres on our southern frontier; it is all that is left to them of their once boundless forest: and still, like the horse-leech, our insatiated cupidity cries, give! give! ... Sir ... Do the obligations of justice change with the color of the skin?

The North was in general against the removal bill. The South was for it. It passed the House 102 to 97. It passed the Senate narrowly. It did not mention force, but provided for helping the Indians to move. What it implied was that if they did not, they were without protection, without funds, and at the mercy of the states.

Now the pressures began on the tribes, one by one. The Choctaws did not want to leave, but fifty of their delegates were offered secret bribes of money and land, and the Treaty of Dancing Rabbit Creek was signed: Choctaw land east of the Mississippi was ceded to the United States in return for financial help in leaving, compensation for property left behind, food for the first year in their new homes, and a guarantee they would never again be required to move. For twenty thousand Choctaws in Mississippi, though most of them hated the treaty, the pressure now became irresistible. Whites, including liquor dealers and swindlers, came swarming onto their lands. The state passed a law making it a crime for Choctaws to try to persuade one another on the matter of removal.

In late 1831, thirteen thousand Choctaws began the long journey west to a land and climate totally different from what they knew. "Marshaled by guards, hustled by agents, harried by contractors, they were being herded on the way to an unknown and unwelcome destination like a flock of sick sheep." They went on ox wagons, on horses, on foot, then to be ferried across the Mississippi River. The army was supposed to organize their trek, but it turned over its job to private contractors who charged the government as much as possible, gave the Indians as little as possible. Everything was disorganized. Food disappeared. Hunger came. Van Every again:

> The long somber columns of groaning ox wagons, driven herds and straggling crowds on foot inched on westward through swamps and forests, across rivers and over hills, in their crawling struggle from the lush lowlands of the Gulf to the arid plains of the west. In a kind of death spasm one of the last vestiges of the original Indian world was being dismembered and its collapsing remnants jammed bodily into an alien new world.

The first winter migration was one of the coldest on record, and people began to die of pneumonia. In the summer, a major cholera epidemic hit Mississippi, and Choctaws died by the hundreds. The seven thousand Choctaws left behind now refused to go, choosing subjugation over death. Many of their descendants still live in Mississippi.

As for the Cherokees, they faced a set of laws passed by Georgia: their lands were taken, their government abolished, all meetings prohibited. Cherokees advising others not to migrate were to be imprisoned. Cherokees could not testify in court against any white. Cherokees could not dig for the gold recently discovered on their land. A delegation of them, protesting to the federal government, received this reply from Jackson's new Secretary of War, Eaton: "If you will go to the setting sun there you will be happy; there you can remain in peace and quietness; so long as the waters run and the oaks grow that country shall be guaranteed to you and no white man shall be permitted to settle near you."

The Cherokee nation addressed a memorial to the nation, a public plea for justice. They reviewed their history:

> After the peace of 1783, the Cherokees were an independent people, absolutely so, as much as any people on earth. They had been allies to Great Britain. ... The United States never subjugated the Cherokees; on the contrary, our fathers remained in possession of their country and with arms in their hands. ... In 1791, the treaty of Holston was made. ... The Cherokees

acknowledged themselves to be under the protection of the United States, and of no other sovereign. ... A cession of land was also made to the United States. On the other hand, the United States ... stipulated that white men should not hunt on these lands, not even enter the country, without a passport; and gave a solemn guarantee of all Cherokee lands not ceded. ...

They discussed removal:

We are aware that some persons suppose it will be for our advantage to remove beyond the Mississippi. We think otherwise. Our people universally think otherwise. ... We wish to remain on the land of our fathers. We have a perfect and original right to remain without interruption or molestation. The treaties with us, and laws of the United States made in pursuance of treaties, guarantee our residence and our privileges, and secure us against intruders. Our only request is, that these treaties may be fulfilled, and these laws executed. ...

Now they went beyond history, beyond law:

We intreat those to whom the foregoing paragraphs are addressed, to remember the great law of love. "Do to others as ye would that others should do to you." ... We pray them to remember that, for the sake of principle, their forefathers were compelled to leave, therefore driven from the old world, and that the winds of persecution wafted them over the great waters and landed them on the shores of the new world, when the Indian was the sole lord and proprietor of these extensive domains—Let them remember in what way they were received by the savage of America, when power was in his hand, and his ferocity could not be restrained by any human arm. We urge them to bear in mind, that those who would not ask of them a cup of cold water, and a spot of earth ... are the descendants of these, whose origin, as inhabitants of North America, history and tradition are alike insufficient to reveal. Let them bring to remembrance all these facts, and they cannot, and we are sure, they will not fail to remember, and sympathize with us in these our trials and sufferings.

Jackson's response to this, in his second Annual Message to Congress in December 1830, was to point to the fact that the Choctaws and Chickasaws had already agreed to removal, and that "a speedy removal" of the rest would offer many advantages to everyone. For whites it "will place a dense and civilized population in large tracts of country now occupied by a few savage hunters." For Indians, it will "perhaps cause them, gradually, under the protection of the Government and through the influence of good counsels, to cast off their savage habits and become an interesting, civilized, and Christian community."

He reiterated a familiar theme. "Toward the aborigines of the country no one can indulge a more friendly feeling than myself. ..." However: "The waves of population and civilization are rolling to the westward, and we now propose to acquire the countries occupied by the red men of the South and West by a fair exchange. ..."

Georgia passed a law making it a crime for a white person to stay in Indian territory without taking an oath to the state of Georgia. When the white missionaries in the Cherokee territory declared their sympathies openly for the Cherokees to stay, Georgia militia entered the territory in the spring of 1831 and arrested three of the missionaries, including Samuel Worcester. They were released when they claimed protection as federal employees (Worcester was a federal postmaster). Immediately the Jackson administration took away Worcester's job, and the militia moved in again that summer, arresting ten missionaries as well as the white printer of the *Cherokee Phoenix.* They were beaten, chained, and forced to march 35 miles a day to the county jail. A jury tried them, found them guilty. Nine were released when they agreed to swear allegiance to Georgia's laws, but Samuel Worcester and Elizur Butler, who refused to grant legitimacy to the laws repressing the Cherokees, were sentenced to four years at hard labor.

This was appealed to the Supreme Court, and in *Worcester v. Georgia,* John Marshall, for the majority, declared that the Georgia law on which Worcester was jailed violated the treaty with the Cherokees, which by the Constitution was binding on the states. He ordered Worcester freed. Georgia ignored him, and President Jackson refused to enforce the court order.

Georgia now put Cherokee land on sale and moved militia in to crush any sign of Cherokee resistance. The Cherokees followed a policy of nonviolence, though their property was being taken, their homes were being burned, their schools were closed, their women mistreated, and liquor was being sold in their churches to render them even more helpless.

The same year Jackson was declaring states' rights for Georgia on the Cherokee question in 1832, he was attacking South Carolina's right to nullify a federal tariff. His easy reelection in 1832 (687,000 to 530,000 for his opponent Henry Clay) suggested that his anti-Indian policies were in keeping with popular sentiment, at least among those white males who could vote (perhaps 2 million of the total population of 13 million). Jackson now moved to speed up Indian removal. Most of the Choctaws and some of the Cherokees were gone, but there were still 22,000 Creeks in Alabama, 18,000 Cherokees in Georgia, and 5,000 Seminoles in Florida.

The Creeks had been fighting for their land ever since the years of Columbus, against Spaniards, English, French, and Americans. But by 1832 they had been reduced to a small area in Alabama, while the population of Alabama, growing fast, was now over 300,000. On the basis of extravagant promises from the federal government, Creek delegates in Washington signed the Treaty of Washington, agreeing to removal beyond the Mississippi. They gave up 5 million acres, with the provision that 2 million of these would go to individual Creeks, who could either sell or remain in Alabama with federal protection.

Van Every writes of this treaty:

The interminable history of diplomatic relations between Indians and white men had before 1832 recorded no single instance of a treaty which had not been presently broken by the white parties to it ... however solemnly embellished with such terms as "permanent," "forever," "for all time," "so long as the sun shall rise." … But no agreement between white men and Indians had ever been so soon abrogated as the 1832 Treaty of Washington. Within days the promises made in it on behalf of the United States had been broken.

A white invasion of Creek lands began—looters, land seekers, defrauders, whiskey sellers, thugs—driving thousands of Creeks from their homes into the swamps and forests. The federal government did nothing. Instead it negotiated a new treaty providing for prompt emigration west, managed by the Creeks themselves, financed by the national government. An army colonel, dubious that this would work, wrote:

> They fear starvation on the route; and can it be otherwise, when many of them are nearly starving now, without the embarrassment of a long journey on their hands. … You cannot have an idea of the deterioration which these Indians have undergone during the last two or three years, from a general state of comparative plenty to that of unqualified wretchedness and want. The free egress into the nation by the whites; encroachments upon their lands, even upon their cultivated fields; abuses of their person; hosts of traders, who, like locusts, have devoured their substance and inundated their homes with whiskey, have destroyed what little disposition to cultivation the Indians may once have had. … They are brow beat, and cowed, and imposed upon, and depressed with the feeling that they have no adequate protection in the United States, and no capacity of self-protection in themselves.

Northern political sympathizers with the Indian seemed to be fading away, preoccupied with other issues. Daniel Webster was making a rousing speech in the Senate for the "authority of law … the power of the general government," but he was not referring to Alabama, Georgia, and the Indians—he was talking about South Carolina's nullification of the tariff.

Despite the hardships, the Creeks refused to budge, but by 1836, both state and federal officials decided they must go. Using as a pretext some attacks by desperate Creeks on white settlers, it was declared that the Creek nation, by making "war," had forfeited its treaty rights.

The army would now force it to migrate west. Fewer than a hundred Creeks had been involved in the "war," but a thousand had fled into the woods, afraid of white reprisals. An army of eleven thousand was sent after them. The Creeks did not resist, no shots were fired, they surrendered. Those Creeks presumed by the army to be rebels or sympathizers were assembled, the men manacled and chained together to march westward under military guard, their women and children trailing after them. Creek communities were invaded by military detachments, the inhabitants driven to assembly points and marched westward in batches of two or three thousand. No talk of compensating them for land or property left behind.

Private contracts were made for the march, the same kind that had failed for the Choctaws. Again, delays and lack of food, shelter, clothing, blankets, medical attention. Again, old, rotting steamboats and ferries, crowded beyond capacity, taking them across the Mississippi. "By midwinter the interminable, stumbling procession of more than 15,000 Creeks stretched from border to border across Arkansas."

Starvation and sickness began to cause large numbers of deaths. "The passage of the exiles could be distinguished from afar by the howling of trailing wolf packs and the circling flocks of buzzards," Van Every writes.

Eight hundred Creek men had volunteered to help the United States army fight the Seminoles in Florida in return for a promise that their families could remain in Alabama, protected by the federal government until the men returned. The promise was not kept. The Creek families were attacked by land-hungry white marauders—robbed, driven from their homes, women raped. Then the army, claiming it was for their safety, removed them from Creek country to a concentration camp on Mobile Bay. Hundreds died there from lack of food and from sickness.

When the warriors returned from the Seminole War, they and their families were hustled west. Moving through New Orleans, they encountered a yellow fever plague. They crossed the Mississippi—611 Indians crowded onto the aged steamer *Monmouth*. It went down in the Mississippi River and 311 people died, four of them the children of the Indian commander of the Creek volunteers in Florida.

A New Orleans newspaper wrote:

> The fearful responsibility for this vast sacrifice of human life rests on the contractors ... The avaricious disposition to increase the profits on the speculation first induced the chartering of rotten, old, and unseaworthy boats, because they were of a class to be procured cheaply; and then to make those increased profits still larger, the Indians were packed upon those crazy vessels in such crowds that not the slightest regard seems to have been paid to their safety, comfort, or even decency.

The Choctaws and Chickasaws had quickly agreed to migrate. The Creeks were stubborn and had to be forced. The Cherokees were practicing a nonviolent resistance. One tribe—the Seminoles—decided to fight.

With Florida now belonging to the United States, Seminole territory was open to American land-grabbers. They moved down into north Florida from St. Augustine to Pensacola, and down the fertile coastal strip. In 1823, the Treaty of Camp Moultrie was signed by a few Seminoles who got large personal landholdings in north Florida and agreed that all the Seminoles would leave northern Florida and every coastal area and move into the interior. This meant withdrawing into the swamps of central Florida, where they could not grow food, where even wild game could not survive.

The pressure to move west, out of Florida, mounted, and in 1834 Seminole leaders were assembled and the U.S. Indian agent told them they must move west. Here were some of the replies of the Seminoles at that meeting:

We were all made by the same Great Father, and are all alike His Children. We all came from the same Mother, and were suckled at the same breast. Therefore, we are brothers, and as brothers, should treat together in an amicable way.

Your talk is a good one, but my people cannot say they will go. We are not willing to do so. If their tongues say yes, their hearts cry no, and call them liars.

If suddenly we tear our hearts from the homes around which they are twined, our heart-strings will snap.

The Indian agent managed to get fifteen chiefs and subchiefs to sign a removal treaty, the U.S. Senate promptly ratified it, and the War Department began making preparations for the migration. Violence between whites and Seminoles now erupted.

A young Seminole chief, Osceola, who had been imprisoned and chained by the Indian agent Thompson, and whose wife had been delivered into slavery, became a leader of the growing resistance. When Thompson ordered the Seminoles, in December 1835, to assemble for the journey, no one came. Instead, the Seminoles began a series of guerrilla attacks on white coastal settlements, all along the Florida perimeter, striking in surprise and in succession from the interior. They murdered white families, captured slaves, destroyed property. Osceola himself, in a lightning stroke, shot down Thompson and an army lieutenant.

That same day, December 28, 1835, a column of 110 soldiers was attacked by Seminoles, and all but three soldiers were killed. One of the survivors later told the story:

It was 8 o'clock. Suddenly I heard a rifle shot ... followed by a musket shot. ... I had not time to think of the meaning of these shots, before a volley, as if from a thousand rifles, was poured in upon us from the front, and all along our left flank. ... I could only see their heads and arms, peering out from the long grass, far and near, and from behind the pine trees. ...

It was the classic Indian tactic against a foe with superior firearms. General George Washington had once given parting advice to one of his officers: "General St. Clair, in three words, beware of surprise. ... again and again, General, beware of surprise."

Congress now appropriated money for a war against the Seminoles. In the Senate, Henry Clay of Kentucky opposed the war; he was an enemy of Jackson, a critic of Indian removal. But his Whig colleague Daniel Webster displayed that unity across party lines which became standard in American wars:

The view taken by the gentleman from Kentucky was undoubtedly the true one. But the war rages, the enemy is in force, and the accounts of their ravages are disastrous. The executive government has asked for the means of suppressing these hostilities, and it was entirely proper that the bill should pass.

General Winfield Scott took charge, but his columns of troops, marching impressively into Seminole territory, found no one. They became tired of the mud, the swamps, the heat, the sickness, the hunger—the classic fatigue of a civilized army fighting people on their own land. No one wanted to face Seminoles in the Florida swamps. In 1836, 103 commissioned officers resigned from the regular army, leaving only forty-six. In the spring of 1837, Major General Jesup moved into the war with an army of ten thousand, but the Seminoles just faded into the swamps, coming out from time to time to strike at isolated forces.

The war went on for years. The army enlisted other Indians to fight the Seminoles. But that didn't work either. Van Every says: "The adaptation of the Seminole to his environment was to be matched only by the crane or the alligator." It was an eight-year war. It cost $20 million and 1,500 American lives. Finally, in the 1840s, the Seminoles began to get tired. They were a tiny group against a huge nation with great resources. They asked for truces. But when they went forward under truce flags, they were arrested, again and again. In 1837, Osceola, under a flag of truce, had been seized and put in irons, then died of illness in prison. The war petered out.

Meanwhile the Cherokees had not fought back with arms, but had resisted in their own way. And so the government began to play Cherokee against Cherokee, the old game. The pressures built up on the Cherokee community—their newspaper suppressed, their government dissolved, the missionaries in jail, their land parceled among whites by the land lottery. In 1834, seven hundred Cherokees, weary of the struggle, agreed to go west; eighty-one died en route, including forty-five children—mostly from measles and cholera. Those who lived arrived at their destination across the Mississippi in the midst of a cholera epidemic and half of them died within a year.

The Cherokees were summoned to sign the removal treaty in New Echota, Georgia, in 1836, but fewer than five hundred of the seventeen thousand Cherokees appeared. The treaty was signed anyway. The Senate, including northerners who had once spoken for the Indian, ratified it, yielding, as Senator Edward Everett of Massachusetts said, to "the force of circumstances ... the hard necessity." Now the Georgia whites stepped up their attacks to speed the removal.

The government did not move immediately against the Cherokees. In April 1838, Ralph Waldo Emerson addressed an open letter to President Van Buren, referring with indignation to the removal treaty with the Cherokees (signed behind the backs of an overwhelming majority of them) and asked what had happened to the sense of justice in America:

> The soul of man, the justice, the mercy that is the heart's heart in all men, from Maine to Georgia, does abhor this business ... a crime is projected that confounds our understandings by its magnitude, a crime that really deprives us as well as the Cherokees of a country for how could we call the conspiracy that should crush these poor Indians our government, or the land that was cursed by their parting and dying imprecations our country any more? You, sir, will bring down that renowned chair in which you sit into infamy if your seal is set to this instrument of perfidy; and the name of this nation, hitherto the sweet omen of religion and liberty, will stink to the world.

Thirteen days before Emerson sent this letter, Martin Van Buren had ordered Major General Winfield Scott into Cherokee territory to use whatever military force was required to move the Cherokees west. Five regiments of regulars and four thousand militia and volunteers began pouring into Cherokee country. General Scott addressed the Indians:

> Cherokees—the President of the United States has sent me with a powerful army, to cause you, in obedience to the treaty of 1834, to join that part of your people who are already established in prosperity on the other side of the Mississippi. … The full moon of May is already on the wane, and before another shall have passed every Cherokee man, woman, and child … must be in motion to join their brethren in the far West. … My troops already occupy many positions in the country that you are about to abandon, and thousands and thousands are approaching from every quarter, to tender resistance and escape alike hopeless. … Chiefs, head men, and warriors—Will you then, by resistance, compel us to resort to arms? God forbid. Or will you, by flight, seek to hide yourselves in mountains and forests, and thus oblige us to hunt you down?

Some Cherokees had apparently given up on nonviolence: three chiefs who signed the Removal Treaty were found dead. But the seventeen thousand Cherokees were soon rounded up and crowded into stockades. On October 1, 1838, the first detachment set out in what was to be known as the Trail of Tears. As they moved westward, they began to die—of sickness, of drought, of the heat, of exposure. There were 645 wagons, and people marching alongside. Survivors, years later, told of halting at the edge of the Mississippi in the middle of winter, the river running full of ice, "hundreds of sick and dying penned up in wagons or stretched upon the ground." Grant Foreman, the leading authority on Indian removal, estimates that during confinement in the stockade or on the march westward four thousand Cherokees died.

In December 1838, President Van Buren spoke to Congress:

> It affords sincere pleasure to apprise the Congress of the entire removal of the Cherokee Nation of Indians to their new homes west of the Mississippi. The measures authorized by Congress at its last session have had the happiest effects.

CHAPTER 2

MULTICULTURAL EMERGENCE

THE NINETEENTH CENTURY, PART I: CONQUEST AND DISPOSSESSION

MARIO BARRERA

Westward the course of Empire wends its Way.

—slogan favored by
William Blackmore,
British land speculator
in the Southwest

In the nineteenth century the area that is now the Southwest was incorporated into the United States through a war of conquest. With the Southwest came a population of former Mexican citizens who were now granted American citizenship by the Treaty of Guadalupe Hidalgo. These were the original Chicanos. During the remainder of the century a social and economic structure crystallized in the Southwest in which Chicanos and other racial minorities were established in a subordinate status. It is into this structure that succeeding generations of Chicanos have been fitted during the twentieth century, with some modifications.

There were certain key developments affecting the Chicano's social and economic status in the nineteenth century. The first of these was the Mexican American War. In considering this topic, my main concern has been with the identification of the interests that motivated that war, since such an analysis has an important bearing on subsequent developments. The second key factor was the displacement of Chicanos from the land in the various areas of the Southwest. The third was the emergence of a labor system in which Chicanos and other minorities constituted a clearly subordinate segment, which I call a colonial labor force. It is my contention that the processes affecting the land and labor showed important continuities with the interests underlying the Mexican American War. A consideration of all three developments reveals an intricate interplay between class and race factors in the Southwest.

This chapter deals with the first two of these three topics, the war and the land. The next chapter outlines the development of the colonial labor system.

Events up to 1848

The Spanish settlements in the area that is now the Southwest date from the late sixteenth and early seventeenth centuries. The earliest settlements were in the area now known as New Mexico, where Santa Fe was founded in 1609. Over the next 200 years there were additional settlements, and by the early nineteenth century there were three main areas of concentration: the New Mexico territory, southern and southeastern Texas, and the California coast. With the independence of Mexico in 1821, these areas became part of the new Mexican republic. These territories were thinly populated and relatively isolated from each other and from the major centers of Mexican population. The bulk of the population was *mestizo,* a mixture of Mexican Indian, European, and African stocks, and the predominant economic activities were mining, ranching, and agriculture. Vast areas of the Southwest were still controlled by various Native American groups, such as the Apaches, Pueblos, Navajos and Comanches.

It was during the first half of the nineteenth century that regular contacts were made between merchants and traders of the United States and the people of northern Mexico. Regular trade between St. Louis and northern New Mexico was initiated with the blazing of the Santa Fe Trail in 1822, leading to a lively trade in furs, silver, and other goods. One result was the weakening of the economic ties between northern New Mexico and the rest of Mexico, as the area came more into the orbit of the Missouri merchants (Lamar, 1970, p. 48). By the 1840s there was a sizable number of American businessmen in the cities of Taos and Santa Fe, whose economic activities were paralleled by their efforts to increase their political influence. In addition to trading, Anglos in New Mexico engaged in land speculation.

In California, Yankee maritime traders had established a presence going back to the late eighteenth century, built around their interests in sea-otter furs and whaling. During the 1820s an important trade developed around the exchange of California cattle products (the hide-and-tallow trade) for manufactured goods from New England (Billington, 1974, p. 474). In 1830 an overland route was established from Santa Fe to California which became known as the Old Spanish Trail. In addition to the exchange of California primary products for American processed goods, the trial served as a conduit for commodities brought to the California coast from Asia. In a recent paper, Almaguer has emphasized the manner in which these developments linked California to the United states and the broader world-economy (Almaguer, 1977).

The penetration of Texas by settlers from the United States was more thorough than in the other areas of northern Mexico. Here the Spanish and later the Mexican governments had made vigorous attempts to populate the area through a series of land grants, some of which had gone to Anglo colonizers. The most famous of these was the Austin Colony, but there were others. While the Mexican government realized to some extent the dangers of settling the area with non-Mexicans, there was considerable danger in allowing this territory to remain very thinly populated. In any case, by the 1830s only the area around and south of San Antonio could be said to be distinctly Mexican in character (Meinig, 1969, pp. 35ff.).

The main economic activities in the Texas area were subsistence agriculture and cattle raising, although, starting in the 1820s, cotton became increasingly important. Eastern Texas in particular had very close economic ties with Louisiana and looked much more to the United States than to Mexico as far as trade was concerned.

It was in Texas, of course, that the first major political development took place that foreshadowed the incorporation of northern Mexico into the United States. There was a history of unrest and tension between the Anglo settlers in Texas and the Mexican government, as exemplified in the shortlived Fredonia Revolt in 1826. There was also a long-standing effort by the United States to purchase the Texas area from Mexico. As presidents, both John Quincy Adams and Andrew Jackson made offers to the Mexican government for the acquisition of Texas, and these overtures made Mexico suspicious of American intentions toward the area.

Mexican anxieties had also been aggravated by the continued influx of Anglo settlers (many of them "illegal aliens"), which resulted by 1830 in a ratio of some 25,000 Anglos to 4,000 Spanish-speaking Mexicans in that area (Meier and Rivera, 1972, p. 58). As a result, there had been sporadic attempts by Mexico to curb Anglo-American influence in Texas. In 1830, for example, the Mexican government passed a Colonization Law which prohibited the importation of more slaves into Texas and also attempted to cut off further Anglo settlement. Texas at this time was part of the state of Coahuila-Texas. The law was ineffective and was repealed in 1833, but it indicates the concern of Mexican officials over the situation.

Specific economic interests were clearly involved in the conflict. On the one hand, many of the Anglo settlers were interested in cotton cultivation and desired the free importation of slaves to work in the cotton fields. Mexico had abolished slavery, and its policy toward the movement of slaves into Texas was ambivalent but obviously negative. In addition, Anglos with commercial interests wanted to engage in free trade with the United States, and resented Mexican efforts to enforce the national customs laws. (Meir and Rivera, 1972, p. 59).

The decisive revolt for an independent Texas came about during a period of considerable internal conflict within Mexico. Federalists and Centralists were contesting for national power, with the Centralists, led by Santa Anna, gaining the upper hand. Resistance to the Centralist regime broke out in several provinces, and it was in this context that the conflict in Texas was converted into a revolt among the Anglo settlers against any form of Mexican authority over the area. With the success of the revolt, the Republic of

Texas was established in 1836. During the course of the armed conflict the official position of the United States was neutrality, but considerable support for the separatist cause flowed into Texas unofficially.

The new authorities in Texas promptly sought to be annexed to the United States, but annexation was rejected by the United States because of complications over the issue of slavery. Texas would have come in as slave territory, and the entire issue thus became embroiled in the American sectional conflict as well as in the competition between the two major parties, the Democrats and the whigs. Texas thus remained a republic until 1845, during which time the Anglo population greatly increased through immigration.

The subject of the annexation of Texas came up again in 1844, and when annexation was rejected by the Congress the issue became important in the presidential campaign of 1844. In this campaign the Democratic candidate, James K. Polk, ran on a strongly annexationist platform and defeated the more ambivalent Whig nominee, Henry Clay. With the results of the election known, the outgoing president, Tyler, managed to get a joint resolution through Congress providing for the addition of Texas to the union. This act led Mexico, which had never formally recognized the independence of Texas, to break off diplomatic relations with the United States. In this charged atmosphere it became increasingly clear that Polk had broader territorial ambitions.

Shortly after the annexation of Texas, an American emissary, Slidell, was sent to Mexico to settle the Texas matter, but also to attempt to purchase the areas of New Mexico and California. With the failure of the Slidell Mission, the stage was set for the outbreak of hostilities. Polk had ordered American troops into Texas, and these had advanced to the Rio Grande, although the southern area between the Nueces River and the Rio Grande had always been a contested area between Texas and Mexico, in which there were no Texas settlements. In April 1846 the United States blockaded the mouth of the Rio Grande, which historian Glenn Price points out constituted an act of war even if the river had been the agreed-upon international boundary (Price, 1967, p. 153). In that same month an armed clash between Mexico and American troops along the river provided the incident which quickly led the United States to declare war against Mexico. Polk's war message to Congress was based on the claim that Mexican troops had invaded the territory of the United States and attacked American forces. But price argues that Polk had concluded that his territorial aims could not be achieved peacefully, and that he had thus engaged in a series of actions designed to provoke an incident that could be used to stir up popular support for war.

The Mexican American War which resulted from these events lasted from 1846 to 1848, and the Treaty of Guadalupe Hidalgo, signed in the latter year, added a vast territory to the United States. Mexico lost one-third of its territory and the United States gained an area that was to become the states of California, New Mexico, Arizona, Nevada, Utah, and part of Colorado, as well as all of Texas. The former citizens of Mexico who remained in this area became American citizens and constituted the original Chicanos. In light of the preceding discussion, their incorporation into the United States must be seen as the product of an imperial war.

The interests that underlay the conquest of the Southwest have been a subject of considerable debate among historians, and a number of motivations have been put forth which need to be reviewed and assessed. One interpretation that has enjoyed considerable popularity is that Southern slaveowners were instrumental in instigating the conflict. According to this argument, they stood to gain in that the Southwest would provide room for expansion of cotton agriculture. Also, the addition of more slave states would aid the Southern planters in their conflict with Northern industrialists for control of the government (see Rhodes, 1907, p. 79). That political considerations led many in the South to push for the annexation of Texas is admitted even by those who play down the Southern conspiracy thesis (for example, see Boucher, 1921, p. 22). The economic argument also makes sense, in that cotton agriculture, as it was practiced at the time, tended to exhaust the land rapidly, and there was a continuous move westward from the old cotton states in search of more land suitable for plantations. The fact that most Southern planters were Democrats and that the national administration was Democratic also seems to add weight to this thesis.

However, the limitations of the argument need to be carefully noted. In the first place, there seems to be a consensus among historians that Polk did not act as a sectional president, in spite of his Southern origins. Rather, his thinking seems to have run primarily along national lines. In addition, it was already clear at the time of the Mexican American War that most of the Southwest was not suitable for cotton agriculture. Southerners, clearly, had little to gain from seeing more free territory enter the Union, and it was this consideration that led them to oppose the trend toward the annexation of all of Mexico that developed once the Mexican American War was under way (Fuller, 1969). Thus, while it seems clear that Southerners were active in pushing the demand for Texas, their interests do not explain the acquisition by the United States of the rest of the Southwest as well.

A second explanation for the expansion of the United States into the Southwest has been couched in terms of Manifest Destiny. This explanation is the most widely held among historians, including Mexican American historians. According to this explanation, Anglo-Americans were possessed of a vision of history in which they were divinely chosen to populate the North American continent and to bring the blessings of democracy and progress to this area. Their expansion into the Southwest was simply an expression of this conviction.

While it is true that there was strong popular support for expansionism in the United States, especially in the West and in some portions of the Northeast, various considerations severely limit the usefulness of Manifest Destiny as a fundamental motive for expansion into the Southwest. It may be more accurate to say that the fervor behind the idea of Manifest Destiny was the product of a campaign of ideological manipulation. Such a hypothesis is reinforced by the timing of the phenomenon:

> The date at which the doctrine emerged as a force to be reckoned with in politics is important to ascertain. … It can be ascertained only approximately, for many facets were present in this complex phenomenon and some of them came into prominence sooner than others. Some editorial voices proclaiming the full doctrine were heard already during the campaign of 1844.

They were voices crying in the wilderness. The date when the full chorus proclaimed the doctrine came after the election, as late even as the closing months of the Tyler administration. It came after the annexation of Texas had emerged as a good prospect in politics. [Merk, 1963, p. 41]

The suddenness with which the doctrine emerged and spread inevitably arouses suspicions, as does the fact that the annexation of Texas was a contested political issue and that one of the major parties, the Democratic party, was strongly identified with the issue. As Merk points out, "In party affiliation, journals of Manifest Destiny views were Democratic. Organs of the Polk administration were strongly represented among them" (Merk, 1963, p. 35). From Merk's account, there was a large-scale selling effort by many newspapers for the doctrine.

A second major objection to Manifest Destiny as a fundamental explanation is that the doctrine was too vague and diffuse to serve as an adequate explanation of the expansion. It does not explain why certain areas were taken over and others were not. As Merk points out, "In some minds it meant expansion over the region to the Pacific; in others, over the North American continent; in others, over the hemisphere" (Merk, 1963, p. 24). Historian Norman Graebner puts it this way:

> Manifest destiny persists as a popular term in American historical literature to explain the expansion of the United States to continent-wide dimensions in the 1840's. Like most broad generalizations, it does not bear close scrutiny. ... The concept of manifest destiny, as a democratic expression, represented an expanding, not a confining or limiting, force. As an ideal, it was not easily defined in terms of precise territorial limits. ... Some suggested that American laws be extended to include the downtrodden peons of South America. ... In their enthusiasm to extend the "area of freedom," many even looked beyond the continental limits to Cuba, the Sandwich Islands, the far-flung regions of the Pacific, and even to the Old World itself. This was a magnificent vision for a democratic purpose, but it hardly explains the sweep of the United States across the continent. [Graebner, 1955, pp. 217–18]

As others have pointed out, the concept of Manifest Destiny fit in very well with the All-of-Mexico movement, but all of Mexico was not taken.

Another objection to this type of explanation can be raised in terms of a general theory of history. Materialist theories in particular argue (and I would agree) that political movements are motivated fundamentally by interests rather than disembodied ideas. Ideas and concepts which "catch on" enter into political debate largely as expressions or justifications of specific interests, rather than as free-floating concepts and doctrines. In the case at hand, elites in the form of politicians and journalists played a major part in popularizing the doctrine, and the role of interests does not appear to be too difficult to identify.

In summary, then, Manifest Destiny was essentially a manipulated appeal and an attempt to secure broad popular support for an expansionist policy of particular benefit to certain political and economic interests. The specific nature of those interests will become clearer as we examine other explanations.

Some writers have argued that the incorporation of the Southwest into the United States should be understood in terms of economic and commercial interests of various types. To assess this argument we have to look at the three major areas of the Southwest: Texas, California, and New Mexico (which at that time included what is now Arizona). In the case of Texas (described above) there was clearly a desire on the part of cotton-growing interests in expanding into that area. California, however, appears to be the key to understanding commercial interests in expansion. The interest in California was particularly keen among the merchant and manufacturing interests of the American Northeast, generally represented in the Whig party. According to Robert Cleland,

> A second reason for the belief that the annexation of California was not a slavery measure is the fact that the movement found its strongest popular favor in the north. Most of the contemporary newspaper and magazine articles which advocated the acquisition of this portion of Mexican territory first appeared in New York or New England. [Cleland, 191 4–15, p. 250]

Cleland also notes an 1846 article in the *American Review* ("Text Book of the Whig Party") detailing the rich resources of California and urging its immediate annexation, provided it could be done peacefully. He goes on to state:

> Yet the interest with which the commercial states of the north regarded the future of California was unquestionably greater than that of any other section of the country, with the possible exception of the extreme west. For it was natural that those who had important trade relations not merely with California, but with India, China, and the Sandwich Islands, beside extensive whale fisheries, should of all others desire most eagerly a harbor and territory on the Pacific. [Cleland, 1914–51, p. 251]

The thesis that ports on the Pacific were the most important factor in explaining the conquest of the Southwest has been extensively developed by Norman Graebner. According to him,

> The essential fact [is] that the expansion of the United States was a unified, purposeful, precise movement that was ever limited to specific maritime objectives. It was the Pacific Ocean that determined the territorial goals of all American presidents from John Quincy Adams to Polk. From the beginning, travelers, traders, and officials who concerned themselves with the coastal regions had their eyes trained on ports. The goal of American policy was to control the great harbors of San Francisco, San Diego, and Juan de Fuca Strait. With their acquisition, expansion on the coastline ceased. [Graebner, 1955, pp. v-vi]

Two of these three Pacific ports were in the California territory. The other was in the Oregon territory, which the United States acquired at about the same time after a contest with Great Britain. San Diego at that time was the center of the hide trade. San Francisco was also involved in that trade, and was seen as a major future trade link with Asia. In his message to Congress in December 1847, Polk declared that the California ports "would afford shelter for our navy, for our numerous whale ships, and other merchant vessels employed in the Pacific ocean, [and] would in a short period become the marts of an extensive and profitable commerce with China, and other countries of the East" (quoted in Graebner, 1955, p. 225).

American interest in New Mexico can also be interpreted in economic terms. For one thing, the New Mexico area served as an overland route between California on the one hand and Texas and the American Midwest on the other. Significant trade routes crossed this territory and had been in existence for some time. Santa Fe served as the overland link between California and St. Louis in a trade route that followed the Old Spanish Trail. Over this route passed manufactured goods, silver, livestock, and commodities from Asia (Billington, 1974, p. 477). Howard Lamar, in speaking of the New Mexico conquest, puts the matter this way:

> It was not an expression of land hunger or slavery extension; and it was only partly prompted by that vaguer expansionist sentiment called Manifest Destiny. Rather, American conquest meant regularizing and securing rich trade and safe transportation routes for a previously erratic, uncertain enterprise. It was, in short, a conquest of merchants who worried little about extending the glories of free government to their captive customers. [Lamar, 1970, p. 63]

The evidence thus seems clearly to support the argument that the American intrusion into the Southwest was motivated by several important economic considerations, perhaps most importantly in California. One objection that has been raised to this thesis has to do with the role of the Whigs in the national debate with regard to American expansionism during that period. While both Whigs and Democrats represented commercial interests, the Whigs were preeminently the party of Northeastern merchants and manufacturers, and they were for the most part vociferous critics of Polk and the conduct of the Mexican American War. From this fact some critics have argued against the kind of emphasis Graebner and Cleland have given to California and its ports as a motivation for the war. According to these critics, if that thesis was correct the Whigs should have been enthusiastic supporters of the war, since they represented economic interests that stood to benefit from it (see Zwelling, 1970).

There are several answers to this criticism. Whigs were not opposed to the acquisition of California, but they apparently felt that it could be done without necessarily resorting to war (Merk, 1963, p. 39). Whigs were also critical of the war for other reasons. They were not enthusiastic about the acquisition of Texas because of the slavery question and their fears of creating splits within their party and within the nation (ibid., p. 153). It should also be kept in mind that the war provided an issue which the Whigs were trying to turn to partisan advantage (Graebner, 1955, pp. 171–72, 188). At any rate, as Graebner has pointed out, Whig congressmen continued to vote financial support for the war while trying to make political hay by criticizing Polk's conduct of it. That this was a sound political strategy was indicated by their political gains in the elections of 1848.

Another interpretation of the Mexican American War that is sometimes found in the historical literature has to do with the pioneer movement. According to this view, the Anglo pioneers who had moved into the northern provinces of Mexico constituted an important force behind the American annexation of this area, acting as a kind of latter-day Trojan Horse. In assessing this argument, it seems fair to say that Anglo settlers played an important role in Texas but were not a major force elsewhere. These settlers had of course been the prime movers behind the splitting of Texas from Mexico and the establishment of the Texas Republic, and this paved the way for the incorporation of Texas into the United States. However, there was only a sprinkling of Anglo settlers in California and the New Mexico area, and they did not play a central role in the Mexican American War.

Yet another factor that entered into the American move into the Southwest was the role played by foreign countries, especially England. England, seeing the United States as a potentially formidable competitor economically and politically, was doing what it could to limit American influence on the North American continent and to increase its own. While contesting the Oregon territory with the United States, England was attempting to prevent the annexation of Texas and was supporting the Mexican government in its efforts to hold on to the rest of its northern provinces. England apparently considered that an independent Texas would constitute a receptive market for British goods, as well as an ally in limiting American growth and power. At the same time, England was interested in exercising as much control as possible over the Pacific coast and its ports, although it was in no position to think of taking over California. The maneuvers and ambitions of Britain were well known in Washington, and were undoubtedly a source of anxiety to national policymakers. In attempting to assess the role this factor played, however, it may be best to quote a historian's opinion:

> The degree to which Polk's moves to acquire California were influenced by concern over British designs can be—and have been—easily exaggerated, for he was wise enough to realize that the jingoistic ambitions of a few English empire-builders did not constitute official policy. He was also aware, however, that those ambitions provided him an effective tool to manipulate American opinion toward favoring peaceful annexation, and Polk used that tool well. [Billington, 1974, p. 485]

Another dimension to American expansion into the Southwest is curiously missing or seriously underemphasized by historians. In the various interpretations that have been written there is rarely a discussion of the dynamics and level of development of the American economy as a whole during this period. It may be that a closer examination of this dimension will further clarify the motivations behind the Mexican American War.

The American economy during the first half of the nineteenth century was marked by a distinct regional pattern. The South, which had been a diversified agricultural area, was becoming more and more specialized as a cotton-growing region. The West was primarily a grower of foodstuffs. The Northeast, an area of incipient manufacturing, also provided important services in shipping and trade. According to the classic account by Douglass C. North (North, 1966), prior to the 1830s it was not clear that the United States would be able to develop into a major industrial country. The internal market was not highly developed, and the export sector was less than dynamic. The urban areas were relatively small, and the West was relatively isolated from the Northeast by natural geographic barriers. Starting around 1830, however, there was a major expansion in the value of the goods the United States was able to export. The earnings derived from exports then became the key factor in the economic development of the country, and particularly in manufacturing and regional integration. Of the various components that went into the export trade, cotton was by far the leading element.

The effects of this growth in exporting were many and interrelated. With growth in the demand for cotton, more land in the South was devoted to that crop, and the search for land suitable for cotton cultivation was intensified. However, a great deal of the cotton earnings flowed to the Northeast, since that region provided the services to finance, transport, and market the South's cotton. Some of these resources went into the establishment of a textile industry in the Northeast, and this in turn led to the development of an industry that produced machinery, first for the textile industry and then more generally. with the growth of urban industrial centers, the demand for western-grown foods increased, and this stimulated the economy of the west and accelerated the developments of transportation links between the Northeast and the West. As North notes, "it was industrialization in the Northeast and the opening up of the West and Far West which was primarily responsible for the growth of the 1840's and 1850's" (North, 1966, p.71)

From this perspective, some of the interests and motivations reviewed above take on added significance. The boom in the demand for cotton and the key role this played in the economy of the entire country help explain the strong interest in Texas. The interest of the Southern ruling class in that area was also stimulated by the economic and population gains being made in the Northeast and West, since this tended to undercut their relative power at the national level. The booming economy of that period also heightened the interest of Northeastern commercial elites in California, with its ports and its potential role in future trade with Asia. The New Mexico territory, with its natural resources and its trade routes, also took on added significance. At the same time, the fact that the United States was more and more becoming an economic competitor helps explain England's concern with limiting American territorial growth, and made the United States even more eager to establish the base for its future role as a major world power.

The other side of the coin is that the economic and technological growth of the period made it possible for the United States to act on its ambitions. As Frederick Merk puts it,

The steam engine had come into its own in river, ocean, and land travel. From distant territories to the center of government travel time by water had been sensationally reduced. On land railroads had proved themselves practical. But even more remarkable than the actual achievements of these agencies in contracting space was the stimulus given to the expansion of thought. In the mid-1840's projects to build transcontinental railroads to the Pacific by northern, central, and southern routes were on the lips of all. [Merk, 1963, pp. 51–52]

In summary, then, a variety of interests can be seen to have played a role in the American penetration into the Southwest, some of major importance and some distinctly secondary. But at the heart of the phenomenon were a number of economic interests closely tied to the dynamic expansion of American capitalism from the 1830s on. These interests included those of Southern agricultural capitalists, based on the plantation system, but more importantly those of the Northern industrialists and men of commerce who were on the ascendance nationally.

The Land

With the termination of the Mexican American War, a process of transferring Southwestern land from Mexican American to Anglo hands was set in motion—in spite of provisions in the Treaty of Guadalupe Hidalgo guaranteeing the new citizens the security of their property. The pace of dispossession varied from area to area because of a variety of factors, but the general trend was everywhere consistent. Still, it would be an oversimplification to deal with this topic in strictly ethnic or racial terms. Class factors strongly influenced the process, as I emphasize in the following account. Given the uneven pace of land transfer, it is necessary to look at developments by geographic area.

California

In 1851 the U.S. Congress passed a Land Law that established a commission to review the validity of claims to the land in California based on grants made during the Spanish and Mexican periods. Attention has usually focused on the resulting adversary process, and the conflict over the land has been perceived as pitting the native Spanish-speaking Californios, as the land-grant claimants, against Anglo settlers who were often squatters on the land. While this was an important part of what was going on, several complicating factors need to be added to the picture.

On the Californio side, account needs to be taken of the fact that land-ownership in California had been highly unequal. Much of the desirable California land was held in the form of land grants that had been made by the Spanish and Mexican governments. Among the Californios was a small class of large landowners and a much larger group of people who lived on a more modest scale. Among these were agricultural laborers, small farmers, servants, artisans, and small merchants. Laborers were the majority and were very poor. Thus all Californios did not have the same immediate stake in the question of who should control the land. According to Leonard Pitt, reports in 1849 showed that 200 California families owned 14 million acres (Pitt, 1970, p.86).

There are complications as well on the Anglo side. In the first place, not all of the land grants had been made to Californios. There was a group of Anglos who had been recipients of grants prior to the Mexican American War. Among them were such well-known figures as Abel Stearns and John C. Fremont. Many of the Anglo landholders of this period were in the central valley of California, but several of the most important were in southern California (Robinson, 1948, pp. 63–64). Many of these men blended into Californio culture and had intermarried with Californios.

Another complicating factor arises from the fact of land transference through mechanisms that had little to do with the Land Commission. According to Paul Gates, "before 1851, 42 percent of the claims were in the hands of non-Mexicans and in the years thereafter an increasing number were lost to the hard-driving, better-financed Americans who began to develop their grants" (Gates, 1975, p. 159). Richard Morefield comments on this situation as follows:

> The process [of land transfer] had begun as soon as the first foreigner had set foot in California. ... A breakdown of the figures gives an idea of how much of the land had already passed from [Californio] control. Of the 813 cases presented to the Commission, 521 were confirmed by the time the Commission adjourned in 1856; this number was raised to 604 by successful appeals to the courts. Of these 604 cases only 330 were confirmed to Californians of Mexican descent. [Morefield, 1971, p. 26]

This transfer was not being made to small Anglo settlers, as Gates makes clear:

> When sales were made, it was to new men with financial backing who were able to develop some portions of their purchases, even to lay out towns and cities on them. Thus, the early non-Mexican owners of great ranchos such as Thomas O. Larkin, John Bidwell, William A. Dana, Nicholas Den, W. E. P. Hartness, and Abel Stearns were joined by a group of new millionaires whose wealth had been or was being made in banking, shipping, the cattle trade, mining, and railroads. This new group became owners of numerous ranchos or parts of ranchos running into hundreds of thousands of acres. [Gates, 1975, p. 159]

Thus while it was true that Californios were being displaced from the land, many Californios owned no land from which to be displaced. While it was true that Anglos were taking over the land, some had been there earlier, and the new masters of the land were increasingly likely to be men of means rather than the average Anglo newcomer.

The process of displacing the Californios from the land was more rapid in northern than in southern California. The reason for this is that the Gold Rush in northern California attracted large numbers of

Anglos into that area during and after 1848. With the influx of Anglos, land values in northern California skyrocketed (Gates, 1962, p. 100). Pitt and others have discussed various factors that facilitated the transfer of land. One was that the requirements for proof of ownership under American law were different and more stringent than under Mexican law. The Land Law of 1851 put the burden of proof squarely on the shoulders of the land-grant claimants. In addition, unfamiliarity with American law and the English language put many of the claimants at the mercy of Anglo lawyers, many of whom had designs on the land (Pitt, 1970, pp. 91, 97; Cleland, 1951, p. 39). Gates notes that "a fairly common practice was for lawyers prosecuting claims to charge a contingent fee of one quarter of the land if successful" (Gates, 1958, p. 235). The shortage of capital often forced the claimants to pay their lawyers entirely in land. The high legal fees and other costs led many landowners to borrow money at high interest rates, so that even if they won their case they frequently had to sell their land to meet their debts (Pitt, 1970, p. 1001; Cleland, 1951, p. 40; Robinson, 1948, p. 106). In addition, land claimants in northern California were faced with a particularly strong surge of squatters on their land. These settlers formed associations to exert political pressure on behalf of their interests. Not infrequently, they exercised intimidation and coercion on the grant claimants (Pitt, 1970, pp. 95ff.)

> In the north of California … the basis of landownership had changed drastically by 1856. Through armed struggle, legislation, litigation, financial manipulation, outright purchase, and innumerable other tactics, Yankees had obtained a good deal of interest in the land. The transfer of property destroyed the irenic vision provided by the Treaty of Guadalupe Hidalgo, which guaranteed the Californios the "free enjoyment of their liberty and property"—an obligation that did not worry many Yankees. [Ibid., p. 103]

The process operated at a slower pace in southern California, largely because the northern area was more dynamic economically in the first two decades following the Mexican American War. In the south there were few newcomers to speed the transfer of land. Other factors, however, intervened. The Gold Rush and population increase in the north stimulated the cattle industry of the south, which boomed in the early 1850s. But the boom was short-lived. By 1856 the cattle industry had peaked and started to decline (Cleland, 1951, p. 110). Overexpansion and poor investment practices had undermined the stability of the cattle ranches, and a severe drought in the 1860s brought about the downfall of many Californio rancheros (ibid., pp. 130ff.).

> Before the catastrophe, practically all land parcels worth more than $10,000 had still been in the hands of old families; by 1870, these families held barely one-quarter. A mean and brassy sky thus did in the south of California what lawyers and squatters had accomplished in the north—the forced breakup of baronial holdings, their transfer to new owners, and the rise of a way of life other than ranching. [Pitt, 1970, p. 248]

The finishing touches were added by the events associated with the coming of the railroads of southern California in the late 1870s and early 1880s. With the railroads came a monumental land boom that largely completed the erosion of the California-held lands. The immigration of large numbers of Anglos reduced the Californios in the southern part of the state to a small minority, as it had earlier in the north. Combined with the other factors cited above, the economic expansion of the 1880s reduced the Californios' holdings to a small fraction of their former possessions.

The situation of the Californios in San Diego County has been described by García (1975a) and Hughes (1975). Hughes stresses the role of legal fees and associated court costs in eroding the financial position of San Diego landowners. Land taxes also played an important role here, as in other parts of southern California.

> Since state laws exempted much of the northern mining industry, the brunt of the property tax fell on the large property owners of southern California who were primarily Californios. Most of the state's population resided in the North and worked in the mines or in related occupations. Their representatives dominated state government and attempted to use taxation to break up the large land holdings. [Hughes, 1975, p. 18]

In the Santa Barbara area, important changes in landownership took place during the 1860s, according to a study by Camarillo (1975a, 1975b). The downturn in the fortunes of the pastoral economy seems to have played an important role here as well. A comparison of censuses taken in 1860 and 1870 shows a dramatic decline in the number of Spanish-surname rancheros and farmers in the Santa Barbara area during that period (Camarillo, 1975a, p. 6).

In summary, a number of factors had gone into the process that resulted in dispossession from the land of the Californio elite and some small farmers.

Among these were:

Imposition of a different legal system with different standards of proof of ownership
Placing the burden of proof on the land-grant claimant to demonstrate that the claim was legitimate
Legal chicanery by Anglo lawyers dealing with culturally different clients
Manipulations of the tax system on land
High legal fees and court costs, combined with a shortage of capital and the necessity to borrow money at high interest rates (see Cleland, 1951, p. 114; Pitt, 1970, p. 100)
Coercion and intimidation (e.g., on the part of squatters)
Anti-Californio biases by elected and appointed government officials
Natural calamities, such as drought
Overextension of the cattle industry following the boom of the 1850s

All this is not to say that legitimate transfers of land through proper sales at fair prices did not take place. Nevertheless, a distinct discriminatory aspect was present, not only in the attitudes of individuals but in the effects of the institutional mechanisms that were set up to deal with the problem. While "institutional racism" is a relatively recent concept, it should be applied to the situation in California with respect to the land in the nineteenth century.

At the same time, the conflict between the interests of the Californio landowners and the Anglo newcomers should not obscure the fact that racial divisions were only part of the story. As mentioned earlier, Anglos found themselves on both sides of the conflicts over land, as many land-grant claimants were Anglos. In addition, there appears to have been a considerable amount of intra-Anglo class conflict over the land. Paul Gates has documented the process from 1860 to 1900 through which agricultural capitalists accumulated large holdings at the expense of small settlers.

> Statistics of the number of new farms being created in California between 1860 and 1900— 55,826—offer little support for the notion that the great ranchos were being subdivided into many small farms. During this period 147,000 homestead and preemption applications were filed. These might have led to small farms but did not for, as is seen later, many were filed by men acting as dummies for large engrossers. … Prominent Californians seemed determined to bring about the greatest possible concentration of land in large ownerships and bent their energies to shape state and federal legislation to contribute to that end while paying lip service to the small-family-farm concept. From the election of John C. Fremont as its first senator in 1850 … the state was represented in Washington by men closely identified with the great landowners and railroad tycoons. …
>
> Much unhappiness was expressed at the speed with which the 500,000 acres were grabbed up by capitalists who were accused of making their entries on lands being improved by settlers who were waiting for the enactment of a free homestead measure. … Meetings of squatters were held at which "raging excitement" was expressed at the land speculators who had entered land on which settlers had commenced their homestead. [Gates, 1975, pp. 160–61, 163]

Or as Pitt puts it:

> No set pattern emerges in these land transformations, but the eroded claims of the original claimants washed away steadily and flowed into the hands of the newcomers—financiers, railroad developers, town promoters, cooperative colonizers, and irrigation companies. [Pitt, 1970, p. 275]

In the long run, then, the main beneficiaries of the displacement of Californios from the land were those who had the financial resources and the political clout to reconcentrate the land in their own hands. The benefits were disproportionately capitalists, speculators, and financiers whose interests had most strongly motivated the Mexican American War.

New Mexico

During the nineteenth century the bulk of the Chicano population of the Southwest was concentrated in New Mexico. Here, as in California, settlement of the land had taken place through Spanish and Mexican grants. In the southern part of the state, the common pattern was haciendas established by grantees who became patrons and brought in settlers to do the work. The haciendas were largely self-sufficient and were usually organized around a system of debt peonage. The haciendas grew their own food and were also engaged in pastoral activities. Sheep were the main export. Trade was carried on largely with Mexico, until the Santa Fe Trail was opened and American economic penetration of the area began.

The northern part of the state was characterized by "communal" villages which were organized on the basis of grants that had been given to the community as a whole. Here homesteads and farming lands were owned privately, whereas grazing and other land was owned in common and grazing and water rights were assigned by community councils (Zeleny, 1944, p. 68). Economic life revolved around subsistence agriculture and sheep raising. There was little manufacturing in the area. Northern New Mexico was more densely settled by Hispanos than the southern area.

The pace of Anglo economic penetration in New Mexico was more like that of southern than northern California, and the tempo of land transfer was correspondingly slow, although steady. In the mid-nineteenth century the economic penetration took the form of movement into agriculture and expansion of the commercial sector.

Initially, the Anglo conquest of New Mexico resulted in a limited expansion of the area occupied by the Spanish-speaking New Mexicans, or Hispanos. The reason for this is that the American military presence served to decimate the nomadic Indians who had previously resisted encroachments on their territory (Meinig, 1971, p. 32). The Hispano expansion, however, was halted in the 1870s as Anglo cattlemen and farmers increasingly moved into the area. As Meinig puts it:

> The Hispano hold upon much of their newly acquired country was necessarily thin, discontinuous, and at times no more than seasonal. The vanguard of their herders was often repelled and confined to the poorer lands, the outermost of their settlements were often soon enclaved within Anglo cattle country. The actual stabilization of the patterns of the two peoples was a long and complicated process which resulted neither in simple areal boundaries nor simple contrasts in activities (increasingly, Hispano shepherds tended Anglo-owned flocks), but it was a process which relentlessly strengthened the dominance of the one over the other. [Ibid., pp. 34–35]

As in southern California, the coming of the transcontinental railroads had a significant impact in New Mexico. New Mexico was fully connected with the transcontinental system in the late 1870s and early 1880s, and with the transportation system came an economic boom and an influx of Anglos. "The notion of migration to New Mexico was boosted by promoters of development of the West and by financial interests in the East which stood to profit by such migration" (Zeleny, 1944, p. 143). The 1880s saw a rapid increase in the number of Anglo-owned cattle companies (Westphall, 1965, p. 56). With the economic boom and the movement of Anglos into the state, the pressure on the land increased. From that point on, the process of land transfer accelerated. According to Zeleny, the process went faster in the southern part of the state, where the hacienda pattern had been dominant. Presumably, the denser Hispano population in the north and the pattern of communal holdings acted to retard the transfer to some extent (Zeleny, 1944, pp. 186–87).

Clark Knowlton has provided a detailed list of the mechanisms by which the transfer of land took place in the New Mexico area. In general, the processes were much like those in California. Only two or three aspects of the transfer process warrant a more extended discussion, and one of them has to do with the impact of land taxes. Knowlton notes that under the Mexican system the land had been free of taxation—taxes were levied on the products of the land rather than on the land itself. "In an area where the income from agriculture fluctuates irregularly according to climatic conditions, a fixed land tax in bad years places heavy burdens upon farmers and ranchers. A small Spanish-American subsistence farmer living in the villages was singularly unprepared to adjust to a fixed land-tax system. Cultivating his land to feed his family, he seldom ever possessed enough actual cash to pay taxes requiring money payments" (Knowlton, 1967, p. 7). According to New Mexico law, anyone can pay delinquent taxes on land and receive a title to that land. "Probably no other Anglo-American measure has had a harsher impact upon Spanish-American property than the fixed land tax" (ibid.). Knowlton argues that the county land tax was also subject to extensive fraud and manipulation, to the detriment of the Hispano population. McWilliams notes the same phenomenon:

> In many cases, the Spanish-Americans could not pay land taxes of $1.50 an acre, or more, levied against grazing lands. Anglo-Americans would then buy up the lands at tax sales and promptly have the land tax reduced to thirty or forty cents an acre. [McWilliams, 1968, p. 77]

In many cases it appears that the new owners of the land engaged in an unwarranted enlargement of the grant boundaries.

> A number of grants have had their boundaries stretched and areas marvelously expanded. But this has been done mostly by Yankee and English purchasers and not by the original Mexican owners. Where boundaries were made by natural landmarks, such as a "white rock," a "red hill," or a "lone tree," another rock, hill or tree of like description could always be found a league or two farther off, and claimed to be the original landmark described in the grant documents.

[Wilbur F. Stone, associate justice of the Court of Private Land Claims, cited in Westphall, 1973, p. 36]

In New Mexico, also, the role of the government and its use of land became an important factor—increasingly so toward the end of the century. Without compensation, the National Forest Service has taken millions of acres from the northern villages for the creation of national forests. Hispanos must now pay grazing fees on land that once belonged to the villages (Knowlton, 1967, p. 10).

> The creation of forest reserves by the Federal Government has likewise withdrawn large portions of the public domain from free grazing lands of the Spanish-Americans. The Santa Fe National Forest was created in 1892, and the Cibola and Carson National Forests were established in 1906 ... they combined with other factors in confining the Spanish-Americans to a smaller and smaller land base. Grants made by the government to railroads during the period of their construction also withdrew substantial portions of the public domain from the free use of the old residents. [Zeleny, 1944, p. 171]

Malcolm Ebright has described the process in relation to the San Joaquin del Rio de Chama grant in northern New Mexico, originally made in 1808 to a group of Mexican families:

> There was never any serious question regarding the validity of the grant nor of the nature of the grant as one made to a community. The only real question which the U.S. officials who were responsible for its adjudication asked was, how big was it. In 1861 when approximately 400 of the grantees and their heirs petitioned for confirmation of the grant, its size was estimated at 184,320 acres. But when surveyed in 1878 it turned out to contain 472,736 acres. It appears that the rejection of 471,314 acres of the grant, most of which eventually wound up in the Santa Fe National Forest, was based on the simple fact that the grant was too big and would unreasonably deplete the U.S. public domain. [Ebright, 1976, p. 3]

Of course, even if a different determination had been made by the court, there was no guarantee that the land would remain under the control of the villagers, given the various processes that were acting to concentrate the land in the hands of large companies and land speculators.

It was not until 1891 that a Court of Private Land Claims was established for New Mexico. Prior to that time, conflicts over claims were handled by the state surveyor general, subject to congressional confirmation. The Court of Private Land Claims was empowered to deal with all Spanish and Mexican land claims in the areas of New Mexico, Colorado, and Arizona. Because of the biases of the rules and procedures the court was to follow, similar to those of the California Land Commission, the results were highly disadvantageous to the Hispanos.

The court [of Private Land Claims] was set up with five judges selected from other parts of the United States, a United States Attorney, and other court officials. The members of the court were Anglo-American legal officials with little knowledge of Spanish and Mexican law and no knowledge of Spanish-American land-owning customs. Court decisions were based upon a rigid interpretation of Anglo legal precepts. [Knowlton, 1967, p. 6]

In the years from 1891 until 1904, when the Court was disbanded, decisions were made settling the currently urgent land claims. In this time about two-thirds of the claims examined were rejected; the court confirmed the grants to 2,051,526 acres, and rejected claims to 33,439,493 acres. … The stipulation that no grant be confirmed unless there was strict legal authority in the granting powers was the basis for the rejection of many claims. … The decisive action taken by the court in its years of activity actually relegated the Spanish-Americans to a position of greater disadvantage than they had occupied prior to its establishment. … The conflicts over land were turned over to a supposedly impersonal third party, the Court, which technically fulfilled the Anglo-American conception of "justice" but at the same time proceeded to fix the Spanish-American in a position of subordination. [Zeleny, 1944, pp. 166–67]

The result was that eventually Anglos came to own four-fifths of the former grant areas (Brayer, 1974, p. 19; Meier and Rivera, 1972, p. 107). The loss of the community lands, from an original 2 million acres to 300,000 by 1930, was a major blow to the economic viability of the villages (Harper, Córdova, and Oberg, 1943, p. 62).

The emphasis in the litigation decisions was clearly on ascertaining if there was legal authority in the original granting process. Although this may seem a proper norm of justice, it must be emphasized it was a norm of Anglo justice being applied to the *traditional legal process of another* sovereign state (either Spain or Mexico) which functioned in a different cultural and legal framework. Moreover, it applied current norms to a previous circumstance, which to the Mexican Americans could reasonably be considered an ex post facto application. It can certainly be argued that the determination of legitimacy in the granting process was an important aspect of the legal question, but the overriding importance placed on this single norm, relative to the reasonableness of the acceptance of the original grantors and the appropriate communities or individuals of the legality of the grants by their traditional expressions of legality (occupation and use) and the long time lag between the grants and their validity determination seems a clear bias against the Mexican Americans. [Jim Johnson, 1975, memo prepared for this study]

A number of the grants in New Mexico had been made under terms in which the members of the local community were to use the land under the condition of usufruct. "It is the nature of usufruct that it is a perpetual right attached to the land, a right effective not only against the owner of the land, but also against all others. Usufruct can be owned in common, but the owners do not possess the land; they possess the right to use it" (Rock, 1976, p. 54). The right is intended to be perpetual, as long as the grantees live up to their obligations to maintain the land. This right was supposed to be protected by the Treaty of Guadalupe Hidalgo, but the courts of New Mexico have refused to depart from a rigid adherence to Anglo legal norms in deciding land grant cases, and these norms do not include the right of usufruct (ibid., pp. 56–61).

At the same time, there is evidence that violence and intimidation played a considerable role in the economic changes that were taking place. "Hand in hand with the vast expropriation of lands went a wave of violence and terrorism which caused many Hispanos to leave the San Luis Valley. Family histories in the San Juan Basin relate incidents of covert shootings and public lynchings over land and political control" (Swadesh, 1974, p. 80; see also Ganaway, 1944, p. 102).

As in the case of California, dispossession from the land was largely effected through the "normal workings" of the institutions which were set up by Anglo society. The process illustrates the way in which institutional discrimination can operate in an apparently color-blind manner.

> The situation of the Spanish-Americans was made even more difficult by the establishment of only two federal land offices in New Mexico during much of the territorial period. ... The very existence of these offices, let alone their functions, was unknown to the Spanish-American village population. On the other hand, the Americans, who lived in the larger urban centers of the Territory, possessed far better means of traveling and of communicating with each other and with the land offices. As political alliances were established, often with the personnel of the land office, they were able to note which land grants were registered and which were not and thus to take appropriate action to register many unregistered grants in their own names. [Knowlton, 1967, p. 6]

The overall result was a steady decline in the economic and political fortunes of the Hispanos, with the land playing a key role.

> The struggle between the Spanish-Americans and Anglo-Americans taking place in New Mexico during this period was one in which the defeat of the Spanish-Americans was pre-ordained because of certain critical advantages which the Anglo-Americans possessed. In the struggle economic and political factors were inter-related in such a manner as to produce a shift in power from the hands of the numerically preponderant Spanish-American group to those of the invading Anglos. (Zeleny, 1944, p. 159]
>
> The accommodation which was effected in the economic sphere through land displacement and competition resulted essentially in a relationship of superordination and subordination between the two competing ethnic groups. [Ibid., p. 196]

The loss of lands by the Hispanos is only one aspect of the situation, however. If anything, the class dimension to the economic penetration and transfer of land in New Mexico was even more apparent than in other parts of the Southwest. Zeleny notes that

> New Mexico did not at first attract many of the regular settler class, but rather was a field for exploitation by American commercial enterprise and American and European capital. [Ibid., p. 159]

The activities of the Santa Fe Ring and its various component rings in the nineteenth century exemplify this class dimension. The ring consisted of a group of Anglo merchants, lawyers, bankers, politicians, and ranchers who dominated the territory during the last two decades of the century. With headquarters in Santa Fe, they exercised great influence in the territorial and national capitals. While engaged in every facet of commercial and political life, the biggest impact of the ring was probably in manipulating the land and concentrating it in their hands through a variety of sharp practices (Larson, 1968, pp. 137ff.; see also Lamar, 1970, chap. 6).

Frances Swadesh has provided us with a description of the manner in which Thomas Catron, one of the leaders of the ring, gained control of the large Tierra Amarilla grant. According to this account, his methods included the manufacture of evidence, collecting large legal fees in the form of land, and defrauding the original grant claimants (Swadesh, 1974, pp. 84–85). By the 1880s, he was one of the largest landowners in the United States, with the Tierra Amarilla grant alone totaling some 600,000 acres. In the process of developing this area, Hispano communities were disrupted and much of the land was "clean cut" by lumber companies (ibid., pp. 88–89). Brayer's extended account of the activities of the British capitalist and speculator, William Blackmore, in gaining control over several grants in the northern New Mexico–southern Colorado area also highlights the class dimension in the transfer of land titles.

One of the more interesting aspects of this process stands out clearly in the Santa Fe Ring, which was able to exercise power effectively because of the alliance it forged with the wealthy Hispano elite, the *ricos* (McWilliams, 1948, p. 122; Knowlton, 1967, p. 5; Larson, 1968, p. 144). In effect, there was an interethnic class alliance, which, however, was dominated by the Anglos. Actually, such an alliance had long been in existence. Brayer has described the manner in which Cornelio Vigil and Ceran St. Vrain, prominent residents of Taos, combined to petition Governor Armijo for a substantial grant of land in 1843. The grant was made in that same year. Within two months, the two recipients of the grant had deeded a one-sixth interest to Armijo, to Donanciano Vigil (Armijo's territorial secretary), and to Charles Bent and Eugene Leitensdorfer, important merchants and traders (Brayer, 1974, pp. 127–29).

In another example, Guadalupe Miranda and Charles Beaubien were placed in possession of a large grant of northern New Mexico land in 1841 by Governor Armijo. The curate of Taos, Father Martinez, protested that much of the land belonged to the people of Taos and had long been used as common grazing land, but to no avail (Keleher, 1964, pp. 13–15).

The role of the ricos in the post-Mexican American War period was to provide their Anglo partners with political support through their influence with the Hispano population. In return, they hoped to be safeguarded to some extent in retaining control of their lands (Zeleny, 1944, p. 160). In the long run, however, the bargain turned out badly for many of the ricos. Rodman Paul has given us an assessment of the effects of the alliance on the Hispano elite:

> Whether Hispanos really were the big gainers from the operations of either the Ring or the early business houses may be doubted. One suspects that their Anglo associates were too resourceful for that. And in any event, while some of the Hispano upper class were prospering, many of their cousins ... were losing ownership of the land that had been the traditional basis of their power. So at best only a portion of even the favored class were better off at the end of the century than they had been in 1848. [Paul, 1971, p. 39]

Another aspect of the class dimension as it affected the land (already seen in California) was class conflict within the Anglo population. Keleher provides a vivid account of the formation on the Maxwell land grant of groups of Anglo settlers determined to wage a struggle against the promoters and capitalists who had gained control of the grant. In the end, their efforts were largely unsuccessful (Keleher, 1964, pp. 84–107). Westphall has documented the fraudulent manipulation of the land by land and cattle companies, along the same lines as the practices described by Gates for California (Westphall, 1965, pp. 64, 81, 100ff.).

In summary, it is possible to see in New Mexico, even more clearly than in California, the interrelated nature of ethnic and class factors in the dispossession of the land and its reconcentration in the hands of an Anglo-dominated economic and political elite.

Texas

Texas differs from the other areas of the Southwest in that here there was a pattern of extensive Anglo settlement of the land. A substantial amount of land had been granted to Anglos through the Mexican government's *empresario* grants, particularly in southeastern Texas.

Perhaps in part because of this, little has been written about the displacement of Mexicans and Chicanos from the land in this region. Yet this process appears to have started quite early. During the war that resulted in the independent Republic of Texas in 1836, Spanish-speaking residents were apparently driven out of certain areas, notably in Bexar County, where San Antonio is located (Meinig, 1969, p. 46). Joseph Nance adds that Texas Anglo raiders "forced the abandonment of many of the Mexican ranches between the Neuces and the Rio Grande" in the late 1830s (Nance, 1963, p. 547). Meinig notes that "east of Victoria nearly all of the few Hispanos who had not fled in 1836 were harassed and driven out in 1845 or shortly thereafter" (Meinig, 1969, p. 55).

The process continued after the termination of the Mexican American War. Speaking of south central Texas, Meinig states that "by 1860 the Anglos had gotten control, by fair means or foul, of nearly every ranch worth having north of the Neuces" (Meinig, 1969, p. 54). As in other areas, force and fraud were not the only mechanisms used to facilitate the transfer of land. The Texas historian Fehrenbach describes the situation in this way, with an unconscious touch of irony:

> There is some truth that many Mexican landowners, especially the small ones, were robbed in south Texas by force, intimidation, or chicanery. But what is usually ignored is the fact that the hacendado class, as a class, was stripped of property perfectly legally, according to the highest traditions of U.S. law. [Fehrenbach, 1968, p. 510]

The Espíritu Santo grant in the Rio Grande Valley provides one example of a Chicano-held grant that was validated by the courts but in which the land was lost because of the prohibitive costs of the litigation (Acuña, 1972, pp. 43–44). "The imposition of American law infuriated most Mexican landowners. They had to defend their ancient titles in court, and they lost either way, either to their own lawyers or to the claimants" (Fehrenbach, 1968, p. 511). Acuña notes that an 1860 census showed that 263 Texans owned over $100,000 in real property, and that only two of these were Chicanos (Acuña, 1972, p. 44).

Paul Taylor has provided us with a more intensive look at the situation in the southern Gulf Coast county of Neuces. He states that by 1835 all of the county had been granted in large tracts to Mexicans, who used the area for cattle. By 1859 all but one of the grants had passed to Anglo hands (Taylor, 1971, p. 179). The process of transfer started in 1840, through sales. Taylor addresses himself to whether the sales could be considered fair and free:

> When the Mexicans first sold to Americans they were under stress to sell. They were not simply individual holders of property selling of their free will; they were selling *because they were Mexicans* who, in a time of chaos, could no longer occupy their land, and who saw the imminent American military and political domination. ... It was under the pressure of these conditions that the grants passed to Americans, who as bargainers took advantage of them in varying degrees. (Ibid., pp. 182–83)

Taylor's insights into the psychological pressure on the Mexican landholders undoubtedly apply to other areas of the Southwest as well.

As in other parts of the Southwest, land transfer in Texas was strongly affected by the economy. The boom in cattle that followed the American Civil War led to greater pressure on the land, as did the economic development stimulated by the coming of the railroads. According to Meier and Rivera, "as a result of the cattle boom after the Civil War ... the loss of land by tejanos to Anglos was accelerated. In many cases these lands were acquired by forced sales for nonpayment of taxes, with Anglo speculators often obtaining tejano lands at only a few cents per acre" (Meier and Rivera, 1972, pp. 93–94).

Again, the class factor in this process needs to be emphasized. In spite of the fact that there was strong antispeculator sentiment in Texas, speculating in land was a major economic factor even before the establishment of the Republic of Texas. Several important land speculation ventures began in the early 1830s, including those of the notorious Galveston Bay and Texas Land Company. Such famous names as General (later Texas President) Sam Houston and Jim Bowie were closely linked with these activities (Hogan, 1946, pp. 83–85). According to Fehrenbach, "the land maps of virtually every central Texas county show that the best lands, with their precious water rights, passed into private ownership between ten and thirty years before these counties were settled by whites" (Fehrenbach, 1968, p. 283). Alwyn Barr, in his study of late nineteenth-century Texas, makes references to west Texas county-based land rings, and quotes Texas land commissioner Charles Rogan to the effect that

> while the laws were enacted ostensibly for the benefit of the actual settler, he has derived but little benefit from them. The chief beneficiaries have been land agents, speculators and bonus hunters, and finally the ranch men. [Barr, 1971, p. 84]

According to Barr, Rogan's "statement may well stand as a summary of Texas land policy for the last two decades of the nineteenth century" (Ibid., p. 84).

LAND TRANSFER IN THE SOUTHWEST

Perhaps the key point that emerges from this review of the land situation in the nineteenth century is that the subordinate status of Chicanos in the Southwest put them in a particularly vulnerable economic position. Anglo capitalists and land speculators were best able to take advantage of this vulnerability to dispossess Chicanos of the land they had previously controlled. Certain factors, such as class status, population density, or geographic isolation, had an effect on the pace of dispossession, but eventually it affected all or nearly all Chicanos.

While it is true that Anglo settlers were also adversely affected by the increasing concentration of land in the hands of large Anglo landowners, there was an important difference in degree. As Brayer has pointed out for New Mexico, Anglo settlers were better able to defend their claims to the land than Chicanos (Brayer, 1949, pp. 119–20n.). In addition, as Keleher notes, in most cases the Anglo settlers did not have the same long-standing claim to the land that most Chicanos had (Keleher, 1964, p. 23).

Anglo control of the political process appears to have been a key factor in all this (political control is explored further in chapter 6). Zeleny describes the situation in New Mexico:

> The land situation, and the control exercised by the Anglo-American officials in land decisions, were important factors in producing this shift in power. In the political field the Spanish-Americans, whose numerical superiority had given them an advantage in territorial politics, rapidly became the victims of corrupt American practices and machine politics. Politics in the

territory were soon in the hands of a political combination … which succeeded in controlling appointments made through both the territorial and federal governments in New Mexico. [Zeleny, 1944, pp. 159–60]

The link between loss of political control and loss of the land has also been recognized by other writers. Swadesh points out that "officials appointed by the federal government helped deprive the land grant heirs of their rights" (Swadesh, 1974, p. 69), and Fehrenbach, writing of Texas, states that "the law added injury to insult, because it failed to protect the Mexicans and actually was the chief instrument of their dispossession" (Fehrenbach, 1968, p. 510).

Dispossession from the land, in turn, depleted the economic base of Chicanos and put them in an even less favorable position to exercise influence over the political process. In addition, it had other far-ranging consequences, including facilitating the emergence of a colonial labor system in the Southwest, based in large part on Chicano labor.

IMMIGRATION AND LIVELIHOOD, 1840S TO 1930S

SUCHENG CHAN

Asian immigrants came to the United States primarily to earn a living. Work was available because the entrepreneurs who operated within America's capitalist economy wanted the cheapest labor they could find, so that they could maximize their profits. However, Euro-American workers who felt threatened by the Asian competition and nativists from all classes who felt hostile toward them for racist reasons agitated to stop their coming. With the exception of Koreans, members of each immigrant group managed to enter without restriction for only two or three decades before they were excluded.

Though there were many similarities in the occupational history of the five major Asian immigrant groups, differences also existed. Hawaii and California were frontiers in the early 1850s, when the Chinese came; they were undergoing rapid economic transformation in the 1880s, when the Japanese entered; and were becoming mature capitalist economies by the early twentieth century, when Asian Indians, Koreans, and Filipinos arrived. Given the shortage of Euro-American workers in California during the 1850s and 1860s, the Chinese there found work in a wide range of occupations. But as more and more Euro-Americans settled along the Pacific Coast after the first transcontinental railroad was completed in 1869, they wanted the better jobs for themselves. Through a variety of means—including discriminatory legislation and taxes, boycotts, and barring nonwhites from unions and consequently unionized jobs—they increasingly confined the Chinese and the other Asians who came after them to low-status menial work.

The first Asians to set foot in the New World came with the Manila galleon trade. Filipino and Chinese sailors and stewards were employed in the specially constructed ships that carried cargoes of Chinese luxury goods between Manila and Acapulco from 1565 to 1815. A number of Filipinos apparently had settled in Acapulco by the late sixteenth century, while some Chinese merchants had set up shop in Mexico City by the seventeenth. Marina E. Espina and Fred Cordova have surmised that the Filipinos known as Manilamen found in the marshlands of Louisiana's Barataria Bay (about thirty miles south of New Orleans) in the 1760s were descendants of sailors who had worked on the Manila galleons.[1]

The historical record is clearer with regard to the earliest Chinese arrival in Hawaii. Several Chinese artisans being taken by a British sea captain to build ships in Nootka Sound in British Columbia touched shore at the mid-Pacific islands in 1789—only 11 years after Captain James Cook first landed there and named them the Sandwich Islands. Ships engaged in the China trade soon began calling at Hawaiian ports and took sandalwood, which grew abundantly in the islands, to sell in China. For that reason, Chinese have called the Hawaiian islands Tanxiangshan (Tanheungsan, "the Sandalwood Mountains") from the time they learned of their existence.

The first Chinese to reside in Hawaii for any length of time were men skilled at sugar making. According to Tin-Yuke Char, long before the first sugar plantation was established in 1835, a Chinese "sugar master" had reportedly reached Hawaii by 1802 on a ship engaged in the sandalwood trade, bringing with him boiling pans and other paraphernalia for sugar making.[2] That he should have done so is not surprising, as Guangdong province is one of China's major sugar-producing areas. By the 1830s several Chinese sugar companies were in operation on the islands of Maui and Hawaii. At least half a dozen Chinese sugar masters and their mills were at work in the 1840s. The first sizable batch of Chinese—195 contract laborers recruited from the city of Amoy in Fujian province—arrived in 1852, imported into Hawaii in response to fundamental changes occurring in the kingdom.

When plantations were first organized, their managers relied on Hawaiian labor, but since many of the local people still had subsistence plots to depend on for survival, they did not take readily to the harsh work regime that sugarcane cultivation required. More important, the indigenous population was declining rapidly: its size in 1860 was at most a fifth of what it had been in 1778 when Captain Cook appeared. This sharp decline had multiple causes. Many Hawaiians with no immunity to the diseases brought by Americans and Europeans died from them, while others succumbed to cold and exposure as they went up the mountains to cut sandalwood. The commercialization of the islands' economy—in particular, a new system of land tenure urged upon the king by his American advisers—also deprived an increasing number of commoners of their traditional means of livelihood.

The alienation of land occurred very rapidly, as Edward D. Beechert has documented.[3] In the 1840s the king first made informal grants to Westerners, then signed formal leases with them, and finally allowed them to buy land outright. The changes culminated in the Great Mahele or land redistribution of 1848.

Land that hitherto had been communally held could thenceforth be sold. This enabled more and more missionary-entrepreneurs to acquire large tracts for sugar plantations.

Because sugarcane cultivation is so labor-intensive, however, before plantations could materialize a sufficient and dependable labor supply had to be secured. Several pieces of legislation were passed in 1850 toward this end. In that year, because Hawaiians, like other people from around the world, were joining the California gold rush, a law was enacted to forbid them to leave the islands without permission. Another law made it illegal for them to sign on as sailors on outbound ships. Finally, "An Act for the Governance of Masters and Servants" specified how apprentices and contract laborers were to be treated, while a judicial and administrative apparatus with penal sanctions was set up to implement it. In 1850 also, the Royal Hawaiian Agricultural Society came into being for the purpose of obtaining labor needed for land development. It was succeeded by the Planters' Society and a Bureau of Immigration in 1864.

As cane acreage expanded—albeit slowly at first—and as the Hawaiian population dwindled, an attempt was made to import Chinese laborers. The group that came in 1852 had five-year contracts. Each man received free passage and three dollars a month, including food and lodging. No more Chinese were brought in under contract again until 1865, but a handful of free immigrants entered every year in the interim. The renewed attempt to import contract laborers was a reflection of the fact that sugar production had increased greatly during the American Civil War, when sharply rising prices boosted Hawaii's output from under 600 to almost 9,000 tons. The 1865 arrivals were paid eight dollars a month; each man was supplied with two suits of clothing, a warm jacket, a pair of shoes, a bamboo hat, a mat, a pillow, and a blanket. A greater leap in numbers occurred after 1876, following the signing of the Reciprocity Treaty, which allowed Hawaiian-grown sugar to enter the United States duty-free. According to figures compiled by Ronald Takaki, sugar tonnage rose to 32,000 in 1880, 130,000 in 1890, 300,000 in 1900, and more than 500,000 in 1910.[4] Whereas only 151 Chinese had entered in 1875, 1,283 did so in 1876. Arrivals averaged more than 2,000 a year for the next decade. A very large percentage came in under contract, but there were also some who paid their own way. Altogether, around 50,000 Chinese set foot on Hawaiian soil between 1852 and the end of the nineteenth century.

As the number of Chinese increased, different groups of people began to find fault with them. Though the plantation owners considered the Chinese satisfactory workers, the fact that most of them declined to sign on for a second term after their contracts expired posed a problem. The Chinese left the sugar plantations as soon as they could because the luna (overseers) were abusive and the working conditions extremely unpleasant. Some became peddlers and merchants in towns such as Honolulu and Hilo, while others went into independent rice farming (some as owner-operators, others as tenants) and truck gardening. For several decades, rice was the second most important source of income in the Hawaiian economy, and Chinese were its main cultivators.[5] Rice acreage rose from about 1,000 acres in 1875 to almost 7,500 in 1890 to over 9,000 by 1900. A good portion of the crop grown in Hawaii was shipped to California to help feed the Chinese there.

Meanwhile, as Edward C. Lydon has recounted, the native Hawaiians, as well as missionaries and politicians who claimed to champion their welfare, thought that the increasing Chinese presence endangered the survival of the Hawaiian population. The Chinese were accused of introducing dreaded diseases, such as leprosy and smallpox, and immoral habits, such as opium smoking and gambling. Though some Chinese men had married or cohabited with Hawaiian women, their critics did not consider them a desirable vehicle for replenishing the islands' declining population. When Walter Murray Gibson, a Mormon missionary-turned-politician and an opponent of Chinese immigration, became simultaneously minister of foreign affairs and premier under King Kalakaua in 1882, he issued one regulation after another to restrict the Chinese influx, which finally ended in 1886. The planters did not protest because before stopping the flow of Chinese, Gibson had made sure a supply of Japanese would be forthcoming.[6] The Hawaiians also welcomed the change, as they considered the Japanese a more compatible "cognate" race for the purpose of repopulating the kingdom.

Far more Chinese landed in California than did in Hawaii because of the gold rush. In 1852—the same year that the first 200 or so Chinese contract laborers set foot in Hawaii—more than 20,000 Chinese passed through the San Francisco Customs House enroute to the gold fields in the Sierra Nevada foothills. Fewer than 5,000 stepped ashore in 1853, partly because California had imposed a Foreign Miners' Tax, which greatly reduced the income of non-American prospectors, but also because news of the gold discovery in Australia had by then reached Guangdong province, causing thousands to rush southward instead of eastward. However, more than 16,000 came in 1854. For the next decade, arrivals in California fluctuated between 2,000 and 9,000 a year. Then between 1867 and 1870, partly in response to recruitment efforts by the Central Pacific Railroad Company, which was building the western section of the first transcontinental railroad, some 40,000 Chinese poured into the country.

The singular importance of gold to the early immigrants in California is reflected in the folk memory of many Chinese around the world to this day: until quite recently, they called San Francisco Jiujinshan (Gaogamsan, "the Old Gold Mountain"), while Australia is known as Xinjinshan (Sungamsan, "the New Gold Mountain"). A few statistics will also illustrate the significance of gold in Chinese American history. The 1860 census takers found that virtually 100 percent of the Chinese in the continental United States were still living in California. The state continued to hold a majority of the nation's Chinese population until the turn of the century: 78, 71, 67, and 51 percent of them lived in California in 1870, 1880, 1890, and 1900, respectively. Within the state itself, 84, 45, 32, 13, and 12 percent of them were found in the mining counties in 1860, 1870, 1880, 1890, and 1900, respectively.[7] Unlike the independent white prospectors, most of whom had left the mining regions by the late 1850s, sizable numbers of Chinese remained there until the 1880s.

In terms of occupational distribution, in 1860, when surface deposits had already been depleted, fully 85 percent of the Chinese in the mining counties were still panning or digging for gold. A decade later, 65 percent of them were doing so, while in 1880, 59 percent persisted in prospecting. Since the manuscript schedules of the 1890 census were lost in a fire, no computation can be made with regard to how many Chinese miners were still at work that year, but census takers counted over 2,000 Chinese miners in California in 1900—a year when the overall Chinese population was 45,753 in the state and 89,863 in the nation.

Three principal methods were used for obtaining the precious metal: placer, hydraulic, and deep-shaft or quartz mining. The vast majority of the Chinese worked only placer claims. In the early years, when surface deposits were abundant, many miners, including Chinese, used nothing more complicated than a pan, into which they placed a small amount of gold-bearing dirt, swirling it to wash the lighter earth off the rim while letting the gold settle at the bottom. A more efficient contraption was the rocker or cradle—a wooden box with cleats (called riffles) nailed across the bottom and mounted on rockers. "Pay dirt" was placed with water into the box, which was then rocked back and forth. Such motion separated the heavier gold dust and nuggets from the rest of the dirt; as water flowed over the mixture, the gold was caught by the cleats at the bottom, while the nonauriferous dirt flowed out the open end. Another device, the long-torn, was a longer rocker that remained stationary. Mounted at an angle with a continuous stream of water flowing through it, it could handle a large volume of dirt with a minimal amount of human labor. Sluices—a series of open troughs with cleats—evolved from long-toms, requiring large volumes of water for their proper functioning.

Chinese miners used all of the above devices and also introduced some implements of their own. The most notable was the waterwheel, similar to those used by farmers in China. Mounted with buckets to scoop water from a stream or river, the wheel, as it turned slowly, emptied the buckets of water into a trough that carried the water to where it was needed. Chinese were also skilled at building wing dams that diverted water either from a small tributary or one section of a river, in order to expose the riverbed for mining. Perhaps they resorted to such ingenious contrivances because, as J. D. Borthwick observed in the early 1850s, they did not seem to like standing in water for long periods. Borthwick thought that the way Chinese mined resembled "scratching": instead of pushing their shovels forcefully into the ground as Euro-American miners did, they scraped its surface to loosen the gravel.[8]

Only a small number of Chinese attempted hydraulic mining. The most likely reason is that this method, which shot powerful jets of water against ore-bearing hillsides to wash down the dirt, required considerable capital. Since Chinese miners were periodically subjected to violence, investing a lot of money in heavy equipment was simply too risky. Those who did engage in hydraulic mining did so in rather remote areas, largely in the Siskiyou and Trinity mountains of northwestern California.

Documentation regarding Chinese participation in quartz mining—digging tunnels into the mountains that contained veins of ore—is conflicting. Some accounts suggest that no Chinese could be hired by the mining companies extracting gold this way because unionized Euro-American miners—particularly imported ones from Cornwall, who were the world's most skillful deep-shaft operators—stopped any attempts by the companies to employ Chinese. Other sources claim that a large number of Chinese miners worked for companies from the late 1860s on, and although their authors do not indicate the mining methods these companies used, they could not have been exploiting placer claims, which had been completely depleted by then.

The presence of so many miners among the Chinese influenced what other Chinese did for a living. Wherever groups of miners congregated, merchants opened stores to provision them and to serve their social and recreational needs.[9] Merchants imported a variety of ingredients needed for Chinese cooking.

Invoices of Chinese import–export firms found at San Francisco's Custom House in the early 1850s list rice, noodles, beans, yams, sugar, tea, vinegar, peanut oil, dried vegetables, bamboo shoots, dried mushrooms, ginger, cured eggs, sweetmeats, sausages, salted fish, dried shrimp and oysters, dried bean curd, and dried as well as fresh fruits. The immigrants' diet was supplemented with vegetables grown by local Chinese truck gardeners, with meat from pigs, ducks, and chickens raised by Chinese farmers, and with fish caught by Chinese fishermen. Once in a while, they also ate American canned sardines and ham, as well as fresh beef purchased from Euro-American butchers.

In addition, merchants brought in Chinese textiles and clothing, although [] pants. As shown in many photographs taken of them, another item of American apparel they seemed to fancy was felt hats, although men working in the countryside continued to depend on imported conical bamboo hats.

Merchants made it possible for Chinese immigrants to be surrounded by all the essential and familiar items of their material culture. Even rice paper and Chinese ink and brushes found their way across the Pacific, as did matches, firecrackers, joss sticks (made from Hawaiian sandalwood), washbasins, pots and pans, Chinese-style weights and measures, and a large array of herbs. Opium entered without restriction during the early years, but it was not the only recreational drug the Chinese used: most Chinese stores, even those in remote mountain areas, also stocked American cigarettes and whiskey.

Merchants played such a critical role that they became the wealthiest members and most important leaders of the community, even though in the rural areas and small towns they usually comprised only about 3 percent of the population. The larger the urban center, however, the more numerous they were. In San Francisco, not counting the gamblers, brothel owners, and other underworld entrepreneurs, merchants hovered around 10 percent of the gainfully employed.

One development that affected both Chinese miners and merchants was the building of the western half of the first transcontinental railroad—a project that employed more than 10,000 Chinese workers at its peak, many of whom were former miners.[10] In fact, the railroad company's effort to recruit Chinese laborers provided the impetus that finally took large numbers of Chinese away from the mines. Meanwhile, Chinese merchants profited from the construction project, since they served as labor contractors who gathered the men into gangs, charged each one a commission for finding him work, and provisioned the whole lot.

Proposals for a transcontinental railroad had been made since the 1840s, but it took the Civil War to spur Congress finally to pass a bill that made the construction possible. To enable private entrepreneurs to finance such a momentous undertaking, the federal government issued bonds on behalf of and granted public land to the railroad companies—land they were supposed to sell to raise the capital needed. The amount of land granted depended on the miles of tracks laid and on the difficulty of the terrain traversed. The Union Pacific Railroad Company got the contract to build westward from the Missouri River, while the Central Pacific Railroad Company, formed by four Sacramento merchants, was to build eastward from that city. Unlike the Union Pacific, which could lay one mile of track a day across open plains using cheap Irish immigrant labor, the Central Pacific had to traverse several ranges of high mountains and had, moreover, to deal with the fact that California had the nation's highest wages.

First hired as an experiment to do grading in 1865, Chinese workers numbered 3,000 by the end of the year. Despite the skepticism that was expressed about their physical strength, Chinese soon became the backbone of the company's construction crews, providing the bulk of the labor not only for unskilled tasks but for highly demanding and dangerous ones as well. Regardless of the nature of the work they did, however, all Chinese were paid the same wage, which was considerably lower than what Euro-American skilled workers received.

The first true test the Chinese faced was a huge rock outcrop called Cape Horn, around which no detour was possible. To carve a ledge on the rim of this granite bulk, Chinese were lowered by rope in wicker baskets from the top of cliffs. While thus dangled, they chiseled holes in the granite into which they stuffed black powder. Fellow workers pulled them up as the powder exploded. Those who did not make it up in time died in the explosions.

As the road ascended into the high Sierras, it often took 300 men a month to clear and grub a bare three miles. Grading the way thus cleared took even more effort. As the crew neared the crest of the mountain range, they began the almost impossible task of drilling a tunnel through solid granite. Before they got very far, winter came and snow fell. Nevertheless, the company decided to press on, conscious that its rival was racing across the plains and getting the larger share of the land grants. Thousands of Chinese worked underground in snow tunnels around the clock through the winter of 1866. It took all summer and fall to grade the route thus created, but before tracks could be laid, winter descended again with even heavier snowfalls. As one of the Central Pacific's engineers admitted years later, "a good many men" (i.e., Chinese) were lost during the terrible winter of 1867.[11] The bodies of those buried by avalanches could not even be dug out until the following spring. Once the tracks descended the eastern slopes of the Sierras, the Chinese crews sped across the hot, dry plateaus of Nevada and Utah until the two ends of the railroad joined at Promontory Point, Utah in 1869. Despite their heroic feat, the Chinese were not invited to the jubilant ceremonies that marked the completion of America's first transcontinental railroad, hailed as one of the most remarkable engineering feats of its time.

But the railroad was more than a technological wonder: it transformed the American West, especially California. Before its completion, California was geographically isolated from the rest of the country. Immigrants had to come by wagon train, while manufactured goods from the eastern United States arrived by ship around the tip of South America. The state's exports—primarily wheat from the 1860s through the 1880s—traveled by the same long route to Atlantic seaboard and British ports. The railroad's full effect was not felt for more than a decade after its completion because high passenger and freight rates limited its usage. In the mid-1880s, after a second transcontinental railroad was built, the two engaged in a cutthroat rate war. The fares they charged became so cheap that hordes of people rode the trains to California—if not to settle, then at least to sightsee.

The manner in which railroad construction was financed also affected California's development. The railroad company was supposed to have sold most of the land the federal government granted it—some 9 to 11 million acres, depending on how one counts—but it never did so, keeping the land, instead, for speculation. Because prices were so high, few settlers in California could afford to buy land. They blamed the railroad, on the one hand, and the Chinese, on the other, for their plight. As Varden Fuller has argued, in their eyes, were it not for the availability of Chinese "cheap labor," owners of large tracts would have been forced to subdivide and sell the plots at affordable prices.[12] But there was little that angry citizens could do to break the railroad company's power: with its enormous economic assets, it controlled state politics for decades.

Ironically for the Chinese, the completion of the railroad affected them negatively. The company retained several hundred of them for maintenance work, but discharged the rest, thereby instantaneously rendering almost 10,000 Chinese jobless. These former employees were not even allowed to ride the trains free of charge back to California. Instead, they straggled on foot westward in small groups, finding work wherever they could, mostly as common laborers and migrant farmworkers. But as more and more Euro-Americans appeared in California, they began to compete with the Chinese for jobs. Their resentment helped to fan the flames of the anti-Chinese movement.

Discharged Chinese railroad workers could find work in agriculture because California in the 1870s was one of the world's leading producers of wheat, a large percentage of which was shipped to Liverpool, headquarters of the world wheat market. The long and rainless California summers proved to be a real advantage: because the wheat could be thoroughly dried before being loaded in the holds of ships, it did not mold during the long voyage down the South American coast, around Cape Horn through the Straits of Magellan, and across the South and North Atlantic Ocean to Liverpool, where it brought premium prices due to its superior quality. Chinese helped to harvest the wheat but also found employment cultivating, harvesting, and packing a wide variety of other crops.

Farm owners welcomed Chinese workers when they discovered that employing them was convenient: instead of having to deal with individual seasonal laborers, they could simply arrange with a Chinese crew leader or labor contractor to have so many men at a given place on a given date, paying the contractor a lump sum for a specified job. Moreover, the Chinese boarded themselves and even provided their own tents or slept under the stars. Each group of men either chose one of their own to do the cooking or jointly paid the wages of a cook. Some of the contractors were local merchants, who charged each man a small commission for finding him a job and earned sizable profits by selling the crews their provisions.

But harvest labor was not the only kind of agricultural work the Chinese performed. In California's great Central Valley as well as smaller coastal valleys and plains, in Washington's Yakima Valley, Oregon's Hood River Valley, and in arable areas in other states west of the Rocky Mountains, Chinese leased land to become tenant farmers. For the most part, they specialized in labor-intensive vegetables, strawberries and other small fruits, deciduous tree fruits, and nuts. In the Sacramento-San Joaquin Delta, a reclaimed marshland that is one of the most fertile agricultural areas of California, Chinese tenant farmers grew potatoes, onions, and asparagus—leasing large plots, many of which they had earlier helped to drain, dike, and put under the plow. Other Chinese became commission merchants, selling the crops that their fellow countrymen as well as Euro-American farmers produced. Yet others worked as farm cooks, feeding the farm owners' families as well as the workers the latter employed.

Life was quite different for the Chinese in San Francisco, the metropolis of the Pacific Coast, where thousands of Chinese artisans and factory workers lived. Manufacturing occupied some two-fifths of the gainfully employed Chinese in the city in the 1870s and early 1880s. In crowded, poorly lit and ventilated sweatshops and factories, they made shoes, boots, slippers, overalls, shirts, underwear, woolen blankets, cigars, gunny sacks, brooms, and many other items. In other towns along the Pacific Coast, Chinese also worked in a few nascent manufacturing industries, but they did so only in very small numbers: before such places as Sacramento, Stockton, Marysville, Portland, or Seattle could develop into industrial centers, Chinese had already been driven out of light manufacturing as a result of anti-Chinese sentiment and activities. Boycotts against Chinese-made goods in the second half of the 1880s effectively eliminated them from the market.

One occupation that acquired a special significance in Chinese American history is laundering.[13] Large numbers of Chinese eventually became laundry-men, not because washing clothes was a traditional male occupation in China, but because there were very few women—and consequently virtually no washerwomen of any ethnic origin—in gold-rush California. The shortage was so acute that shirts were sent all the way from San Francisco to Honolulu to be washed and ironed at exorbitant prices in the early 1850s.

According to one anecdotal account related by Paul C. P. Siu, the first Chinese laundryman to appear in San Francisco was Wah Lee, who hung a sign, "Wash'ng and Iron'ng," over his premises at the corner of Dupont Street (now Grant Avenue) and Washington Street in 1851.[14] By 1860 there were 890 Chinese laundrymen in California, comprising 2.6 percent of the total employed Chinese in the state. By 1870 almost 3,000 Chinese in California (6 percent of the gainfully employed) were washing and ironing clothes for a living. A decade later, the number had increased to more than 5,000, representing 7.3 percent of the working Chinese in the state. There were still almost 4,800 laundrymen (11 percent of the gainfully employed Chinese) in California at the turn of the century, even though the overall Chinese population had declined drastically from the peak it had reached in the early 1880s.

Important as they were in California, laundries were even more significant in other parts of the United States, for laundering was one of four "pioneer" occupations that enabled Chinese to move eastward across the continent. Just as mining drew Chinese to the Pacific Northwest and the northern tier of the states in the Rocky Mountains and Great Plains, and railroad construction introduced Chinese first to Nevada and Utah and then to Arizona, New Mexico, and Texas, so operating laundries and restaurants allowed them to find an economic niche for themselves in towns and cities of the Midwest and along the Atlantic seaboard. By rendering a much needed service, Chinese laundrymen found a way to survive wherever they settled.

Siu's detailed study of laundries in Chicago gives an idea of how they grew. The first Chinese laundry in the city opened in 1872. Eight years later, there were 67; in 1883, 199; and ten years later, 313. The peak was reached in 1918 with 523; after that, the numbers declined. More interesting than the numerical increase was the spatial spread and the kind of people who made use of Chinese laundries. At first, the laundries were confined to the periphery of the central business district, but they soon became established in more outlying residential neighborhoods. Young married couples with both spouses employed in white-collar salaried jobs and single men and women living in rooming houses were the laundries' two main groups of customers. Relatively few laundries existed in neighborhoods with single-family dwellings; an even smaller number was found in industrial areas occupied by recent European immigrants.

Laundries both sustained and entrapped those who relied on them for survival. On the one hand, washing and ironing clothes was one of the few occupations the host society allowed the Chinese to follow after the 1880s. On the other hand, as one person interviewed by Siu observed: "white customers were prepared to patronize him as a laundryman because as such his status was low and constituted no competitive threat. If you stop to think about it, there's a very real difference between the person who washes your soiled clothing and the one who fills your prescription. As a laundryman he occupied a status which was in accordance with the social definition of the place in the economic hierarchy suitable for a member of an 'inferior race.'"[15]

Precisely because laundering was deemed an "inferior" occupation, those who relied on it for a living were isolated from and subservient to the larger community. Though Chinese laundries were located primarily in white neighborhoods, their occupants lived in a self-contained world. A great deal of both their business and social needs were met by people who came to their doors. Agents of laundry supply companies visited them regularly to take and deliver their orders; drivers of "food wagons" brought them cooked food, fresh produce, and staples; tailors came to take their measurements for custom-tailored suits that they could pay for by installment; jewelers tried to sell them gold watches and diamond rings (two of the conspicuous-consumption items that Chinese laundrymen seemed to fancy); and, on occasion, prostitutes dropped by to see if they felt in need of sex. Most laundrymen left their stores only on Sunday afternoons to eat, gamble, or visit friends in Chinatown.

Restaurants likewise enabled Chinese to settle and survive in communities with few of their fellow countrymen, for their business did not depend solely on a Chinese clientele. In gold-rush California, which was filled with men but had few women, men of any nationality willing to cook and feed others found it relatively easy to earn a living. A few observant Chinese quickly realized that cooking could provide a more steady income than many other occupations. In time, thousands of Chinese worked as cooks—in private homes, on farms, in hotels and restaurants—all over the American West. In the late nineteenth century, Chinese started moving to other parts of the country to open restaurants. Establishments in the larger towns and cities generally served only Chinese food and used only fellow Chinese as waiters and busboys, but those in the smaller communities dished up large plates of American-style beef stew, pork chops, or fried chicken as well as Chinese spare ribs, sweet and sour pork, fried rice, or chow mein, and relied on Euro-American waitresses for help.

One feature common to Chinese enterprises—be they mining claims, groceries, laundries, or restaurants—was that a large number of the people who worked in them owned shares in the business, and were thus partners, albeit often unequal ones. This practice, together with the fact that the men were often bound by kinship ties and lived in the same premises, modulated whatever conflicts might have arisen between the "bosses" and the "workers." The ability to get along with each other in close quarters was crucial: given the inhospitability of the larger society in which they found themselves, "ethnic confinement" was an important survival mechanism.

Chinese—and the other Asian immigrant groups who came after them—could find economic niches that sheltered them because of the nature of American capitalism. In the late nineteenth century, as firms became bigger and more oligopolistic through mergers and the growth of new industrial sectors, independent artisans found it more and more difficult to survive. This development was by no means universal, however: there has always been considerable room in the less-developed parts of the economy for small businesses to operate. Chinese laundries persisted until the 1950s and restaurants to this day because they fill needs unmet by the corporate structure.

At the turn of the century, the emerging capitalist structure affected not only industries but also agriculture. In the development of the large-scale cultivation and marketing of specialty crops for the export market, Hawaii and California led the nation. By the 1880s neither region was a frontier any longer, and immigration into each was dictated in large part by the needs of the agribusiness that became the very foundation of both their economies. But Hawaii and California did differ in one important way: Hawaii's economy has been based on one crop, sugar, and has been dominated by five big companies, while that in California has been more diverse, in terms of what crops are grown as well as the pattern of landownership and the marketing of crops. The capital to develop both places, however, came initially from the eastern United States and, to a smaller extent, from Great Britain.

Sugar production increased rapidly in Hawaii between 1876, when the Reciprocity Treaty was signed, and 1891, when the McKinley tariff eliminated the duty-free status of Hawaiian sugar and restored protection to American producers on the mainland. Important as the Reciprocity Treaty was, the Hawaiian sugar boom could not have occurred without the importation of a new group of Asian laborers, the Japanese.[16] The newcomers soon outnumbered Hawaiians and Chinese, up to that time the mainstays of the plantation labor force. Although Hawaiians and part-Hawaiians still comprised a majority of the workers, their numbers were declining. Chinese, meanwhile, were coming both from China and the Pacific Coast, but these arrivals were barely sufficient to replace the Chinese leaving the plantations after their contracts expired. Thus, new labor supplies had to be found if the Hawaiian sugar industry was to take advantage of the preferential treatment conferred by the Reciprocity Treaty.

By the time Japanese started coming, commercial sugar production was concentrated in what historians of Hawaii have called "industrial plantations"—a more efficient, large-scale system that enabled the yield per acre to increase from just under 6,500 pounds in 1895 to almost 8,700 pounds in 1900. The importation of Japanese laborers for these plantations was much more organized than it had been for the Chinese. Under the Irwin Convention, before each Japanese worker left home, he or she signed a contract that specified which plantation he or she would be assigned to. With the exception of the first two shipments, all the emigrants sailed to Hawaii on Japanese ships. Family groupings were kept intact, and more often than not, people from the same villages ended up in the same plantations.

After Irwin stopped supervising labor emigration, private companies took over. They operated under close government supervision between 1894 and 1908. Their representatives negotiated with plantation owners for the number of workers the latter desired, the terms of the contracts, as well as the amount ($30 in the 1890s) the companies would receive for each worker brought to the islands. After the 1900 Organic Law made Hawaii a formal U.S. territory, the entry of contract laborers became illegal. Thereafter, arriving passengers had to prove they were free immigrants, each with a minimum of $50 in his or her pocket.

Furthermore, Japanese ships no longer monopolized the Yokohama-Honolulu traffic. Japan's fleet was tied up during the Sino-Japanese War (1894–95), which gave American lines such as the Pacific Mail Steamship Company (the major carrier of Chinese passengers to the United States) and the Occidental and Oriental Steamship Company a chance to enter the Japanese steerage-passenger business. From the late 1890s on, American vessels dominated the Japanese passenger traffic to both Hawaii and the mainland. The emigration companies' agents, along with representatives of the Planters' Labor and Supply Company (which became the Hawaiian Sugar Planters' Association in 1895) and officials of the Bureau of Immigration (and after 1900, federal immigration officers), met each incoming shipload. Inspectors, doctors, and interpreters all participated in the landing process. Before the workers could be distributed to the plantations, each of them had to register with the Japanese consulate in Honolulu. Japanese destined for plantations in Oahu were transported there without further ado, while those intended for the other islands had to reboard inter-island steamers for the final leg of their journey.

Living conditions on the plantations were primitive. On most plantations, workers of various national origins were segregated in different camps. Single men slept in bunkhouses on wooden shelves several feet above the ground, while families were assigned cottages where these were available. On plantations without such separate dwellings, families were crammed into rooms created in bunkhouses with partitions that went up only to the rafters, thus offering no auditory privacy. Sometimes women with crying babies were told to leave the bunkhouse; they had to spend the night in the cane fields so others could sleep. Campsites in general, and the water supply in particular, were frequently unsanitary. Neither cooking nor recreational facilities were available in the early years. These were built only after laborers repeatedly engaged in work stoppages and strikes to demand improved working conditions, and after rising desertion rates alarmed the planters.

Plantation work was both regimented and unpleasant. A 5 a.m. whistle roused the camps each morning. After a quick breakfast, laborers divided into gangs, each led by a luna, and set off for the fields at 5:30. These luna supervised each step in the production process, frequently on horseback. Some were infamous for their cruelty: they not only verbally abused the laborers but on occasion hit and kicked them to maintain discipline and to keep up the pace of production. They did not allow the workers to talk in the fields or even to stand up to stretch while hoeing weeds.

During different stages of the cane's growth cycle, workers performed different tasks in the fields and mills: plowing and cultivating the fields in preparation for planting; planting, watering, and otherwise caring for the growing cane; hoeing the earth between the rows of cane to get rid of weeds; digging ditches for irrigation and maintaining them; stripping dead leaves from the stalks before the 12-foot-tall cane was cut and harvested; loading the stalks onto carts or trams running on movable single-gauge tracks; transporting the loads to the mills and unloading them; placing the cane into crushers to extract the juice; boiling the liquid to make molasses; and desiccating the thick syrup into coarse brown sugar. The final process of turning the moist, brown lumps into dry, white granules was usually carried out somewhere else, often in refineries on the mainland. Because cane leaves have tiny, sharp bristles, the field workers wore several layers of clothing to protect their hands and bodies, despite the humid heat under which they labored. The dust during harvesting was also awful, clogging nostrils and windpipes. Given such harsh working conditions, it is little wonder, then, that plantation laborers were not eager to renew their contracts or to stay on the plantations if they had saved up sufficient funds to leave.

When the 1900 Organic Law made all contracts null and void in Hawaii, labor recruiters from the mainland, working in conjunction with Japanese boardinghouse owners in both the ports of departure and arrival, descended on Hawaii to lure Japanese workers away with the prospect of higher wages. Railroad companies, lumber mills, and farmers in the Pacific Northwest and in California all desired Japanese labor. (The recruiters did not try to entice Chinese because Chinese exclusion, as chapter 3 recounts, had been in effect in the United States since 1882.) Between the beginning of 1902 and the end of 1906, almost 34,000 Japanese left the islands for Pacific Coast ports. To plug this leakage, plantation owners successfully urged the territorial government to pass a law in 1905 requiring each recruiter to pay a $500 license. Two years later, President Theodore Roosevelt signed an executive order to prohibit Japanese holding passports for Hawaii, Mexico, or Canada from remigrating to the continental United States. As a result, the Japanese exodus to the continental United States soon became a mere trickle. By the 1910s a vast majority of the Japanese departing from Hawaii was headed for Japan, and not the mainland United States.

The lives of Korean and Filipino plantation workers were no different from those of Japanese. By the late 1920s Filipinos had become the largest ethnic group in the plantation labor force, working in plantations whose average size had grown steadily from an average of slightly over 400 acres in 1880 to almost 2,500 acres in 1900 to over 5,300 acres by 1930. Along with the size increase came improvements in housing, recreational facilities, and sanitation conditions. Plantation owners and managers had learned by then that they could better control and keep workers by small acts of kindness than by harsh treatment.

Japanese, Korean, Asian Indian, and Filipino immigrants along the Pacific Coast likewise performed farm work, but because Hawaiian plantations and mainland agribusiness are organized differently, the lives of Asian farm workers in the islands and on the mainland were dissimilar in one fundamental way: plantation workers remained in one place, while mainland farm workers moved with the crops. Given the great variety of crops grown along the Pacific Coast, something is being harvested virtually every month of the year, but each harvest lasts only two to six weeks. Once it is over, the farm workers must move on, a migrant labor force constantly in search of work. Nevertheless, despite the fact that a migratory existence was, in many ways, even harsher than plantation life, the mainland offered a better chance for climbing up the so-called agricultural ladder, whereby laborers save up enough money to lease land as tenant farmers and eventually to buy land as farm owner-operators. The Japanese, in particular, had a penchant to use this channel of advancement.[17]

The fact that Japanese immigrants were able to benefit from the rapid growth in the production of specialty crops in the western United States is reflected in immigration statistics. Before 1908 only 55,000 Japanese had come to the mainland, compared to the more than 150,000 landing in Hawaii. But between 1908 and 1924 more than 120,000 arrived at Pacific Coast ports, in contrast to the 48,000 entering the islands. Japanese first entered the California migrant farm labor force in 1888, when several dozen students harvested crops during their summer vacation in the Vaca Valley of Solano County, located to the northeast of San Francisco. Two years later, several hundred Japanese appeared as grape pickers in the Fresno area of the San Joaquin Valley. From this modest beginning, Japanese farm workers eventually found their way to all the other major agricultural regions up and down the Pacific Coast and into the Southwest and the intermountain states. During the first years of the twentieth century, fully two-thirds of the Japanese in California (about 16,000 individuals) earned a living as farm laborers.[18] That number remained stable for the next decade as a result of a change in the pattern of immigration: although the Gentlemen's Agreement cut off any further influx of male laborers, immigrants found a loophole by sending for brides and younger relatives known as *yobiyose* (those "called" abroad by kinsmen), who worked for their husbands or elder relatives after arrival.

By saving their wages and by pooling resources, many immigrants scraped together the funds needed to lease small plots usually to grow strawberries, medium-size tracts to plant tomatoes, celery, onions, and a wide variety of other vegetables and fruits, or even rather large acreages to cultivate row and field crops. By 1913, when California passed its first alien land law, more than 6,000 Japanese had become tenant farmers. This number increased to 8,000 four years later. The growth of Japanese tenant farming was likewise highly visible in Oregon and Washington and to a lesser degree in the other western states. In Utah and Colorado many Japanese produced and harvested beets on contract. Those farmers who purchased land in California tended to specialize in grapes—a fact that caused them considerable financial hardship when Prohibition went into effect in 1919.

The agricultural productivity of Japanese immigrants in the western United States reached its zenith in 1917, when the United States finally entered World War I, greatly increasing the country's need for food while simultaneously removing male citizens from their farms for military service. In that year Japanese in California produced almost 90 percent of the state's output of celery, asparagus, onions, tomatoes, berries, and cantaloupes; more than 70 percent of the floricultural products; 50 percent of the seeds; 45 percent of the sugar beets; 40 percent of the leafy vegetables; and 35 percent of the grapes.[19]

The achievements of Korean and Asian Indian tenant farmers were less spectacular simply because there were far fewer of them.[20] Unlike Japanese farmers, who were found virtually everywhere, Korean tenant farmers worked largely in the San Joaquin Valley around the towns of Reedley and Dinuba, where they specialized in deciduous fruit; in the Sacramento-San Joaquin Delta, where they grew row crops; and in the upper Sacramento Valley, where they cultivated rice. A handful of Koreans also grew sugar beets on contract in Colorado and Utah. Small numbers of Asian Indian tenant farmers were found in scattered locations, but the bulk of them congregated in the Imperial and Coachella valleys in southern California, where they raised cotton, cantaloupes, and winter lettuce, after irrigation works made the desertlike land there arable.

Filipinos became the largest group of Asian farm laborers along the Pacific Coast in the 1920s, but they never managed to climb the agricultural ladder for reasons related to the timing of their arrival.[21] First, various anti-alien land laws had been passed by the time they came in large numbers. Whereas the Chinese, Japanese, Koreans, and Asian Indians—either by virtue of having American-born children in whom alien parents could vest title to whatever land they owned, or by relying on relationships they had formed earlier with landowners who continued to lease to them—found ways to continue farming, the newly arrived Filipinos could use no such loopholes. Second, farm prices were falling drastically in the early 1920s, following the prosperity agriculture had enjoyed during World War I. So, even if there had been no legal obstacles, Filipinos would have found it difficult to become tenant farmers or independent owner-operators in those years. Finally, by the time Filipinos came, the defenders of Euro-American supremacy had had more than half a century to refine and perfect mechanisms for keeping nonwhites in their place. In short, by the 1920s economic niches such as those the Chinese and Japanese had carved out for themselves were much harder to find.

Two other outdoor occupations that had sustained tens of thousands of Chinese—gold mining and railroad construction—provided a living to only a few of the later-arriving Asian immigrant groups, again because the latter entered an economy that was considerably more mature than the one that had greeted the Chinese. By the late 1880s and early 1890s, when Japanese started coming, the gold rush in California, the Pacific Northwest, and the Dakotas was over. However, several thousand Japanese and dozens of Koreans did work as wage laborers in mining companies.[22] As for the railroads, their trunk lines had been completed. Workers were now needed not so much for laying track as for maintaining what had been built. Accordingly, more than 12,000 Japanese and smaller numbers of Koreans and Asian Indians labored as section hands.[23]

Unlike mining, fishing is an extractive industry whose resource is less easily depleted. Following the footsteps of the Chinese, who had been among the pioneer fishermen of the Pacific Coast—catching not only fish but also shrimp and abalone, which they dried and exported to China—many Japanese operated their own small fleets all the way from Baja California in the south to Alaska in the north. Meanwhile, thousands of Japanese and Filipinos (alongside some Chinese) worked in the salmon canneries of Oregon, Washington, British Columbia, and Alaska every summer.[24]

In towns and cities, similarities and differences also existed in the occupational history of the various Asian immigrant groups. Large numbers of Japanese entered the labor market as domestic servants, just as the Chinese had done. In fact, Japanese first competed successfully against the Chinese by accepting lower wages. There were three kinds of Japanese domestics. "School boys"—young men from poor families who worked as live-in servants while attending school part-time—usually received free room and board plus a token weekly or monthly salary. Day workers cleaned houses, washed windows, prepared meals, washed and ironed clothes, or tended yards and gardens for a daily wage, while living in Japanese-operated boardinghouses. The third kind of domestic workers found long-term employment in restaurants and

Japanese-owned companies, performing whatever tasks their employers desired. By the end of the first decade of the twentieth century, the U.S. Immigration Commission estimated that 12,000 to 15,000 Japanese in the western United States earned a living in domestic service.[25]

Filipino boys and men were also readily hired as household servants, as janitors in office buildings and other institutional facilities, as bellhops and doormen in hotels, and as waiters and cooks in restaurants and other eating facilities. Few Koreans or Asian Indians, however, relied on domestic service for their livelihood, for reasons that have not yet been studied.

Unlike the Chinese who actively pursued manufacturing for a quarter century in San Francisco, only a few Japanese immigrants and an even smaller handful of Koreans, Asian Indians, or Filipinos did so. In 1886 Euro-Americans launched a boycott of merchandise made by Chinese, which drove the latter out of producing merchandise for the wider market. Thereafter, Asian entrepreneurs were confined to manufacturing ethnic foodstuffs. Chinese and Japanese made soy sauce and tofu (soybean cake) and germinated bean sprouts; Japanese made miso (bean paste for seasoning broth and other dishes) and *kamaboko* (fish cake); and Koreans made *kimchi* (hot pickled vegetables).

Like the Chinese, many Japanese became merchants, importing cooking ingredients for fellow immigrants, and curios and art goods such as lacquerware, china, parasols, fans, scrolls, tea, and silk goods for Euro-American customers. One special group of Japanese merchants were silk importers in New York, who worked hard over several decades to capture a share of the silk trade between Japan and the United States. According to Scott Miyakawa, the pioneers in this venture landed in New York in 1876, only four years after a Japanese consulate had been established in that city. At that time, all silk from Japan that entered the United States came via Europe, Japanese silk export being entirely in the hands of Western merchants. When the Japanese merchants showed samples of the silk threads spun in Japan that they had brought with them to some of New York's largest silk importers, they were told that their threads were neither strong enough nor uniform enough in size for the fast machinery then in use in America. Only after years of effort, as well as a vast improvement in the quality of their merchandise, did these Japanese silk merchants succeed in setting up direct shipments of silk from Japan to the United States. In time, silk became the most valuable item in the trade between the two countries.[26]

Very few Koreans and almost no Asian Indians or Filipinos became merchants in the United States for a variety of reasons. Though the earliest Koreans to enter the continental United States were ginseng (a medicinal root) merchants, few persons with a business background came during the brief period of Korean mass emigration to Hawaii. Then after Japan declared Korea its protectorate in 1905, and especially after it colonized the country in 1910, Japanese officials prohibited Koreans from engaging in the import–export trade. Moreover, given the small size of the immigrant community, there was no ready-made ethnic market to speak of. Koreans in Hawaii who went into business kept boardinghouses and bathhouses or ran used furniture and clothing stores.

No study has yet been done to discover why Asian Indian immigrants did not become merchants. One likely reason is that most of them were *jats,* members of a farming caste. The Indian caste system prescribed what occupations various groups could follow, so people rarely took up work that was not traditional among their ancestors. Even though Sikhs, as members of a separate religion, did not subscribe to Hindu beliefs and were theoretically outside of the caste system, they nevertheless adhered to certain broad cultural norms, which, though based on the tenets of Hinduism, affected Hindus and non-Hindus alike.

In the case of Filipinos, history provides an answer to why so few of them entered business in the United States. Since Spanish colonial days, retail trade in the Philippines had been in the hands of immigrant Chinese merchants, so relatively few of the indigenous people acquired experience in trade. Those who did so tended to be Filipinas, and not Filipinos. In the United States, Filipinos ran only very small operations: cigar stalls, candy stands, and barbershops. In Hawaii, they were barbers, tailors, grocers, and importers of Philippine consumer goods.

Quite apart from the cultural baggage that various groups of immigrants brought with them, and the different timing of their entry, differences in the regional economies of the United States have also affected the manner in which each has been incorporated into American society. During the late nineteenth and early twentieth centuries, while millions of European immigrants found jobs in the growing metallurgical, chemical, and electrical industries of eastern and midwestern cities, hundreds of thousands of incoming Asians worked in the fields, orchards, households, laundries, and restaurants of the American West. Each new group of European immigrant industrial workers initially experienced economic exploitation, but in time, most of them managed to secure a measure of protection through unionization. In contrast, wage earners in agriculture and in the service sector, regardless of their ethnic origins, have been extremely difficult to organize, as their work is seasonal, migratory, or part-time. To this day, farm and service workers, the vast majority of whom are either nonwhite or female, remain trapped in nonunionized, dead-end jobs. Ironically, as will be seen in chapter 5, even when Asian immigrant workers did try to organize, their petitions for affiliation with national unions were rejected.

Economic factors alone, however, do not account fully for the obstacles the early Asian immigrants encountered. Social, political, and legal barriers, which became increasingly clearly defined vis-à-vis Asians as the nineteenth century progressed, have also played a significant role in delimiting the world in which they lived. That is why, although Chinese initially found work in many sectors of the economy and over a wide geographic area, they eventually had to retreat to urban enclaves. Most members of the later-arriving groups likewise found themselves relegated to the lowest echelons of the labor market. Briefly put, racial discrimination is what separates the historical experience of Asian immigrants from that of Europeans, on the one hand, and makes it resemble that of enslaved Africans and dispossessed Native Americans and Mexican Americans, on the other hand.

THE MAKING OF RADICAL RECONSTRUCTION

ERIC FONER

I t was a peculiarity of nineteenth-century politics that more than a year elapsed between the election of a Congress and its initial meeting. The Thirty-Ninth Congress, elected in 1864 in the midst of war, assembled in December 1865 to confront the crucial issues of Reconstruction: Who would control the South? Who would rule the nation? What was to be the status of the emancipated slave? In both houses, Republicans outnumbered Democrats by better than three to one. The interaction between the Republican party's distinctive factions would effectively determine the contours of Congressional policy.

The Radical Republicans

On the party's left stood the Radical Republicans, a self-conscious political generation with shared experiences and commitments, a grass-roots constituency, a moral sensibility, and a program for Reconstruction. At the core of Congressional Radicalism were men whose careers had been shaped by the slavery controversy: Charles Sumner, Benjamin Wade, and Henry Wilson in the Senate; Thad-deus Stevens, George W. Julian, and James M. Ashley in the House. With the exception of Stevens they represented constituencies centered in New

Eric Foner, "The Making of Radical Reconstruction," *A Short History of Reconstruction 1863–1877*, pp. 104–123. Copyright © 1990 by HarperCollins Publishers. Reprinted with permission.

England and the belt of New England migration that stretched across the rural North through upstate New York, Ohio's Western Reserve, northern Illinois, and the upper Northwest. Here lay rapidly growing communities of family farms and small towns, where the superiority of the free labor system appeared self-evident, antebellum reform had flourished, and the Republican party commanded overwhelming majorities.

The preeminent Radical leaders, Thaddeus Stevens and Charles Sumner differed in personality and political style. The recognized floor leader of House Republicans, Stevens was a master of Congressional infighting, parliamentary tactics, and blunt speaking. One contemporary called him "a rude jouster in political and personal warfare." Sumner, disliked by Senate colleagues for egotism, self-righteousness, and stubborn refusal to compromise, acted as the voice, the embodiment, of the New England conscience. Unconcerned with the details of committee work and legislative maneuvering, his forte lay in lengthy, erudite speeches in which he expounded the recurrent theme of his political career: equality before the law. Abolitionists considered him *their* politician. So too did ordinary blacks, North and South, who deluged him with requests for advice and accounts of their grievances. "Your name," wrote a black army veteran in 1869, "shall live in our hearts for ever."

Uniting Stevens, Sumner, and the other Radicals in 1865 was the conviction that the Civil War constituted a "golden moment" for far-reaching change. The driving force of Radical ideology was the Utopian vision of a nation whose citizens enjoyed equality of civil and political rights secured by a powerful and beneficent national state. For decades, long before any conceivable political benefit derived from its advocacy, Stevens, Sumner, and other Radicals had defended the unpopular cause of black suffrage and castigated the idea that America was a "white man's government" (a doctrine, Stevens remarked, "that damned the late Chief Justice [Roger B. Taney] to everlasting fame; and, I fear, to everlasting fire"). There was no room for a legally and politically submerged class in the "perfect republic" that must emerge from the Civil War.

To Radical egalitarianism, the Civil War wedded a new conception of the powers and potentialities of the national state. More fully than other Republicans, the Radicals embraced the wartime expansion of national authority, determined not to allow federalism and states' rights to obstruct a sweeping national effort to define and protect the rights of citizens. For Stevens, the war had created its own logic and imperatives. "We are making a nation," he told the House. The vanquished Southern states had sacrificed their constitutional standing and could be treated by Congress as conquered provinces. Yet Stevens's disregard for constitutional niceties denied him broad support. Other Radicals turned to a different reservoir of federal power, the Constitution's clause guaranteeing to each state a republican form of government. Sumner called the provision "a sleeping giant ... never until this recent war awakened, but now it comes forward with a giant's power. There is no clause in the Constitution like it. There is no other clause which gives to Congress such supreme power over the states." A government that denied any of its citizens equality before the law and did not rest fully on the consent of the governed, he insisted, ceased to be republican.

Reconstruction Radicalism was first and foremost a civic ideology, grounded in a definition of American citizenship. On the economic issues of the day no distinctive or unified Radical position existed. Stevens, himself a small iron manufacturer, favored an economic program geared to the needs of aspiring entrepreneurs, including tariff protection, low interest rates, plentiful greenback currency, and promotion of internal improvements. On the other hand, Radicals like Charles Sumner and *Nation* editor E. L. Godkin, men attuned to orthodox laissez-faire economic theory, favored a low tariff, the swift resumption of specie payments, and minimal government involvement in the economy. Generally, Congressional Radicals viewed economic issues as secondary to those of Reconstruction. "No question of finance, or banks, or currency, or tariffs," declared Illinois Sen. Richard Yates, "can obscure this mighty moral question of the age." Nor did capitalists agree among themselves on Reconstruction. Bostonian John Murray Forbes, a leading investor in Midwestern railroads, viewed black suffrage as essential to creating the political conditions necessary for Northern investment in a reconstructed South. Radicals also won support among manufacturers who saw upwardly mobile blacks as a new market for their products. But other businessmen, especially those with ties to the cotton trade or who hoped to invest in the South, feared Radical policies would "disrupt the cheap Southern labor force" and interfere with the resumption of cotton production.

Radical Republicanism did possess a social and economic vision, but one that derived from the free labor ideology rather than from any one set of business interests. The South, Radicals believed, should be reshaped in the image of the small-scale competitive capitalism of the North. "My dream," one explained in 1866, "is of a model republic, extending equal protection and rights to all men. ... The wilderness shall vanish, the church and school-house will appear; ... the whole land will revive under the magic touch of free labor." In such a society, the freedmen would enjoy the same economic opportunities as white laborers. A correspondent of Sumner's, describing how New York City hotels denied his black servant accommodations, strikingly articulated the Radical ideal of equal opportunity regardless of race:

> Is not this state of things a disgrace to America, as a land of liberty and freedom? Must the black man—as free—be insulted and humiliated at every step? ... The white servant is deemed not on an equality with his employer—yet recognized in the right to rise to that equality. Neither is the black servant on an equality with his employer—yet has an equal right with the white servant to gain it.

The idea of remaking Southern society led a few Radicals to propose that the federal government overturn the plantation system and provide the former slaves with homesteads. In a speech to Pennsylvania's Republican convention in September 1865, Stevens called for the seizure of the 400 million acres belonging to the wealthiest ten percent of Southerners:

> The whole fabric of southern society *must* be changed, and never can it be done if this opportunity is lost. ...How can republican institutions, free schools, free churches, free social intercourse exist in a mingled community of nabobs and serfs? If the South is ever to be made a safe republic let her lands be cultivated by the toil of the owners.

Confiscation, Stevens believed, would break the power of the Souths traditional ruling class, transform the Southern social structure, and create a triumphant Southern Republican party composed of black and white yeomen and Northern purchasers of planter land.

Even among the Radicals, however, only a handful stressed the land question as uncompromisingly as did Stevens. Most deemed land for the freedmen, though commendable, not nearly as crucial to Reconstruction as black suffrage. In a free-labor South, with civil and political equality secured, black and white would find their own level, and, as Benjamin Wade put it, "finally occupy a platform according to their merits." The key was that all must be given "a perfectly fair chance."

Yet whatever Radicals' indecision as to the economic future of the postwar South, the core of their ideology—that a powerful national state must guarantee blacks equal political standing and equal opportunity in a free-labor economy—called for a striking departure in American public life. As Congress assembled, no one knew how many Republicans were ready to advance this far. The growing perception of white Southern intransigence, and President Johnson's indifference to the rights of blacks, helped propel the party's center of gravity to the left. Radicalism, however, possessed a dynamic of its own, based above all on the reality that in a time of crisis, Radicals alone seemed to have a coherent sense of purpose. The "one body of men who had any positive affirmative ideas," Texas Senator-elect Oran M. Roberts discovered upon arriving in Washington, was "the vanguard of the radical party. They knew exactly what they wanted to do, and were determined to do it." Repeatedly, Radicals had staked out unpopular positions, only to be vindicated by events. Uncompromising opposition to slavery's expansion; emancipation; the arming of black troops—all these had, at first, little support, yet all finally found their way into the mainstream of Republican opinion. "These are no times of ordinary politics," declared Wendell Phillips. "These are formative hours: the national purpose and thought grows and ripens in thirty days as much as ordinary years bring it forward."

Origins of Civil Rights

From the day the Thirty-Ninth Congress assembled, it was clear the Republican majority viewed Johnson's policies with misgivings. Clerk of the House Edward McPherson omitted the names of newly elected Southern Congressmen as he called the roll, and the two houses proceeded to establish a Joint Committee on Reconstruction to investigate conditions in the Southern states and report on whether any were entitled to representation.

Some of Johnson's supporters considered these steps a direct challenge to Presidential authority, but Johnson's annual message to Congress took a conciliatory approach. Essentially, the President insisted, "the work of restoration" was now complete—all that remained was for Congress to admit Southern representatives. On the other hand, he conceded that Congress had the right to determine the qualifications of its members, apparently offering it some role in judging Reconstruction's progress. Most Republicans appear to have accepted the message as an acceptable starting point for discussions of Reconstruction.

Radical proposals to overturn the Johnson governments and commit Congress to black suffrage fell on deaf ears. No party, however strong, could stand a year on this platform," one Republican newspaper commented.

With the Radical initiative in abeyance, political leadership in Congress passed to the moderates. Politically, ideologically, and temperamentally, moderate leaders like James G. Blaine and John A. Bingham in the House and Lyman Trumbull, John Sherman, and William Pitt Fessenden in the Senate differed markedly from their Radical colleagues. While fully embracing the changes brought about by the Civil War, moderate Republicans viewed Reconstruction as a practical problem, not an opportunity to impose an open-ended social revolution on the South. Nor did they believe a break with Johnson inevitable or desirable. If "Sumner and Stevens, and a few other such men do not embroil us with the President," Fessenden insisted, "matters can be satisfactorily arranged … to the great bulk of Union men throughout the States." Nor were moderates enthusiastic about the prospect of black suffrage, seeing it as a political liability in the North and less likely to provide a stable basis for a new Republican party in the South than a political alliance with forward-looking whites.

Nonetheless, moderate Republicans believed Johnson's Reconstruction policies required modification. Alarmed by the numerous "rebels" holding office in the South, they insisted on further guarantees of "loyalty" and hoped Johnson would repudiate talk of party realignment and stop meeting so openly with "obnoxious Democrats." Equally important, while rejecting black suffrage, mainstream Republicans had embraced civil equality for blacks. The moderates' dilemma was that most of the rights they sought to guarantee for blacks had always been state concerns. Federal action to protect these rights threatened an undue "centralization" of power. Rejecting talk of "conquered provinces" or states reverting to territories, moderates adopted a constitutional position not unlike the President's. While indestructible, the states had forfeited some of their rights by attempting secession; for the moment, they remained in the "grasp of war." Johnson had used similar reasoning to appoint provisional governors and require states to ratify the Thirteenth Amendment. Moderates believed the same logic empowered Congress to withhold representation from the South until the essential rights of the freedmen had been guaranteed.

Two bills reported to the Senate in January 1866 by Lyman Trumbull, chairman of the Judiciary Committee, defined the moderates' policy. The first extended the life of the Freedmen's Bureau and authorized agents to take jurisdiction of cases involving blacks and punish state officials denying blacks the "civil rights belonging to white persons." The bill represented a radical departure from traditional federal policy, but as Trumbull assured the Senate, the Bureau was "not intended as a permanent institution." More far-reaching was his second measure, the Civil Rights Bill, which Henry J. Raymond, editor of the *New York Times* and a Congressman from New York, called "one of the most important bills ever presented to this House for its action." This defined all persons born in the United States (except Indians) as national citizens and spelled out rights they were to enjoy equally without regard to racemaking contracts, bringing lawsuits, and enjoying the benefit of "all laws and proceedings for the security of person and property." No state law or custom could deprive any citizen of what Trumbull called these "fundamental rights belonging to every man as a free man.

In constitutional terms, the Civil Rights Bill represented the first attempt to give meaning to the Thirteenth Amendment, to define in legislative terms the essence of freedom. The bill proposed, one Congressman declared, "to secure to a poor, weak class of laborers the right to make contracts for their labor, the power to enforce the payment of their wages, and the means of holding and enjoying the proceeds of their toil." If states could deny blacks these rights, another Republican remarked, "then I demand to know, of what practical value is the amendment abolishing slavery?" But, beyond these specific rights, moderates, like the Radicals, rejected the entire idea of laws differentiating between black and white in access to the courts and penalties for crimes. The shadow of the Black Codes hung over these debates, and Trumbull declared his intention "to destroy all these discriminations."

As the first statutory definition of the rights of American citizenship, the Civil Rights Bill embodied a profound change in federal-state relations and reflected how Radical ideas had entered the party's mainstream. Before the Civil War, James G. Blaine later remarked, only "the wildest fancy of a distempered brain" could envision an act of Congress conferring upon blacks "all the civil rights pertaining to a white man." And although primarily intended to benefit the freedman, the bill invalidated many discriminatory laws in the North. "I admit," said Maine Sen. Lot M. Morrill, "that this species of legislation is absolutely revolutionary. But are we not in the midst of a revolution?"

In fact, however, the bill combined elements of continuity and change, reflecting Republican opinion in early 1866. It honored the traditional presumption that the primary responsibility for law enforcement lay with the states, while creating a latent federal presence to be triggered by discriminatory state laws. Nor did Congress create a national police force or permanent military presence to protect the rights of citizens. Instead it placed the burden of enforcement on the federal courts. And despite its intriguing reference to the role "custom" played in depriving blacks of legal equality, the bill was primarily directed against public, not private, acts of injustice. Moderates perceived discriminatory state laws as the greatest threat to blacks' rights, a questionable assumption when the freedmen faced rampant violence as well as unequal treatment by sheriffs, judges, and juries, often under laws that made no mention of race. And, as Trumbull insisted, the bill contained nothing "about the political rights of the Negro."

Thus, by February 1866, Republicans had united on Trumbull's Freedmen's Bureau and Civil Rights Bills as necessary amendments to Presidential Reconstruction. Meanwhile, the persistent complaints of persecution forwarded to Washington by Southern blacks and white loyalists persuaded Congress that the Southern states could not be trusted to manage their own affairs without federal oversight. Particularly alarming was the testimony gathered by the Joint Committee on Reconstruction. Army officers, Bureau agents, freedmen, and Southern Unionists repeated tales of injustice. Early in February, North Carolina Senator-elect John Pool concluded that Southern members would not gain admission for some time and that the South faced "conditions that would never have been thought of, if a more prudent and wise course had been adopted" by the Johnson governments.

To the surprise and dismay of Congress, the President vetoed the Freedmen's Bureau Bill. Moreover, rejecting a conciliatory draft written by Secretary of State William H. Seward, which criticized the bill's specifics while acknowledging a federal responsibility for the freedmen, Johnson's message repudiated the

Bureau entirely, deriding it as an "immense patronage" unwarranted by the Constitution and unafford-able given "the condition of our fiscal affairs." Congress, he pointed out, had never provided economic relief, established schools, or purchased land for "our own people;" such aid, moreover, threatened the "character" and "prospects" of the freedmen by implying that they did not have to work for a living. These matters, Johnson added, should not be decided while eleven states remained unrepresented, and at any rate the President—"chosen by the people of all the States"—had a broader view of the national interest than members of Congress, elected "from a single district."

This was a remarkable document. In appealing to fiscal conservatism, raising the specter of an im-mense federal bureaucracy overriding citizens' rights, and insisting self-help, not dependence on outside assistance, offered the surest road to economic advancement, Johnson voiced themes that to this day have sustained opposition to federal aid for blacks. At the same time, he falsely accused Congress of intend-ing to make the Bureau "a permanent branch of the public administration" and showed no sympathy whatever for the freedmen's plight. As for Johnson's exalting himself above Congress, this, one Republican remarked, "is modest for a man … made President by an assassin." The veto ensured a bitter political struggle between Congress and the President, for, as Fessenden accurately predicted, "he will and must … veto every other bill we pass" concerning Reconstruction.

Why did Johnson choose this path? The President had been remarkably successful in retaining support among Northerners and Southerners, Republicans and Democrats, but the Freedmen's Bureau Bill forced him to begin choosing among his diverse allies. Johnson knew Southern whites disliked the Bureau and Northern Democrats clamored for its destruction. He seems to have interpreted moderate Republican efforts to avoid a split as evidence that they feared an open breach in the party. And he was convinced the Radicals were conspiring against him.

Johnson, reported William H. Trescot, hoped the Republican mainstream would "form a new party with the President," excluding the Radicals. Unfortunately for this strategy, Johnson's belief that only the Radicals were concerned about the freedmen's rights caused him to misconstrue divisions within Republican ranks. The Senate vote on overriding his veto ought to have given him pause, for although the bill fell two votes short of the necessary two-thirds, thirty of thirty-eight Republicans voted for repassage. Trescot now recognized that Republicans might well unite against the President, inaugurating "a fight this fall such as has never been seen." But Johnson refused to believe that the majority of Republicans would insist on federal protection for the freedmen. The day after the Senate vote, the President continued his assault upon the Radicals. In an impromptu Washington's Birthday speech, he equated Stevens, Sumner, and Wendell Phillips with Confederate leaders, since all were "opposed to the fundamental principles of this Government." He even implied that they were plotting his assassination.

Attention now turned to the Civil Rights Bill. Republican opinion, Johnson's supporters warned him, insisted that the freedmen must have "the same rights of property and person" as whites. But this premise Johnson rejected. His veto message repudiated both the specific terms of the Civil Rights Bill and its underlying principle. The assertion of national power to protect blacks' civil rights, he insisted, violated "all our experience as a people" and constituted a "stride towards centralization, and the concentration of all legislative powers in the national Government." Most striking was the message's blatant racism. Somehow, the President had decided that giving blacks full citizenship discriminated against whites—"the distinction of race and color is by the bill made to operate in favor of the colored and against the white race." Johnson even invoked the specter of racial intermarriage as the logical consequence of Congressional policy.

For Republican moderates, the Civil Rights veto ended all hope of cooperation with the President. In a biting speech, Trumbull dissected Johnson's logic, especially the notion that guaranteeing blacks civil equality impaired the rights of whites. Early in April, for the first time in American history, Congress enacted a major piece of legislation over a President's veto. A headline in one Republican newspaper summed up the political situation: "The Separation Complete."

Johnson's rejection of the Civil Rights Bill has always been viewed as the most disastrous miscalculation of his political career. If the President aimed to build a new political coalition without the Radicals, he could not have failed more miserably. Whatever their differences, all Republicans agreed with the editorial response of the Springfield *Republican:* Protection of the freedmen's civil rights "follows from the suppression of the rebellion. … The party is nothing, if it does not do this—the nation is dishonored if it hesitates in this."

Yet despite the veto's outcome, Johnson's course cannot be explained simply in terms of insensitivity to Northern public opinion. Given the Civil Rights Act's astonishing expansion of federal authority and blacks' rights, it is not surprising that Johnson considered it a Radical measure against which he could mobilize voters. When, during one April speech, Johnson asked rhetorically, "What does the veto mean?" a voice from the crowd shouted: "It is keeping the nigger down." Johnson chose the issue on which to fight—federal protection for blacks' civil rights—and it was an issue on which he did not expect to lose.

The Fourteenth Amendment

As the split with the President deepened, Republicans grappled with the task of embedding in the Constitution, beyond the reach of Presidential vetoes and shifting political majorities, the results of the Civil War. At one point in January, no fewer than seventy constitutional amendments had been introduced. Not until June, after seemingly endless debate and maneuvering, did the Fourteenth Amendment, the most important ever added to the Constitution, receive the approval of Congress. Its first clause prohibited the states from abridging equality before the law. The second provided for a reduction in a state's representation proportional to the number of male citizens denied suffrage. This aimed to prevent the South from benefiting politically from emancipation. Before the war, three-fifths of the slaves had been included in calculating Congressional representation; now, as free persons, all would be counted. Since Republicans were not prepared to force black suffrage upon the South, they offered white Southerners a choice—enfranchise the freedmen or sacrifice representation in Congress. The third clause barred from national and state office men who had sworn allegiance to the Constitution and subsequently aided the

Confederacy. While not depriving "rebels" of the vote, this excluded from office most of the South's prewar political leadership, opening the door to power, Republicans hoped, for true Unionists. The Amendment also prohibited payment of the Confederate debt and empowered Congress to enforce its provisions through "appropriate" legislation.

Because it implicitly acknowledged the right of states to limit voting because of race, Wendell Phillips denounced the amendment as a "fatal and total surrender." Susan B. Anthony, Elizabeth Cady Stanton, and others in the women's suffrage movement also felt betrayed, because the second clause introduced the word "male" into the Constitution. Alone among suffrage limitations, those founded on sex would not reduce a state's representation.

Ideologically and politically, nineteenth-century feminism had been tied to abolition. Feminists now turned Radical ideology back upon Congress. If "special claims for special classes" were illegitimate and unrepublican, how could the denial of women's rights be justified? Should not sex, like race, be rejected as an unacceptable basis for legal distinctions among citizens? Rather than defining Reconstruction as "the negro's hour," they called it, instead, the hour for change: Another generation might pass "ere the constitutional door will again be opened." The dispute over the Fourteenth Amendment marked a turning point in nineteenth-century reform. Leaving feminist leaders with a deep sense of betrayal, it convinced them, as Stanton put it, that woman "must not put her trust in man" in seeking her rights. Women's leaders now embarked on a course that severed their historic alliance with abolitionism and created a truly independent feminist movement.

The Fourteenth Amendment, one Republican newspaper observed, repudiated the two axioms on which the Radicals "started to make their fight last December: dead States and equal suffrage." Yet it clothed with constitutional authority the principle Radicals had fought to vindicate: equality before the law, overseen by the national government. For its heart was the first section, which declared all persons born or naturalized in the United States both national and state citizens and prohibited the states from abridging their "privileges and immunities," depriving any person of life, liberty, or property without "due process of law," or denying them "equal protection of the laws."

For more than a century, politicians, judges, lawyers, and scholars have debated the meaning of this elusive language. But the aims of the Fourteenth Amendment can be understood only within the political and ideological context of 1866: the break with the President, the need to find a measure able to unify all Republicans, and the growing party consensus in favor of strong federal action to protect the freedmen's rights, short of the suffrage. During many drafts, changes, and deletions, the Amendment's central principle remained constant: a national guarantee of equality before the law. This was "so just," a moderate Congressman declared, "that no member of this House can seriously object to it." In language that transcended race and region, the Amendment challenged legal discrimination throughout the nation and changed and broadened the meaning of freedom for all Americans.

On the precise definition of equality before the law, Republicans differed among themselves. Even moderates, however, understood Reconstruction as a dynamic process, in which phrases like "privileges and immunities" were subject to changing interpretation. They preferred to allow both Congress and the federal courts maximum flexibility in implementing the Amendment's provisions and combating the injustices that confronted blacks in much of the South. Indeed, as in the Civil Rights Act, Congress looked to an activist federal judiciary to enforce civil rights—a mechanism preferable to maintaining indefinitely a standing army in the South or erecting a national bureaucracy empowered to oversee Reconstruction.

In establishing a national citizenship whose common rights no state could abridge, Republicans carried forward the nation-building process born of the Civil War. The states, declared Michigan Sen. Jacob Howard, who guided the Amendment through the Senate, could no longer infringe upon the liberties the Bill of Rights protected against federal violation; henceforth, states must respect "the personal rights guaranteed and secured by the first eight Amendments." The Freedmen's Bureau had already tried to protect such basic rights as freedom of speech, the right to bear arms, trial by impartial jury, and protection against cruel and unusual punishment and unreasonable search and seizure, and the Amendment was deemed necessary, in part, precisely because every one of these rights was being systematically violated in the South in 1866.

When Congress adjourned in July, two divisive questions remained unresolved. One was precisely how the Southern states would achieve readmission. Tennessee quickly ratified the Fourteenth Amendment and regained its right to representation, but without Congress explicitly acknowledging that this established a binding precedent. And, for the moment, the vexing question of black voting rights had been laid aside. Henry M. Turner, the black minister and political organizer who had been sent to Washington to lobby for black rights by Georgia's statewide black convention, reported: "Several Congressmen tell me, 'the negro must vote,' but the issue must be avoided now so as 'to keep up a two thirds power in Congress.'" Even conservative Republican Sen. John B. Henderson of Missouri believed black suffrage inevitable: "It will not be five years from today before this body will vote for it. You cannot get along without it."

The Campaign of 1866

On May 1, 1866, two horse-drawn hacks, one driven by a white man, the other by a black, collided on a street in Memphis. When police arrested the black driver, a group of recently discharged black veterans intervened, and a white crowd began to gather. From this incident followed three days of racial violence, with white mobs, composed in large part of the mostly Irish policemen and firemen, assaulting blacks on the streets and invading South Memphis, an area that included a shantytown housing families of black soldiers stationed in nearby Fort Pickering. Before the rioting subsided, at least forty-six blacks and two whites lay dead, five black women had been raped, and hundreds of black dwellings, churches, and schools were pillaged or destroyed by fire.

Twelve weeks later, a similar outbreak rocked New Orleans, although this time the violence arose directly from Reconstruction politics. The growing power of former Confederates under the administration of Gov. James M. Wells had long dismayed the city's Radicals and eventually alarmed Wells himself.

Wells now endorsed a Radical plan to reconvene the Constitutional Convention of 1864 in order to enfranchise blacks, prohibit "rebels" from voting, and establish a new state government. On the appointed day, July 30, only twenty-five delegates assembled, soon joined by a procession of some 200 black supporters, mostly former soldiers. Fighting broke out in the streets, police converged on the area, and the scene quickly degenerated into what Gen. Philip H. Sheridan later called "an absolute massacre." By the time federal troops arrived, thirty-four blacks and three white Radicals had been killed, and well over 100 persons injured. Even more than the Memphis riot, the events in New Orleans discredited Presidential Reconstruction. Many Northerners agreed with Gen. Joseph Holt that Johnson's leniency had unleashed "the barbarism of the rebellion in its renaissance."

The New Orleans riot could not have occurred at a worse time for the President—only two weeks before the National Union convention, a gathering of his supporters, was to assemble in Philadelphia. On the surface, harmony prevailed at the convention. The 7,000 spectators cheered wildly as South Carolina's massive Gov. James L. Orr marched down the main aisle arm-in-arm with the diminutive Gen. Darius N. Couch of Massachusetts, leading a procession of the delegates. Yet behind the scenes, dissension reigned. *New York Times* editor Henry J. Raymond had been persuaded to deliver the convention's main address, but his draft of the platform included guarded praise of the Fourteenth Amendment and oblique criticism of slavery. This proved too much for the Resolutions Committee, which omitted the offending passages. In the end, the convention did not try to establish a new national party, but called for the election of Congressmen who would support Johnson's policies.

The President now decided to take his case to the Northern people. On August 28, accompanied by Ulysses Grant, Adm. David Farragut, and other notables, he embarked on the "swing around the circle," an unprecedented speaking tour aimed at influencing the coming elections. At first things went well, for New York and Philadelphia men of commerce and finance welcomed him with enthusiasm. Then the party traveled through upstate New York and on to the West. When they reached Ohio, Johnson, interrupted by hecklers, responded in kind. At Cleveland, when a member of the audience yelled "hang Jeff Davis," the President replied, "Why not hang Thad Stevens and Wendell Phillips?" Johnson also indulged his unique blend of self-aggrandizement and self-pity. On one occasion, he intimated that Providence had removed Lincoln to elevate Johnson himself to the White House. At St. Louis, he blamed Congress for instigating the New Orleans riot and unleashed a "muddled tirade" against his opponents: "I have been traduced, I have been slandered, I have been maligned. I have been called Judas Iscariot. … Who has been my Christ that I have played the Judas with? Was it Thad Stevens?" Even Johnson's partisans were mortified. "Thoroughly reprehensible," exclaimed the New York *Journal of Commerce.* The President, former Georgia Gov. Herschel V. Johnson declared, had sacrificed "the moral power of his position, and done great damage to the cause of Constitutional reorganization." In mid-September, Andrew Johnson returned to Washington from what one admirer called "a tour it were better had never been made."

Johnson's supporters subsequently contended that a small band of fanatics secured Republican victory by demagogic attacks against "rebels" and "Copperheads" that obscured the real issues, such as the tariff, on which a pro-Johnson majority could ostensibly have been forged. Yet both parties remained divided on economic questions, and voters displayed little interest in them in 1866. More than anything else, the election became a referendum on the Fourteenth Amendment. Seldom, declared the *New York Times,* had a political contest been conducted "with so exclusive reference to a single issue." And the President's supporters went down to a disastrous defeat. In the next Congress, Republicans would possess well over the two-thirds majority required to override a veto.

"This is the most decisive and emphatic victory ever seen in American politics," exclaimed *The Nation.* In its aftermath, the course of prudence seemed plain. The South, warned the *Times,* must ratify and comply with the Fourteenth Amendment and the President must cease to oppose it; otherwise, black suffrage was inevitable. Johnson, however, refused to alter his opposition to the Amendment. Southern newspapers, moreover, consistently misinformed their readers about Northern politics, portraying Johnson's opponents as a band of Radical fanatics who lacked broad popular support and predicting Congress could not possibly do things it then proceeded to do. The election returns came as a shock, but produced no political reassessment. Between October 1866 and the following January, ten Southern legislatures overwhelmingly repudiated the Amendment. All told, only thirty-three Southern lawmakers braved public opposition to vote for ratification. Not for the first time, Southern intransigence played into the Radicals' hands. For, as Benjamin S. Hedrick of North Carolina had warned, "If the Northern people are forced by the South to follow Thad Stevens or the Copperheads, I believe they will prefer the former."

The Coming of Black Suffrage

The Republicans who gathered in December 1866 for the second session of the Thirty-Ninth Congress considered themselves "masters of the situation." Johnson's annual message, pleading for the immediate restoration of the "now unrepresented States," was ignored. The President, declared the New York *Herald,* his erstwhile supporter, "forgets that we have passed through the fiery ordeal of that the pre-existing order of things is gone and can return no more—that a g is before us, and that we cannot escape it."

Black suffrage, it soon became clear, was on the horizon. In mid-Decemb that Congress possessed the authority to "enter these States and hurl from which controls and governs them," an important announcement that moder Johnson governments. In January 1867, a bill enfranchising blacks in the law over the President's veto. Then, Congress extended manhood suffrage radical proposals were in the air, including widespread disenfranchisement, martial law for the South, confiscation, the impeachment of the President. A *Herald* editorial writer apologized to Johnson for the paper's advocacy of his removal: Its editor always went with the political tide, and the tide now flowed toward the Radicals.

Congress, however, found it difficult to agree on a program, a situation not all Republicans regretted. Late in January, George W. Julian warned against precipitous action. What the South needed was not "hasty restoration" or oaths that invited men to commit perjury, but *"government,* the strong arm of power, outstretched from the central authority here in Washington." Only a prolonged period of federal control would enable loyal public opinion to sink deep roots and permit "Northern capital and labor, Northern energy and enterprise" to venture south, there to establish "a Christian civilization and a living democracy." The South, he proposed, should be governed directly from Washington and readmitted only at "some indefinite future time" when its "political and social elements" had been thoroughly transformed.

Julian's speech struck a chord in Congress. The Joint Committee quickly approved a bill to impose military rule on the South. But even as moderates accepted military rule as a temporary expedient, they insisted on clearly specifying how the South could establish new civil governments and regain its standing within the Union. The military bill passed the House, but in the Senate the Republican caucus appointed a committee to lay down conditions of readmission for the entire South. The main point of dispute concerned black suffrage: All agreed it must operate in elections for constitutional conventions, but not on whether to require new constitutions to incorporate it as well. To Sumner, this was crucial, and when the committee failed to mandate black suffrage in the new documents, he appealed to the full caucus. The question of black voting, he said, must be settled, or "every State and village between here and the Rio Grande would be agitated by it." By a margin of two, the Republican caucus overturned the committee's decision. Exclaimed Radical Sen. Henry Wilson; "This is the greatest vote that has been taken on this continent."

And so Republicans decided that blacks must enter the South's body politic. But when the amended bill returned to the House, it touched off a storm of Radical protest. Rebels, charged George Boutwell, had been handed "the chief places in the work of reconstruction," for while establishing military rule, the bill failed to remove the Johnson governments immediately or disenfranchise former Confederates. Two amendments, intended to place the Reconstruction process in the hands of loyal men, made the bill more palatable to its critics. The first barred anyone disqualified from office under the Fourteenth Amendment from electing, or serving as, constitutional convention delegates. The second declared the Johnson governments subject to modification or abolition at any time and prohibited individuals disqualified under the Fourteenth Amendment from voting or holding office under them. No one knew how many "leading rebels" these eleventh-hour changes affected. But for Southern Unionists, they represented a major victory. The larger part of a political generation, men of local influence ranging from prewar postmasters and justices of the peace to legislators and Congressmen, had been temporarily excluded from office and voting. "This Amendment … will prove of vital importance in the work of reconstruction …," declared the Raleigh *Standard.* "We rejoice that there is to be an end to rebel rule."

Throughout these deliberations, Johnson remained silent. Toward the end of February, New York *Evening Post* editor Charles Nordhoff visited the White House. He found the President "much excited," certain "the people of the South … were to be trodden under foot 'to protect niggers.'" Nordhoff had once admired the President; now he judged him a "pig-headed man" governed by one idea: "bitter opposition to universal suffrage." Gone was the vision of a reconstructed South controlled by loyal yeomen. "The old Southern leaders …," declared the man who had once railed against the Slave Power, "must rule the South." When the Reconstruction bill reached his desk on March 2, Johnson returned it with a veto, which Congress promptly overrode. Maryland Sen. Reverdy Johnson was the only member to break party ranks. Whatever its flaws, he declared, the bill offered the South a path back into the Union, and the President should abandon his intransigence and accede to the plainly expressed will of the people. Reverdy Johnson's was the only Democratic vote in favor of any of the Reconstruction measures of 1866–67.

In its final form, the Reconstruction Act of 1867 divided the Confederate states, except Tennessee, into five military districts under commanders empowered to employ the army to protect life and property. And without immediately replacing the Johnson regimes, it laid out the steps by which new state governments could be created and recognized by Congress—the writing of new constitutions providing for manhood suffrage, their approval by a majority of registered voters, and ratification of the Fourteenth Amendment. Simultaneously, Congress passed the Habeas Corpus Act, which greatly expanded citizens' ability to remove cases to federal courts

Like all the decisions of the Thirty-Ninth Congress, the Reconstruction Act contained a somewhat incongruous mixture of idealism and political expediency. The bill established military rule, but only as a temporary measure to keep the peace, with the states assured a relatively quick return to the Union. It looked to a new political order for the South, but failed to place Southern Unionists in immediate control. It made no economic provision for the freedmen. Even black suffrage derived from a variety of motives and calculations. For Radicals, it represented the culmination of a lifetime of reform. For others, it seemed less the fulfillment of an idealistic creed than an alternative to prolonged federal intervention in the South, a means of enabling blacks to defend themselves against abuse, while relieving the nation of that responsibility.

Despite all its limitations, Congressional Reconstruction was indeed a radical departure, a stunning and unprecedented experiment in interracial democracy. In America, the ballot not only identified who could vote, it defined a collective national identity. Democrats had fought black suffrage on precisely these grounds. "Without reference to the question of equality, declared Indiana Sen. Thomas Hendricks, "I say we are not of the same race; we are so different that we ought not to compose one political community." Enfranchising blacks marked a powerful repudiation of such thinking. In some ways it was an astonishing leap of faith. Were the mass of freedmen truly prepared for political rights? Gen. E. O. C. Ord, federal commander in Arkansas, believed them "so servile and accustomed to submit" to white dictation that they would "not dare to present themselves at the polls." Even some Radicals harbored inner doubts, fearing that "demagogues" or their former masters would control the black vote, or that political rights would prove meaningless without economic independence.

In the course of Reconstruction, the freedmen disproved these somber forecasts. They demonstrated political shrewdness and independence in using the ballot to affect the conditions of their freedom. However inadequate as a response to the legacy of slavery, it remains a tragedy that the lofty goals of civil and political equality were not permanently achieved. And the end of Reconstruction came not because propertyless blacks succumbed to economic coercion, but because a tenacious black community, abandoned by the nation, fell victim to violence and fraud.

"We have cut loose from the whole dead past," wrote Wisconsin Sen. Timothy Howe, "and have cast our anchor out a hundred years." His colleague, Waitman T. Willey of West Virginia, adopted a more cautious tone: "The legislation of the last two years will mark a great page of history for good or evil—I hope the former. The crisis, however, is not yet past."

CHAPTER 3

THE CENTURY OF THE "PROBLEM OF THE COLOR LINE"

THE ATLANTA EXPOSITION ADDRESS

BOOKER T. WASHINGTON

THE ATLANTA EXPOSITION, at which I had been asked to make an address as a representative of the Negro race, as stated in the last chapter, was opened with a short address from Governor Bullock. After other interesting exercises, including an invocation from Bishop Nelson, of Georgia, a dedicatory ode by Albert Howell, Jr., and addresses by the President of the Exposition and Mrs. Joseph Thompson, the President of the Woman's Board, Governor Bullock introduced me with the words, "We have with us today a representative of Negro enterprise and Negro civilization."

When I arose to speak, there was considerable cheering, especially from the colored people. As I remember it now, the thing that was uppermost in my mind was the desire to say something that would cement the friendship of the races and bring about hearty cooperation between them. So far as my outward surroundings were concerned, the only thing that I recall distinctly now is that when I got up, I saw thousands of eyes looking intently into my face. The following is the address which I delivered:

Mr. President and Gentlemen of the Board of Directors and Citizens
One-third of the population of the South is of the Negro race. No enterprise seeking the material, civil, or moral welfare of this section can disregard this element of our population

and reach the highest success. I but convey to you, Mr. President and Directors, the sentiment of the masses of my race when I say that in no way have the value and manhood of the American Negro been more fittingly and generously recognized than by the managers of this magnificent Exposition at every stage of its progress. It is a recognition that will do more to cement the friendship of the two races than any occurrence since the dawn of our freedom.

Not only this, but the opportunity here afforded will awaken among us a new era of industrial progress. Ignorant and inexperienced, it is not strange that in the first years of our new life we began at the top instead of at the bottom; that a seat in Congress or the state legislature was more sought than real estate or industrial skill; that the political convention of stump speaking had more attractions than starting a dairy farm or truck garden.

A ship lost at sea for many days suddenly sighted a friendly vessel. From the mast of the unfortunate vessel was seen a signal, "Water, water; we die of thirst!" The answer from the friendly vessel at once came back, "Cast down your bucket where you are." A second time the signal, "Water, water; send us water!" ran up from the distressed vessel, and was answered, "Cast down your bucket where you are." And a third and fourth signal for water was answered, "Cast down your bucket where you are." The captain of the distressed vessel, at last heeding the injunction, cast down his bucket, and it came up full of fresh, sparkling water from the mouth of the Amazon River. To those of my race who depend on bettering their condition in a foreign land or who underestimate the importance of cultivating friendly relations with the Southern white man, who is their next-door neighbor, I would say: "Cast down your bucket where you are"—cast it down in making friends in every manly way of the people of all races by whom we are surrounded.

Cast it down in agriculture, mechanics, in commerce, in domestic service, and in the professions. And in this connection it is well to bear in mind that whatever other sins the South may be called to bear, when it comes to business, pure and simple, it is in the South that the Negro is given a man's chance in the commercial world, and in nothing is this Exposition more eloquent than in emphasizing this chance. Our greatest danger is that in the great leap from slavery to freedom we may overlook the fact that the masses of us are to live by the productions of our hands, and fail to keep in mind that we shall prosper in proportion as we learn to dignify and glorify common labor and put brains and skill into the common occupations of life; shall prosper in proportion as we learn to draw the line between the superficial and the substantial, the ornamental gewgaws of life and the useful. No race can prosper till it learns that there is as much dignity in tilling a field as in writing a poem. It is at the bottom of life we must begin, and not at the top. Nor should we permit our grievances to overshadow our opportunities.

To those of the white race who look to the incoming of those of foreign birth and strange tongue and habits for the prosperity of the South, were I permitted I would repeat what I say to my own race, "Cast down your bucket where you are." Cast it down among the eight millions of Negroes whose habits you know, whose fidelity and love you have tested in days when to have proved treacherous meant the ruin of your firesides. Cast down your bucket among these people who have, without strikes and labor wars, tilled your fields, cleared your forests, built your railroads and cities, and brought forth treasures from the bowels of the earth, and helped make possible this magnificent representation of the progress of the South. Casting down your bucket among my people, helping and encouraging them as you are doing on these grounds, and to education of head, hand, and heart, you will find that they will buy your surplus land, make blossom the waste places in your fields, and run your factories. While doing this, you can be sure in the future, as in the past, that you and your families will be surrounded by the most patient, faithful, law-abiding, and unresentful people that the world has seen. As we have proved our loyalty to you in the past, in nursing your children, watching by the sickbeds of your mothers and fathers, and often following them with tear-dimmed eyes to their graves, so in the future, in our humble way, we shall stand by you with a devotion that no foreigner can approach, ready to lay down our lives, if need be, in defense of yours, interlacing our industrial, commercial, civil, and religious life with yours in a way that shall make the interests of both races one. In all things that are purely social we can be as separate as the fingers, yet one as the hand in all things essential to mutual progress.

There is no defense or security for any of us except in the highest intelligence and development of all. If anywhere there are efforts tending to curtail the fullest growth of the Negro, let these efforts be turned into stimulating, encouraging, and making him the most useful and intelligent citizen. Effort or means so invested will pay a thousand percent interest. These efforts will be twice blessed—"blessing him that gives and him that takes."

There is no escape through law of man or God from the inevitable:

> The laws of changeless justice bind
> Oppressor with oppressed;
> And close as sin and suffering joined
> We march to fate abreast.

Nearly sixteen millions of hands will aid you in pulling the load upward, or they will pull against you the load downward. We shall constitute one-third and more of the ignorance and crime of the South, or one-third its intelligence and progress; we shall contribute one-third to the business and industrial prosperity of the South, or we shall prove a veritable body of death, stagnating, depressing, retarding every effort to advance the body politic.

Gentlemen of the Exposition, as we present to you our humble effort at an exhibition of our progress, you must not expect overmuch. Starting thirty years ago with ownership here and there in a few quilts and pumpkins and chickens (gathered from miscellaneous sources), remember the path that has led from these to the inventions and production of agricultural implements, buggies, steam engines, newspapers, books, statuary, carving, paintings, the management of drugstores and banks, has not been trodden without contact with thorns and thistles. While we take pride in what we exhibit as a result of our independent efforts, we do not for a moment forget that our part in this exhibition would fall far short of your expectations but for the constant help that has come to our educational life, not only from the Southern states, but especially from Northern philanthropists, who have made their gifts a constant stream of blessing and encouragement.

The wisest among my race understand that the agitation of questions of social equality is the extremest folly, and that progress in the enjoyment of all the privileges that will come to us must be the result of severe and constant struggle rather than of artificial forcing. No race that has anything to contribute to the markets of the world is long in any degree ostracized. It is important and right that all privileges of the law be ours, but it is vastly more important that we be prepared for the exercises of these privileges. The opportunity to earn a dollar in a factory just now is worth infinitely more than the opportunity to spend a dollar in an opera house.

In conclusion, may I repeat that nothing in thirty years has given us more hope and encouragement, and drawn us so near to you of the white race, as this opportunity offered by the Exposition; and here bending, as it were, over the altar that represents the results of the struggles of your race and mine, both starting practically empty-handed three decades ago, I pledge that in your effort to work out the great and intricate problem which God has laid at the doors of the South, you shall have at all times the patient, sympathetic help of my race; only let this be constantly in mind, that, while from representations in these buildings of the product of field, of forest, of mine, of factory, letters, and art, much good will come, yet far above and beyond material benefits will be that higher good, that, let us pray God, will come, in a blotting out of sectional differences and racial animosities and suspicions, in a determination to administer absolute justice, in a willing obedience among all classes to the mandates of law. This, this, coupled with our material prosperity, will bring into our beloved South a new heaven and a new earth.

The first thing that I remember, after I had finished speaking, was that Governor Bullock rushed across the platform and took me by the hand, and that others did the same. I received so many and such hearty congratulations that I found it difficult to get out of the building. I did not appreciate to any degree, however, the impression which my address seemed to have made, until the next morning, when I went into the business part of the city. As soon as I was recognized, I was surprised to find myself pointed out and surrounded by a crowd of men who wished to shake hands with me. This was kept up on every street on to which I went, to an extent which embarrassed me so much that I went back to my boarding place. The next morning I returned to Tuskegee. At the station in Atlanta, and at almost all of the stations at which the train stopped between that city and Tuskegee, I found a crowd of people anxious to shake hands with me.

The papers in all parts of the United States published the address in full, and for months afterward there were complimentary editorial references to it. Mr. Clark Howell, the editor of the Atlanta *Constitution*, telegraphed to a New York paper, among other words, the following, "I do not exaggerate when I say that Professor Booker T. Washington's address yesterday was one of the most notable speeches, both as to character and as to the warmth of its reception, ever delivered to a Southern audience. The address was a revelation. The whole speech is a platform upon which blacks and whites can stand with full justice to each other."

The Boston *Transcript* said editorially: "The speech of Booker T. Washington at the Atlanta Exposition, this week, seems to have dwarfed all the other proceedings and the Exposition itself. The sensation that it has caused in the press has never been equalled."

I very soon began receiving all kinds of propositions from lecture bureaus, and editors of magazines and papers, to take the lecture platform, and to write articles. One lecture bureau offered me fifty thousand dollars, or two hundred dollars a night and expenses, if I would place my services at its disposal for a given period. To all these communications I replied that my life work was at Tuskegee; and that whenever 1 spoke it must be in the interests of the Tuskegee school and my race, and that I would enter into no arrangements that seemed to place a mere commercial value upon my services.

Some days after its delivery I sent a copy of my address to the President of the United States, the Hon. Grover Cleveland. I received from him the following autograph reply:

Gray Gables
Buzzard's Bay, Mass.
October 6, 1895

Booker T. Washington, Esq.
My Dear Sir: I thank you for sending me a copy of your address delivered at the Atlanta Exposition.

I thank you with much enthusiasm for making the address. I have read it with intense interest, and I think the Exposition would be fully justified if it did not do more than furnish the opportunity for its delivery. Your words cannot fail to delight and encourage all who wish well for your race; and if our colored fellow-citizens do not from your utterances gather new hope and form new determinations to gain every valuable advantage offered them by their citizenship, it will be strange indeed.

Yours very truly,
Grover Cleveland

Later I met Mr. Cleveland, for the first time, when, as President, he visited the Atlanta Exposition. At the request of myself and others he consented to spend an hour in the Negro Building, for the purpose of inspecting the Negro exhibit and of giving the colored people in attendance an opportunity to shake hands with him. As soon as I met Mr. Cleveland I became impressed with his simplicity, greatness, and rugged honesty. I have met him many times since then, both at public functions and at his private residence in Princeton, and the more I see of him the more I admire him. When he visited the Negro Building in Atlanta he seemed to give himself up wholly, for that hour, to the colored people. He seemed to be as careful to shake hands with some old colored "auntie" clad partially in rags, and to take as much pleasure in doing so, as if he were greeting some millionaire. Many of the colored people took advantage of the occasion to get him to write his name in a book or on a slip of paper. He was as careful and patient in doing this as if he were putting his signature to some great state document.

Mr. Cleveland has not only shown his friendship for me in many personal ways, but has always consented to do anything I have asked of him for our school. This he has done, whether it was to make a personal donation or to use his influence in securing the donations of others. Judging from my personal acquaintance with Mr. Cleveland, I do not believe that he is conscious of possessing any color prejudice. He is too great for that. In my contact with people I find that, as a rule, it is only the little, narrow people who live for themselves, who never read good books, who do not travel, who never open up their souls in a way to permit them to come into contact with other souls—with the great outside world. No man whose vision is bounded by color can come into contact with what is highest and best in the world. In meeting men, in many places, I have found that the happiest people are those who do the most for others; the most miserable are those who do the least. I have also found that few things, if any, are capable of making one so blind and narrow as race prejudice. I often say to our students, in the course of my talks to them on Sunday evenings in the chapel, that the longer I live and the more experience I have of the world, the more I am convinced that, after all, the one thing that is most worth living for—and dying for, if need be—is the opportunity of making someone else more happy and more useful.

The colored people and the colored newspapers at first seemed to be greatly pleased with the character of my Atlanta address, as well as with its reception. But after the first burst of enthusiasm began to die away, and the colored people began reading the speech in cold type, some of them seemed to feel that they had been hypnotized. They seemed to feel that I had been too liberal in my remarks toward the Southern whites, and that I had not spoken out strongly enough for what they termed the "rights" of the race. For a while there was a reaction, so far as a certain element of my own race was concerned, but later these reactionary ones seemed to have been won over to my way of believing and acting.

While speaking of changes in public sentiment, I recall that about ten years after the school at Tuskegee was established, I had an experience that I shall never forget. Dr. Lyman Abbott, then the pastor of Plymouth Church, and also editor of the *Outlook* (then the *Christian Union),* asked me to write a letter for his paper giving my opinion of the exact condition, mental and moral, of the colored ministers in the South, as based upon my observations. I wrote the letter, giving the exact facts as I conceived them to be. The picture painted was a rather black one—or, since I am black, shall I say "white?" It could not be otherwise with a race but a few years out of slavery, a race which had not had time or opportunity to produce a competent ministry.

What I said soon reached every Negro minister in the country, I think, and the letters of condemnation which I received from them were not few. I think that for a year after the publication of this article every association and every conference or religious body of any kind, of my race, that met, did not fail before adjourning to pass a resolution condemning me, or calling upon me to retract or modify what I had said. Many of these organizations went so far in their resolutions as to advise parents to cease sending their children to Tuskegee. One association even appointed a "missionary" whose duty it was to warn the people against sending their children to Tuskegee. This missionary had a son in the school, and I noticed that, whatever the missionary might have said or done with regard to others, he was careful not to take his son away from the institution. Many of the colored papers, especially those that were the organs of religious bodies, joined in the general chorus of condemnation or demands for retraction.

During the whole time of the excitement, and through all the criticism, I did not utter a word of explanation or retraction. I knew that I was right, and that time and the sober second thought of the people would vindicate me. It was not long before the bishops and other church leaders began to make a careful investigation of the conditions of the ministry, and they found out that I was right. In fact, the oldest and most influential bishop in one branch of the Methodist Church said that my words were far too mild. Very soon public sentiment began making itself felt, in demanding a purifying of the ministry. While this is not yet complete by any means, I think I may say, without egotism, and I have been told by many of our most influential ministers, that my words had much to do with starting a demand for the placing of a higher type of men in the pulpit. I have had the satisfaction of having many who once condemned me thank me heartily for my frank words.

The change of the attitude of the Negro ministry, so far as regards myself, is so complete that at the present time I have no warmer friends among any class than I have among the clergymen. The improvement in the character and life of the Negro ministers is one of the most gratifying evidences of the progress of the race. My experience with them, as well as other events in my life, convince me that the thing to do, when one feels sure that he has said or done the right thing, and is condemned, is to stand still and keep quiet. If he is right, time will show it.

In the midst of the discussion which was going on concerning my Atlanta speech, I received the letter which I give below, from Dr. Gilman, the President of Johns Hopkins University, who had been made chairman of the judges of award in connection with the Atlanta Exposition:

Johns Hopkins University
Baltimore
President's Office
September 30, 1895

Dear Mr. Washington: Would it be agreeable to you to be one of the Judges of Award in the Department of Education at Atlanta? If so, I shall be glad to place your name upon the list. A line by telegraph will be welcomed.

Yours very truly,
D. C. Gilman

I think I was even more surprised to receive this invitation than I had been to receive the invitation to speak at the opening of the Exposition. It was to be a part of my duty, as one of the jurors, to pass not only upon the exhibits of the colored schools, but also upon those of the white schools. I accepted the position, and spent a month in Atlanta in performance of the duties which it entailed. The board of jurors was a large one, consisting in all of sixty members. It was about equally divided between Southern white people and Northern white people. Among them were college presidents, leading scientists and men of letters, and specialists in many subjects. When the group of jurors to which I was assigned met for organization, Mr. Thomas Nelson Page, who was one of the number, moved that I be made secretary of that division, and the motion was unanimously adopted. Nearly half of our division were Southern people. In performing my duties in the inspection of the exhibits of white schools I was in every case treated with respect, and at the close of our labors I parted from my associates with regret.

I am often asked to express myself more freely than I do upon the political condition and the political future of my race. These recollections of my experience in Atlanta give me the opportunity to do so briefly. My own belief is, although I have never before said so in so many words, that the time will come when the Negro in the South will be accorded all the political rights which his ability, character, and material possessions entitle him to. I think, though, that the opportunity to freely exercise such political rights will not come in any large degree through outside or artificial forcing, but will be accorded to the Negro by the Southern white people themselves, and that they will protect him in the exercise of those rights. Just as soon as the South gets over the old feeling that it is being forced by "foreigners," or "aliens," to do something which it does not want to do, I believe that the change in the direction that I have indicated is going to begin. In fact, there are indications that it is already beginning in a slight degree.

Let me illustrate my meaning. Suppose that some months before the opening of the Atlanta Exposition there had been a general demand from the press and public platform outside the South that a Negro be given a place on the opening program, and that a Negro be placed upon the board of jurors of award. Would any such recognition of the race have taken place? I do not think so. The Atlanta officials went as far as they did because they felt it to be a pleasure, as well as a duty, to reward what they considered merit in the Negro race. Say what we will, there is something in human nature which we cannot blot out, which makes one man, in the end, recognize and reward merit in another, regardless of color or race.

I believe it is the duty of the Negro—as the greater part of the race is already doing—to deport himself modestly in regard to political claims, depending upon the slow but sure influences that proceed from the possession of property, intelligence, and high character for the full recognition of his political rights. I think that the according of the full exercise of political rights is going to be a matter of natural, slow growth, not an overnight, gourd-vine affair. I do not believe that the Negro should cease voting, for a man cannot learn the exercise of self-government by ceasing to vote any more than a boy can learn to swim by keeping out of the water, but I do believe that in his voting he should more and more be influenced by those of intelligence and character who are his next-door neighbors.

I know colored men who, through the encouragement, help, and advice of Southern white people, have accumulated thousands of dollars' worth of property, but who, at the same time, would never think of going to those same persons for advice concerning the casting of their ballots. This, it seems to me, is unwise and unreasonable, and should cease. In saying this I do not mean that the Negro should truckle, or not vote from principle, for the instant he ceases to vote from principle he loses the confidence and respect of the Southern white man even.

I do not believe that any state should make a law that permits an ignorant and poverty-stricken white man to vote, and prevents a black man in the same condition from voting. Such a law is not only unjust, but it will react, as all unjust laws do, in time; for the effect of such a law is to encourage the Negro to secure education and property, and at the same time it encourages the white man to remain in ignorance and poverty. I believe that in time, through the operation of intelligence and friendly race relations, all cheating at the ballot box in the South will cease. It will become apparent that the white man who begins by cheating a Negro out of his ballot soon learns to cheat a white man out of his, and that the man who does this ends his career of dishonesty by the theft of property or by some equally serious crime. In my opinion, the time will come when the South will encourage all of its citizens to vote. It will see that it pays better, from every standpoint, to have healthy, vigorous life than to have that political stagnation which always results when one-half of the population has no share and no interest in the Government.

As a rule, I believe in universal, free suffrage, but I believe that in the South we are confronted with peculiar conditions that justify the protection of the ballot in many of the states, for a while at least, either by an educational test, a property test, or by both combined; but whatever tests are required, they should be made to apply with equal and exact justice to both races.

OF MR. BOOKER T. WASHINGTON AND OTHERS (1903)

W.E.B. DUBOIS

From birth till death enslaved; in word, in deed, unmanned!
Hereditary bondsmen! Know ye not
Who would be free themselves must strike the blow?
—BYRON

Easily the most striking thing in the history of the American Negro since 1876 is the ascendancy of Mr. Booker T. Washington. It began at the time when war memories and ideals were rapidly passing; a day of astonishing commercial development was dawning; a sense of doubt and hesitation overtook the freedmen's sons—then it was that his leading began. Mr. Washington came, with a simple definite program, at the psychological moment when the nation was a little ashamed of having bestowed so much sentiment on Negroes, and was concentrating its energies on dollars. His program of industrial education, conciliation of the South, and submission and silence as to civil and political rights, was not wholly original; the free Negroes from 1830 up to wartime had striven to build industrial schools, and the American Missionary Association had from the first taught various trades; and Price and others had sought a way of honorable alliance with the best of the Southerners. But Mr. Washington first indissolubly linked these things; he put enthusiasm, unlimited energy, and perfect faith into this program, and changed it from a bypath into a veritable way of life. And the tale of the methods by which he did this is a fascinating study of human life.

It startled the nation to hear a Negro advocating such a program after many decades of bitter complaint; it startled and won the applause of the South, it interested and won the admiration of the North; and after a confused murmur of protest, it silenced if it did not convert the Negroes themselves.

To gain the sympathy and cooperation of the various elements comprising the white South was Mr. Washington's first task; and this, at the time Tuskegee was founded, seemed, for a black man, well-nigh impossible. And yet ten years later it was done in the word spoken at Atlanta: "In all things purely social we can be as separate as the five fingers, and yet one as the hand in all things essential to mutual progress." This "Atlanta Compromise" is by all odds the most notable thing in Mr. Washington's career. The South interpreted it in different ways: the radicals received it as a complete surrender of the demand for civil and political equality; the conservatives, as a generously conceived working basis for mutual understanding. So both approved it, and today its author is certainly the most distinguished Southerner since Jefferson Davis, and the one with the largest personal following.

Next to this achievement comes Mr. Washington's work in gaining place and consideration in the North. Others less shrewd and tactful had formerly essayed to sit on these two stools and had fallen between them; but as Mr. Washington knew the heart of the South from birth and training, so by singular insight he intuitively grasped the spirit of the age which was dominating the North. And so thoroughly did he learn the speech and thought of triumphant commercialism, and the ideals of material prosperity, that the picture of a lone black boy poring over a French grammar amid the weeds and dirt of a neglected home soon seemed to him the acme of absurdities. One wonders what Socrates and St. Francis of Assisi would say to this.

And yet this very singleness of vision and thorough oneness with his age is a mark of the successful man. It is as though nature must needs make men narrow in order to give them force. So Mr. Washington's cult has gained unquestioning followers, his work has wonderfully prospered, his friends are legion, and his enemies are confounded. Today he stands as the one recognized spokesman of his ten million fellows, and one of the most notable figures in a nation of seventy millions. One hesitates, therefore, to criticise a life which, beginning with so little, has done so much. And yet the time is come when one may speak in all sincerity and utter courtesy of the mistakes and shortcomings of Mr. Washington's career, as well as of his triumphs, without being thought captious or envious, and without forgetting that it is easier to do ill than well in the world.

The criticism that has hitherto met Mr. Washington has not always been of this broad character. In the South especially has he had to walk warily to avoid the harshest judgments—and naturally so, for he is dealing with the one subject of deepest sensitiveness to that section. Twice—once when at the Chicago celebration of the Spanish-American War he alluded to the color-prejudice that is "eating away the vitals of the South," and once when he dined with President Roosevelt—has the resulting Southern criticism been violent enough to threaten seriously his popularity. In the North the feeling has several times forced itself into words, that Mr. Washington's counsels of submission overlooked certain elements of true manhood, and that his educational program was unnecessarily narrow. Usually, however, such criticism has not found open expression, although, too, the spiritual sons of the abolitionists have not been prepared to acknowledge that the schools founded before Tuskegee, by men of broad ideals and self-sacrificing spirit, were wholly failures or worthy of ridicule. While, then, criticism has not failed to follow Mr. Washington, yet the prevailing public opinion of the land has been but too willing to deliver the solution of a wearisome problem into his hands, and say, "If that is all you and your race ask, take it."

Among his own people, however, Mr. Washington has encountered the strongest and most lasting opposition, amounting at times to bitterness, and even today continuing strong and insistent even though largely silenced in outward expression by the public opinion of the nation. Some of this opposition is, of course, mere envy; the disappointment of displaced demagogues and the spite of narrow minds. But aside from this, there is among educated and thoughtful colored men in all parts of the land a feeling of deep regret, sorrow, and apprehension at the wide currency and ascendancy which some of Mr. Washington's theories have gained. These same men admire his sincerity of purpose, and are willing to forgive much to honest endeavor which is doing something worth the doing. They cooperate with Mr. Washington as far as they conscientiously can; and, indeed, it is no ordinary tribute to this man's tact and power that, steering as he must between so many diverse interests and opinions, he so largely retains the respect of all.

But the hushing of the criticism of honest opponents is a dangerous thing. It leads some of the best of the critics to unfortunate silence and paralysis of effort, and others to burst into speech so passionately and intemperately as to lose listeners. Honest and earnest criticism from those whose interests are most nearly touched—criticism of writers by readers, of government by those governed, of leaders by those led—this is the soul of democracy and the safeguard of modern society. If the best of the American Negroes receive by outer pressure a leader whom they had not recognized before, manifestly there is here a certain palpable gain. Yet there is also irreparable loss—a loss of that peculiarly valuable education which a group receives when by search and criticism it finds and commissions its own leaders. The way in which this is done is at once the most elementary and the nicest problem of social growth. History is but the record of such group leadership; and yet how infinitely changeful is its type and character! And of all types and kinds, what can be more instructive than the leadership of a group within a group?—that curious double movement where real progress may be negative and actual advance be relative retrogression. All this is the social student's inspiration and despair.

Now in the past the American Negro has had instructive experience in the choosing of group leaders, founding thus a peculiar dynasty which in the light of present conditions is worthwhile studying. When sticks and stones and beasts form the sole environment of a people, their attitude is largely one of determined opposition to and conquest of natural forces. But when to earth and brute is added an environment of men and ideas, then the attitude of the imprisoned group may take three main forms—a feeling of revolt and revenge; an attempt to adjust all thought and action to the will of the greater group; or, finally, a determined effort at self-realization and self-development despite environing opinion. The influence of all of these attitudes at various times can be traced in the history of the American Negro, and in the evolution of his successive leaders.

Before 1750, while the fire of African freedom still burned in the veins of the slaves, there was in all leadership or attempted leadership but the one motive of revolt and revenge—typified in the terrible Maroons, the Danish blacks, and Cato of Stono, and veiling all the Americas in fear of insurrection. The liberalizing tendencies of the latter half of the eighteenth century brought, along with kindlier relations between black and white, thoughts of ultimate adjustment and assimilation. Such aspiration was especially voiced in the earnest songs of Phyllis, in the martyrdom of Attucks, the fighting of Salem and Poor, the intellectual accomplishments of Banneker and Derham, and the political demands of the Cuffes.

Stern financial and social stress after the war cooled much of the previous humanitarian ardor. The disappointment and impatience of the Negroes at the persistence of slavery and serfdom voiced itself in two movements. The slaves in the South, aroused undoubtedly by vague rumors of the Haitian revolt, made three fierce attempts at insurrection—in 1800 under Gabriel in Virginia, in 1822 under Vesey in Carolina, and in 1831 again in Virginia under the terrible Nat Turner. In the free states, on the other hand, a new and curious attempt at self-development was made. In Philadelphia and New York color-prescription led to a withdrawal of Negro communicants from white churches and the formation of a peculiar socioreligious institution among the Negroes known as the African church—an organization still living and controlling in its various branches over a million of men.

Walker's wild appeal against the trend of the times showed how the world was changing after the coming of the cotton gin. By 1830 slavery seemed hopelessly fastened on the South, and the slaves thoroughly cowed into submission. The free Negroes of the North, inspired by the mulatto immigrants from the West Indies, began to change the basis of their demands; they recognized the slavery of slaves, but insisted that they themselves were freemen, and sought assimilation and amalgamation with the nation on the same terms with other men. Thus, Forten and Purvis of Philadelphia, Shad of Wilmington, DuBois of New Haven, Barbadoes of Boston, and others, strove singly and together as men, they said, not as slaves; as "people of color," not as "Negroes." The trend of the times, however, refused them recognition save in individual and exceptional cases, considered them as one with all the despised blacks, and they soon found themselves striving to keep even the rights they formerly had of voting and working and moving as freemen. Schemes of migration and colonization arose among them; but these they refused to entertain, and they eventually turned to the abolition movement as a final refuge.

Here, led by Remond, Nell, Wells-Brown, and Douglass, a new period of self-assertion and self-development dawned. To be sure, ultimate freedom and assimilation was the ideal before the leaders, but the assertion of the manhood rights of the Negro by himself was the main reliance, and John Brown's raid was the extreme of its logic. After the war and emancipation, the great form of Frederick Douglass, the greatest of American Negro leaders, still led the host. Self-assertion, especially in political lines, was the main program, and behind Douglass came Elliot, Bruce, and Langston, and the Reconstruction politicians, and, less conspicuous but of greater social significance Alexander Crummell and Bishop Daniel Payne.

Then came the Revolution of 1876, the suppression of the Negro votes, the changing and shifting of ideals, and the seeking of new lights in the great night. Douglass, in his old age, still bravely stood for the ideals of his early manhood—ultimate assimilation through self-assertion, and on no other terms. For a time Price arose as a new leader, destined, it seemed, not to give up, but to restate the old ideals in a form less repugnant to the white South. But he passed away in his prime. Then came the new leader. Nearly all the former ones had become leaders by the silent suffrage of their fellows, had sought to lead their own people alone, and were usually, save Douglass, little known outside their race. But Booker T. Washington arose as essentially the leader not of one race but of two—a compromiser between the South, the North, and the Negro. Naturally the Negroes resented, at first bitterly, signs of compromise which surrendered their civil and political rights, even though this was to be exchanged for larger chances of economic development. The rich and dominating North, however, was not only weary of the race problem, but was investing largely in Southern enterprises, and welcomed any method of peaceful cooperation. Thus, by national opinion, the Negroes began to recognize Mr. Washington's leadership; and the voice of criticism was hushed.

Mr. Washington represents in Negro thought the old attitude of adjustment and submission; but adjustment at such a peculiar time as to make his program unique. This is an age of unusual economic development, and Mr. Washington's program naturally takes an economic cast, becoming a gospel of work and money to such an extent as apparently almost completely to overshadow the higher alms of life. Moreover, this is an age when the more advanced races are coming in closer contact with the less developed races, and the race-feeling is therefore intensified; and Mr. Washington's program practically accepts the alleged inferiority of the Negro races. Again, in our own land, the reaction from the sentiment of wartime has given impetus to race-prejudice against Negroes, and Mr. Washington withdraws many of the high demands of Negroes as men and American citizens. In other periods of intensified prejudice all the Negro's tendency to self-assertion has been called forth; at this period a policy of submission is advocated. In the history of nearly all other races and peoples the doctrine preached at such crises has been that manly self-respect is worth more than lands and houses, and that a people who voluntarily surrender such respect, or cease striving for it, are not worth civilizing.

In answer to this, it has been claimed that the Negro can survive only through submission. Mr. Washington distinctly asks that black people give up, at least for the present, three things—first, political power; second, insistence on civil rights; and third, higher education of Negro youth—and concentrate all their energies on industrial education, the accumulation of wealth, and the conciliation of the South. This policy has been courageously and insistently advocated for over fifteen years, and has been triumphant for perhaps ten years. As a result of this tender of the palm branch, what has been the return? In these years there have occurred:

The disfranchisement of the Negro.

The legal creation of a distinct status of civil inferiority for the Negro.

The steady withdrawal of aid from institutions for the higher training of the Negro. These movements are not, to be sure, direct results of Mr. Washington's teachings; but his

propaganda has, without a shadow of doubt, helped their speedier accomplishment. The question then comes: Is it possible, and probable, that nine millions of men can make effective progress in economic lines if they are deprived of political rights, made a servile caste, and allowed only the most meager chance for developing their exceptional men? If history and reason give any distinct answer to these questions, it is an emphatic *No*. And Mr. Washington thus faces the triple paradox of his career:

He is striving nobly to make Negro artisans businessmen and property owners; but it is utterly impossible, under modern competitive methods, for workingmen and property owners to defend their rights and exist without the right of suffrage.

He insists on thrift and self-respect, but at the same time counsels a silent submission to civic inferiority such as is bound to sap the manhood of any race in the long run.

He advocates common-school and industrial training, and depreciates institutions of higher learning; but neither the Negro common schools, nor Tuskegee itself, could remain open a day were it not for teachers trained in Negro colleges, or trained by their graduates.

This triple paradox in Mr. Washington's position is the object of criticism by two classes of colored Americans. One class is spiritually descended from Toussaint the Savior, through Gabriel, Vesey, and Turner, and they represent the attitude of revolt and revenge; they hate the white South blindly and distrust the white race generally, and so far as they agree on definite action, think that the Negro's only hope lies in emigration beyond the borders of the United States. And yet, by the irony of fate, nothing has more effectually made this program seem hopeless than the recent course of the United States toward weaker and darker peoples in the West Indies, Hawaii, and the Philippines—for where in the world may we go and be safe from lying and brute force?

The other class of Negroes who cannot agree with Mr. Washington has hitherto said little aloud. They deprecate the sight of scattered counsels, of internal disagreement; and especially they dislike making their just criticism of a useful and earnest man an excuse for a general discharge of venom from small-minded opponents. Nevertheless, the questions involved are so fundamental and serious that it is difficult to see how men like the Grimkes, Kelly Miller, J.W.E. Bowen, and other representatives of this group, can much longer be silent. Such men feel in conscience bound to ask of this nation three things:

The right to vote.

Civic equality.

The education of youth according to ability.

They acknowledge Mr. Washington's invaluable service in counseling patience and courtesy in such demands; they do not ask that ignorant black men vote when ignorant whites are debarred, or that any reasonable restrictions in the suffrage should not be applied; they know that the low social level of the mass of the race is responsible for much discrimination against it, but they also know, and the nation knows, that relentless color-prejudice is more often a cause than a result of the Negro's degradation; they seek the abatement of this relic of barbarism, and not its systematic encouragement and pampering by all agencies of social power from the Associated Press to the Church of Christ. They advocate, with Mr. Washington, a broad system of Negro common schools supplemented by thorough industrial training; but they are surprised that a man of Mr. Washington's insight cannot see that no such educational system ever has rested or can rest on any other basis than that of the well-equipped college and university, and they insist that there is a demand for a few such institutions throughout the South to train the best of the Negro youth as teachers, professional men, and leaders.

This group of men honor Mr. Washington for his attitude of conciliation toward the white South; they accept the "Atlanta Compromise" in its broadest interpretation; they recognize, with him, many signs of promise, many men of high purpose and fair judgment, in this section; they know that no easy task has been laid upon a region already tottering under heavy burdens. But, nevertheless, they insist that the way to truth and right lies in straightforward honesty, not in indiscriminate flattery; in praising those of the South who do well and criticizing uncompromisingly those who do ill; in taking advantage of the opportunities at hand and urging their fellows to do the same, but at the same time in remembering that only a firm adherence to their higher ideals and aspirations will ever keep those ideals within the realm of possibility. They do not expect that the free right to vote, to enjoy civic rights, and to be educated, will come in a moment; they do not expect to see the bias and prejudices of years disappear at the blast of a trumpet; but they are absolutely certain that the way for a people to gain their reasonable rights is not by voluntarily throwing them away and insisting that they do not want them; that the way for a people to gain respect is not by continually belittling and ridiculing themselves; that, on the contrary, Negroes must insist continually, in season and out of season, that voting is necessary to modern manhood, that color discrimination is barbarism, and that black boys need education as well as white boys.

In failing thus to state plainly and unequivocally the legitimate demands of their people, even at the cost of opposing an honored leader, the thinking classes of American Negroes would shirk a heavy responsibility—a responsibility to themselves, a responsibility to the struggling masses, a responsibility to the darker races of men whose future depends so largely on this American experiment, but especially a responsibility to this nation—this common fatherland. It is wrong to encourage a man or a people in evildoing; it is wrong to aid and abet a national crime simply because it is unpopular not to do so. The growing spirit of kindliness and reconciliation between the North and South after the frightful differences of a generation ago ought to be a source of deep congratulation to all, and especially to those whose mistreatment caused the war; but if that reconciliation is to be marked by the industrial slavery and civic death of those same black men, with permanent legislation into a position of inferiority, then those black men, if they are really men, are called upon by every consideration of patriotism and loyalty to oppose such a course by all civilized methods, even though such opposition involves disagreement with Mr. Booker T. Washington. We have no right to sit silently by while the inevitable seeds are sown for a harvest of disaster to our children, black and white.

First, it is the duty of black men to judge the South discriminatingly. The present generation of Southerners are not responsible for the past, and they should not be blindly hated or blamed for it. Furthermore, to no class is the indiscriminate endorsement of the recent course of the South toward Negroes more nauseating than to the best thought of the South. The South is not "solid"; it is a land in the ferment of social change, wherein forces of all kinds are fighting for supremacy; and to praise the ill the South is today perpetrating is just as wrong as to condemn the good. Discriminating and broad-minded criticism is what the South needs—needs it for the sake of her own white sons and daughters, and for the insurance of robust, healthy mental and moral development.

Today even the attitude of the Southern whites toward the blacks is not, as so many assume, in all cases the same; the ignorant Southerner hates the Negro, the workingmen fear his competition, the moneymakers wish to use him as a laborer, some of the educated see a menace in his upward development, while others—usually the sons of the masters—wish to help him to rise. National opinion has enabled this last class to maintain the Negro common schools, and to protect the Negro partially in property, life, and limb. Through the pressure of the moneymakers, the Negro is in danger of being reduced to semi-slavery, especially in the country districts; the workingmen, and those of the educated who fear the Negro, have united to disfranchise him, and some have urged his deportation; while the passions of the ignorant are easily aroused to lynch and abuse any black man. To praise this intricate whirl of thought and prejudice is nonsense; to inveigh indiscriminately against "the South" is unjust; but to use the same breath in praising Governor Aycock, exposing Senator Morgan, arguing with Mr. Thomas Nelson Page, and denouncing Senator Ben Tillman, is not only sane, but the imperative duty of thinking black men.

It would be unjust to Mr. Washington not to acknowledge that in several instances he has opposed movements in the South which were unjust to the Negro; he sent memorials to the Louisiana and Alabama constitutional conventions, he has spoken against lynching, and in other ways has openly or silently set his influence against sinister schemes and unfortunate happenings. Notwithstanding this, it is equally true to assert that on the whole the distinct impression left by Mr. Washington's propaganda is, first, that the South is justified in its present attitude toward the Negro because of the Negro's degradation; secondly, that the prime cause of the Negro's failure to rise more quickly is his wrong education in the past; and, thirdly, that his future rise depends primarily on his own efforts. Each of these propositions is a dangerous half-truth. The supplementary truths must never be lost sight of: first, slavery and race-prejudice are potent if not sufficient causes of the Negro's position; second, industrial and common-school training were necessarily slow in planting because they had to await the black teachers trained by higher institutions—it being extremely doubtful if any essentially different development was possible, and certainly a Tuskegee was unthinkable before 1880; and, third, while it is a great truth to say that the Negro must strive and strive mightily to help himself, it is equally true that unless his striving be not simply seconded, but rather aroused and encouraged, by the initiative of the richer and wiser environing group, he cannot hope for great success.

In his failure to realize and impress this last point, Mr. Washington is especially to be criticized. His doctrine has tended to make the whites, North and South, shift the burden of the Negro problem to the Negro's shoulders and stand aside as critical and rather pessimistic spectators; when in fact the burden belongs to the nation, and the hands of none of us are clean if we bend not our energies to righting these great wrongs.

The South ought to be led, by candid and honest criticism, to assert her better self and do her full duty to the race she has cruelly wronged and is still wronging. The North—her copartner in guilt—cannot salve her conscience by plastering it with gold. We cannot settle this problem by diplomacy and suaveness, by "policy" alone. If worse come to worst, can the moral fiber of this country survive the slow throttling and murder of nine millions of men?

The black men of America have a duty to perform, a duty stern and delicate—a forward movement to oppose a part of the work of their greatest leader. So far as Mr. Washington preaches thrift, patience, and industrial training for the masses, we must hold up his hands and strive with him, rejoicing in his honors and glorying in the strength of this Joshua called of God and of man to lead the headless host. But so far as Mr. Washington apologizes for injustice, North or South, does not rightly value the privilege and duty of voting, belittles the emasculating effects of caste distinctions, and opposes the higher training and ambition of our brighter minds—so far as he, the South, or the nation, does this—we must unceasingly and firmly oppose them. By every civilized and peaceful method we must strive for the rights which the world accords to men, clinging unwaveringly to those great words which the sons of the Fathers would fain forget: "We hold these truths to be self-evident: That all men are created equal; that they are endowed by their Creator with certain unalienable rights; that among these are life, liberty, and the pursuit of happiness."

ON LYNCHINGS

PATRICIA HILL COLLINS

The resurgence of scholarly interest in the long and productive career of Ida B. Wells-Barnett (1862–1931) is long overdue. This reprint of *Southern Horrors, A Red Record, and Mob Rule in New Orleans,* three of Wells-Barnett's important works on lynching, makes important contributions to our understanding of Wells-Barnett's place within African American social and political thought. Within African American historiography, Wells-Barnett has long been remembered primarily as an activist, an irritant to W. E. B. Du Bois, Mary Church Terrell, and similar African American intellectuals. Wells-Barnett *was* an activist, and an extremely effective one for her time. She participated in an impressive constellation of antiracist and women's rights initiatives. Yet Wells-Barnett also used her journalistic career, her speeches, her leadership in political organizations, and her position papers and pamphlets to advance innovative analyses concerning the connections between African American disempowerment and the need for social justice. Unlike contemporary distinctions made between intellectual production and activism, Wells-Barnett managed to do both. Her analysis of the emergence and persistence of lynching simultaneously shaped and was influenced by her more than twenty-year crusade against lynching. As a result of this recursive and synergistic relationship between her ideas and activism, her analyses of race, class, and gender, crystallized in her work on lynching, reflect a breadth and complexity that we have only come to appreciate in the context of a contemporary Black feminism that brought attention to her accomplishments.

Ida B. Wells-Barnett was neither fully accepted nor recognized during her lifetime, and until recently, was generally neglected within historiography of African American social and political thought. Within African American circles, Wells-Barnett's predilection for positions that were often unpopular and her outspokenness fostered an image of her as being unpredictable and therefore uncontrollable. For Wells-Barnett, those who failed to take a stand against lynching, or who remained silent and looked away, were as culpable as those committing the acts.

In sustaining this recursive relationship between her intellectual and political work, Wells-Barnett embraced what were then seen as two contradictory strands within Black political thought. Unlike the much-touted debates between Booker T. Washington and W. E. B. Du Bois on the desirability of separation versus integration as the solution to the social problems confronting African Americans, Wells-Barnett took a more pragmatic approach. She aimed to address the entrenched poverty, political disenfranchisement, substandard housing, underfunded schools, poor health, and other social problems that confronted a people who were, like Wells-Barnett, one generation away from slavery. Recognizing that major social problems required broad-based social action, Wells-Barnett participated in a broad array of social-action strategies that in turn affected her analyses of social problems and their possible solutions.

On the one hand, in Memphis and in Chicago, Wells-Barnett participated in activities designed to develop local African American communities.[1] Almost four decades in Chicago convinced her of the need for community-development strategies that would prepare African Americans for full participation in mainstream society. For example, in 1910 Wells-Barnett catalyzed the founding of the Negro Fellowship League, an African American initiative that eventually led to a Black settlement house in Chicago providing lodging, recreation facilities, a reading room, and employment for Black migrant men. The spark for the Fellowship League lay in Wells-Barnett expressing her frustration to her Sunday school class about a particularly egregious 1908 riot in Springfield, Illinois, where thousands of Blacks fled for their lives. Several young men asked what they could do, and three of them subsequently met with Wells-Barnett and founded the league.[2] Wells-Barnett was also instrumental in founding the Ida B. Wells Club that established the first Black orchestra and the first kindergarten for African American children in Chicago. As a founding member of the national Black Women's Club Movement that emerged in the 1890s to focus on the "racial uplift" of African American girls and boys, Wells-Barnett clearly supported the community development thrust that was the movement's initial focus. The middle-class Black women in the club movement were committed to a community development strategy based on the philosophy of "lift as we climb." But Wells-Barnett refused to be confined by the politics of respectability advanced by its middle-class membership. Her community development politics were complicated. She opposed Booker T. Washington, and her alliances with Marcus Garvey (she once spoke at a Universal Negro Improvement Association meeting), placed her at odds with her peers. Wells-Barnett's participation in local and national community-development endeavors such as these illustrates her recognition that Black nationalist–inspired strategies for Black community development were essential.

At the same time, Ida Wells-Barnett refused to confine her activism to community-development strategies deemed appropriate for women. She traveled widely, lecturing White audiences about the crime of lynching. Wells-Barnett was so passionate about this cause that, during the early days of her antilynching campaign, she traveled with her nursing baby.[3] For Wells-Barnett, participating in interracial political organizations was not always easy, because she did not mince words and thus stepped outside the boundaries established for African American women pursuing a politics of respectability. For example, claiming that African American women needed the vote just as much if not more so than White American women, Wells-Barnett organized the Alpha Suffrage Club, the first Black women's suffrage organization in Illinois. At the National Woman Suffrage Association March on Washington in 1913, to avoid offending White suffragists from the South, Wells-Barnett and her organization were told to march at the back of the parade in the "colored" section. Wells-Barnett appeared to agree, yet when the parade was in progress, slipped into the Illinois delegation and integrated the march. She also participated in the founding of the National Association for the Advancement of Colored People (NAACP), a major civil rights organization that was sparked by White liberal opposition to the 1908 riot in Springfield, Illinois. Three White liberals put out a call for a conference in New York City to discuss possible responses to the riot and the organization itself began as a coalition of White and Black Americans to work against the unfair treatment of African Americans.[4]

As one of two African American women at the founding meeting in 1909, Wells-Barnett delivered a talk titled "Lynching, Our National Crime" that distilled her experience of nearly two decades of activism. The African American leaders of the fledgling NAACP knew they would have to deal with Wells-Barnett. Yet the need to placate its White members pressured these same leaders to attempt to keep her in the subordinate place reserved for all but a few handpicked African American women. Given her tireless activism on lynching, its severity, and her virtually single-handed marshaling of international support for anti-lynching initiatives, Wells-Barnett expected to be included among the Founding Forty members of the NAACP. She was stunned to find out that her name had been omitted. After protest, her name was added, but this deliberate exclusion contributed to Wells-Barnett's growing recognition that she was being pushed to the margins of the historical record. "Wells-Barnett quickly realized that if she was going to establish her place in history, she had better chronicle her own life."[5]

In response to this and other snubs by the political leadership of antiracist and/or women's movements, Wells-Barnett became the first Black woman political activist to write a full-length autobiography. Edited by her daughter and published posthumously,[6] its title, *Crusade for Justice*, encapsulates why Wells-Barnett was able to maintain this synergistic relationship between sound intellectual analyses and sustained, principled activism. Working for social justice required both, and she did both. Moreover, her distinctive biography sheds light on how her unshakable commitment to achieving social justice for African Americans allowed her to confront a diverse array of colleagues from the Woman Suffrage Movement, to the NAACP, and beyond. Whereas many life experiences shaped her ideas and actions, three stand out, namely, the fact that both of her parents had been slaves, her experiences as a teacher and journalist in the South after emancipation, and firsthand knowledge of a lynching that she could not ignore.

Born into slavery on July 16, 1862, in Holly Springs, Mississippi, Ida Wells-Barnett was the eldest of eight children of Jim Wells and Lizzie Warrenton. Her father, the son of a slave woman and her master, was trained as a carpenter. One of ten children, her mother had been separated from her family, auctioned off, and finally ended up working as a cook on the plantation where Jim Wells worked. Both knew firsthand the hardships and injustice of slavery. Her parents married under slavery and, after emancipation, married again and made a home in Holly Springs. Like many newly emancipated African Americans, they believed that education would improve their children's lives and was essential for the betterment of the "race." They sent their children to Shaw University for freed Black students, Wells-Barnett's mother attending school with her children so that she too could learn to read and write. This early history gave Wells-Barnett two types of knowledge—the formal education that granted her literacy and the wisdom of knowing firsthand what it took for African Americans to become literate.

Ida Wells-Barnett's teenaged years and early adulthood in the South demonstrate that survival was a form of resistance for the African American women and men grappling with the aftermath of emancipation.[7] When a yellow fever epidemic killed both of her parents and one of her siblings in 1878, sixteen-year-old Wells-Barnett took on the responsibility of caring for five siblings. She supported them by passing the county teacher's exam and taking a teaching job. A year later, with her two younger sisters in tow, Wells-Barnett moved to Memphis for a better-paid teaching position. There she became a member of a lyceum of public school teachers who, each week, read from the Evening Star. This weekly newspaper reached hundreds of African Americans and provided one of the few sources of communication countering the growing discourse of racism that rendered African Americans as bestial, criminal, and sexually wanton. Because Wells-Barnett found teaching restrictive and her fellow teachers too submissive to the Memphis school board, Wells-Barnett took over the editorship of the *Evening Star*.

Wells-Barnett's activities as a teacher and journalist in Memphis crystallized her ideas about social injustice. Teaching gave her yet another firsthand experience with the mistreatment of African Americans as well as a journalistic outlet for speaking out. Over the next few years, she established herself as a writer by contributing to local and national publications. In 1889 twenty-seven-year-old Ida Wells-Barnett bought a one-third interest in the *Memphis Free Speech and Headlight* and later became its editor. After writing a series of articles revealing how inadequate buildings and improperly trained teachers resulted in poor conditions in local schools for African American children, Wells found herself unemployed. Without income, Wells-Barnett promoted subscriptions for the *Free Speech* and solicited subscriptions from the Delta region in Mississippi, Arkansas, and Tennessee. Her actions are part of a tradition of Black self-help that funded much-needed institutions. Economic self-reliance was especially needed in Memphis, where African Americans were dominated by Whites who resented and suppressed Black entrepreneurial activity.

In 1892, Wells-Barnett learned firsthand the lengths that some White citizens of Memphis were willing to go to maintain African American political and economic subordination. In March, Thomas Moss, Calvin McDowell, and Henry Steward, successful managers of a grocery business in a Black section just outside Memphis, were lynched. Wells-Barnett knew all three men, and knew that they were resented because they successfully competed with a White store in the same neighborhood. This painful personal experience was a turning point in Wells-Barnett's commitment to social justice activism. Outraged that "the city of Memphis has demonstrated that neither character nor standing avails the Negro if he dares to protect himself against the white man or become his rival," Wells urged the African Americans of Memphis to "save our money and leave a town that will neither protect our lives and property, nor give us a fair trial in the courts, when accused by white persons."[8] In addition, she wrote an editorial that, for 1892, advanced a shocking hypothesis about the prevailing wisdom about lynching. Wells-Barnett claimed that not only were African American men often falsely accused of rape, but that because some White women were attracted to Black men, some sexual relations between African American men and White women were consensual.

Fortunately, when the editorial appeared, Wells-Barnett was out of town or she too might have been lynched. Memphis citizens burned down the *Free Speech* and threatened Wells-Barnett's life if she ever returned to Memphis. This marked the beginning of Ida Wells-Barnett's crusade against lynching that included speaking tours, publishing editorials, preparing pamphlets, organizing community services, participating in women's and civil rights groups, and publishing the three pamphlets reprinted in this volume. Despite Wells-Barnett's impressive accomplishments, with the exception of *Crusade for Justice*, her ideas remained largely unexamined. Until the emergence of the modern Black feminist movement in the 1970s, Wells-Barnett remained neglected in African American historiography, largely because African American women's history was neglected. The resurgence of work in African American women's history created a new context for reclaiming neglected figures such as Wells-Barnett. Angela Davis's 1981 edited volume, *Women, Race, and Class,* positioned Wells-Barnett within the burgeoning interest in race, class, and gender studies largely catalyzed by Black feminism. Davis contextualized Wells-Barnett's analysis of lynching within this emerging interpretive framework.[9] The essays on African American women in Bettina Aptheker's *Woman's Legacy: Essays on Race, Sex, and Class in American History* also explored the significance of Wells-Barnett's antilynching campaign to Black women's political activism for women's suffrage.[10] In 1990 Mildred I. Thompson published her monograph, *Ida B. Wells-Barnett: An Exploratory Study of An American Black Woman, 1893–1930.*[11] The first book-length treatment of Wells-Barnett's life, Thompson's volume appeared as part of the *Black Women in United States History* series edited by Darlene Clark Hine and others. In the contemporary context when African American women's history seems so widely published and, for the moment, so well known, it is easy to forget what a monumental effort it took to reclaim African American women's history and Ida B. Wells-Barnett's significance within it.

The historical neglect of Wells-Barnett's work is unfortunate, for in many ways, Wells-Barnett's corpus of intellectual and activist work on lynching reflects core themes in African American intellectual production generally, most recently codified within African American Studies. According to Manning Marable, Black intellectual production has three distinguishing yet interconnected characteristics, all of which find expression within the three pamphlets reprinted here.[12] First, describing the truth of Black lives in ways that give agency to African Americans is a hallmark of African American scholarship. Black intellectual production routinely reclaims the humanity of Black people by resisting the objectifying and pathologizing of people of African descent that characterized mainstream scholarship. In the preface to *Crusade for Justice,* Wells-Barnett explains this responsibility of Black intellectuals. She decided to write her autobiography after conversing with a twenty-five-year-old woman who approached Wells-Barnett and, with embarrassment, asked about the details of her life. The young woman knew that Wells-Barnett was important but didn't know what she had done. As Wells-Barnett recalls, "One reason she did not know was because the happenings about which she inquired took place before she was born. Another was that there was no record from which she could inform herself. I then promised to set it down in writing so that those of her generation could know how the agitation against the lynching evil began."[13] Wells-Barnett's decision to create a record on lynching stems from similar sensibilities. She chooses to detail a group story of the violence needed to maintain social injustice.

In the work on lynching reprinted here, Wells-Barnett describes the horror of lynching. Extracting African American pain from behind the mask of virulent stereotyping justified by scientific racism, Wells-Barnett provides names, dates, and graphic details of the violence inflicted upon African Americans. We feel the pain of those who are lynched and the loved ones left behind—she makes them real. *Mob Rule in New Orleans* provides an especially chilling example of Wells-Barnett's journalistic skills, describing three days of violence and its effects on African American victims. Police officers approached two Black men sitting talking on a doorstep and for no apparent reason decided to arrest them. The men resisted, an altercation ensued, and one of the police officers was hurt. Wells-Barnett envisions how this event looked to Charles, one of the Black men profiled by the New Orleans police:

> In any law-abiding community Charles would have been justified in delivering himself up immediately to the properly constituted authorities and asking a trial by a jury of his peers. He could have been certain that in resisting an unwarranted arrest he had a right to defend his life, even to the point of taking one in that defense, but Charles knew that his arrest in New Orleans, even for defending his life, meant nothing short of a long term in the penitentiary, and still more probable death by lynching at the hands of a cowardly mob. (p. 158)**

In this context, Charles not only ran from the police, he did the unthinkable of fighting back. Charles's resistance to what he perceived as police harassment so incensed a mob of White citizens of New Orleans that "unable to vent its vindictiveness and bloodthirsty vengeance upon Charles, the mob turned its attention to other colored men who happened to get in the path of its fury" (pp. 166–67). Wells-Barnett tells story after story of unsuspecting African Americans who were pulled from trolley cars, chased down streets, and murdered while they slept. Their only crime was being African American and getting in the path of mob fury. *Mob Rule in New Orleans* is especially interesting because, by recording the range of Black reactions to mob violence, it eschews depicting African Americans as passive victims awaiting White salvation. Most Blacks ran, hid, and tried to get away. Others, like Charles, fought back. Charles was eventually killed in a hail of bullets, but Wells-Barnett refuses to portray Charles solely as a victim.

** Pagination in this edition.

Wells-Barnett's work on lynching also addresses a second distinctive feature of Black intellectual production, namely, that such work should aim to challenge distorted historical records that pathologized African Americans as lazy, unintelligent, sexually wanton, and violent. Pursuing knowledge for knowledge's sake was a frivolous exercise in a climate where African Americans were routinely murdered without recourse. Before Wells-Barnett's intervention, the historical record on lynching proposed that Black men deserved to be lynched, in part, because their allegedly animal-like natures compelled them to lust after White women. Wells-Barnett is quite clear about the need for Black intellectual production to correct this analysis, as well as revealing why Whites advanced such ideas. In the preface to *Southern Horrors,* she notes: "The Afro-American is not a bestial race. If this work can contribute in any way toward proving this, and at the same time arouse the conscience of the American people to a demand for justice to every citizen, and punishment by law for the lawless, I shall feel I have done my race a service. Other considerations are of minor importance." Wells-Barnett took a huge risk in challenging conventional wisdom—she was, after all, threatened with death if she ever returned to Memphis. Thus, her caveat that "other considerations are of minor importance" should be read against the context of her times where speaking out could be extremely dangerous.

Wells-Barnett's brilliance lay in her decision to use the data collected by White journalists to challenge the prevailing wisdom on lynching. Wells-Barnett reported the record by assembling an array of newspaper articles on lynching and demonstrating that what appeared to be isolated events were part of a larger pattern of lawlessness. Such data would be difficult to refute because she assembled and presented in a different medium the very information that White journalists reported. In using quantitative analyses to describe social structures, Wells-Barnett was ahead of her times.

Ida Wells-Barnett did not content herself with generating accurate descriptions of lynching or challenging prevailing justifications for its persistence. Instead, her work speaks directly to a third distinctive dimension of Black intellectual production, namely, that such work aims to prescribe solutions to the social problems uncovered through describing the truths of Black lives and challenging historical records that distorted those truths. In the corpus of Wells-Barnett's intellectual and activist endeavors, exemplified via this work on lynching, we see the synergistic relationship between her ideas and activism shaping the strategies she herself followed and those she advocated for others. Her activism was informed by ideas, and her new interpretations of old realities enabled her to chart a unique activist course.

Wells-Barnett clearly sees the task of prodding a large and seemingly uninformed White American and European public to take action against lynching as essential to its eradication. In the *Introduction to Mob Rule in New Orleans,* she states:

> We do not believe that the American people who have encouraged such scenes by their indifference will read unmoved these accounts of brutality, injustice and oppression. We do not believe that the moral conscience of the nation—that which is highest and the best among us—will always remain silent in the face of such outrages ... When this conscience wakes and speaks out in thunder tones, as it must, it will need facts to use as a weapon against injustice, barbarism

and wrong. It is for this reason that I carefully compile, print and send forth these facts. If the reader can do no more, he can pass this pamphlet on to another. (p. 156)

Included within these essays are specific ideas about how to address the crime of lynching through informed, principled activism. The last chapter of *A Red Record,* "The Remedy," asks "what can you do, reader, to prevent lynching, to thwart anarchy and promote law and order throughout our land?" (p. 150). Wells-Barnett's responses guide readers who are differentially positioned to bring about change. She first suggests that readers "disseminate the facts contained in this book by bringing them to the knowledge of every one with whom you come in contact." She believes that public sentiment will change if people are better informed. She suggests that readers encourage their religious organizations to exert moral leadership by sending letters of condemnation to every place where lynchings occur. Wells-Barnett is far from naïve concerning what it would take to spur some individuals to action. For those who care little about African Americans, Wells-Barnett advances arguments that tap vested interests. She suggests that White Southerners need to see how lynchings are "bad for business" in that capital investment cannot occur in a climate of lawlessness. Via these strategies, Wells-Barnett's work incorporates its own policy implications and eschews the contemporary separation of knowledge from politics. She is quite clear that facts can be harnessed to passion for justice, and the lonely path she followed as an antilynching proponent speaks to this passionate rationality put to the service of all dimensions of the Black intellectual tradition.

Situating Wells-Barnett within the framework of African American intellectual traditions is but one way of contextualizing her life and work. In the past two decades Wells-Barnett has generated a great deal of interest because her analyses and actions are so rich and take us in so many different directions. Some say this is what writing history is all about, continually rewriting the past through the lens of the present in order to provide guidance for the future. Within the project of reclaiming the ideas and actions of Ida B. Wells-Barnett, authors typically contextualize her ideas and career within analytical frameworks that reflect their particular concerns. For example, sociologists Mary Jo Deegan[14] and Charles Lemert[15] discuss Wells-Barnett's activities as a sociologist during its formative decades of 1890–1910, Deegan to reclaim a multiracial tradition of female sociologists and Lemert to advance a contemporary multiracial sociology. Both highlight her contributions yet minimize the culpability of sociology in excluding African American intellectuals, especially African American women. Others analyze Wells-Barnett's place within contemporary efforts to theorize White femininity. Vron Ware opens her chapter "To Make the Facts Known: Racial Terror and the Construction of White Femininity" with a quote by Wells-Barnett. Ware explains how the British responses to Ida Wells-Barnett dispels the myth that Wells-Barnett found a natural ally in White women for her antilynching crusade,[16] Angela Davis[17] and Bettina Aptheker[18] both examine Wells-Barnett's contentious relationship within the women's suffrage movement in light of the contentious issues that continue to plague relationships between African American and White American women today. African American scholar Joy James's intellectual project highlights a tradition of Black women's radical activism that might help guide what James sees as an increasingly bankrupt contemporary Black feminism. James situates Wells-Barnett within James's own interpretation of what constitutes African

American women's activism, pointing out that Wells-Barnett's analyses of lynching challenged well-known ideas advanced by W. E. B. Du Bois and other African American intellectuals of her period.[19]

Ida Wells-Barnett cannot be reduced to these or any other one set of claims. In the sections that follow, I situate her work on lynching published here within the traditions of Black feminism. Picking up the strands left by Ida Wells-Barnett and similar activists, the reemergence of modern Black feminism from 1970 reminds us that Black feminism as a social justice project and Black feminist thought as its intellectual center are inextricably linked.[20] How might Black feminist thought shed light on our readings of Wells-Barnett's essays on lynching? Conversely, in what ways does Wells-Barnett's work on lynching illuminate the connections between Black feminism as a social justice project and Black feminist thought?

First, this work on lynching analyzes the sexual politics of Black womanhood, especially the workings of sexual violence, long a core theme in Black feminist thought. As many authors point out, the struggle to control African American women's bodies and sexuality has been a major part of relations of race, class, and gender in the United States and throughout the African Diaspora.[21] What distinguishes Wells-Barnett's position is that her work advances our understanding of Black sexual politics, not through a focus on African American women, but on African American men.

Within contemporary Western feminist emphasis on personal advocacy on one's own behalf as a hallmark of feminism, Wells is often considered to be a "feminist" due to her support for women's suffrage, while her work on antilynching seems more appropriate for African American politics. Wells-Barnett recognized that, under the conditions of harsh racial segregation that she faced, the fate of African American women remained just as closely tied if not more so to the interests of African American men than those of White women. Because her work on lynching examines a form of sexual violence that fell more heavily on African American men, she can be seen as supporting a male-defined ethos of political struggle where the concerns of African American men take precedence over those of African American women. Yet this would be a misreading of her activism because the impetus for African American women's political activism often stems from an other-oriented catalyst—concern for one's children, a loved one, etc.—that in turn fosters distinctive forms of political activism. We find in Wells-Barnett's work an analysis of sexual violence that has great implications for the lives of African American women.

Second, these essays illustrate another distinguishing feature of Black feminist thought, namely, the use of intersectional paradigms to explain social phenomena. Wells-Barnett suggests that the crime of lynching grew less from the individual psyches of individuals in lynch mobs, and more from structural power relations of race, class, gender, and sexuality. Wells-Barnett's analysis of lynching foreshadows contemporary attention to paradigms of intersectionality where race, class, and gender are seen as mutually constructing systems of oppression.[22] The term *intersectionality* describes analyses claiming that systems of race, social class, gender, sexuality, ethnicity, nation, and age form mutually constructing features of social organization, which shape African American experiences with oppression and, in turn, are shaped by African American ideas and actions in response. What is unique about Wells-Barnett is that she not only introduced a much-needed gender analysis into Black political discourse, she did so via the very controversial theme of interracial sexuality.

Wells-Barnett raised a huge controversy when she dared to claim that many sexual liaisons between White women and Black men were in fact consensual, and most were not rape. She indicted White men as the actual perpetrators of crimes of sexual violence against African American men via lynching and African American women via rape. Consider how her comments in *Southern Horrors* concerning the contradictions of laws forbidding interracial marriage place blame on White male behavior and power:

> The miscegenation laws of the South only operate against the legitimate union of the races: they leave the white man free to seduce all the colored girls he can, but is death to the colored man who yields to the force and advances of a similar attraction in white women. While men lynch the offending Afro-American, not because he is a despoiler of virtue, but because he succumbs to the smiles of white women. (p. 31)

In this analysis, she reveals how ideas about gender difference—the seeming passivity of women and the aggressiveness of men—are in fact deeply racialized constructs. Gender had a racial face, whereby African American women, African American men, White women, and White men occupied distinct race/gender categories within an overarching social structure that prescribed their place. Interracial sexual liaisons violated that space. Wells-Barnett foreshadowed contemporary work on the connections between the creation of Du Bois's famous "color line" and ideas about sexuality and its role in the construction of gender during this same period.[23]

Finally, Wells-Barnett's work on lynching illustrates key elements of Black feminist epistemology.[24] One such element is the valorization of lived experience as a criterion of meaning. Such theorizing argues that, for oppressed people, trusting one's own experiences is of value in resisting oppression. Valorizing lived experiences requires centering on the needs of a particular group harmed by social injustice and finding a prominent place for analyses advanced by victims within the research process. During Wells-Barnett's era, the harm done to the individual African American men, women, and children who were lynched and the harm done to African Americans as a collectivity living with the threat of violence served as daily reminders that victims of lynching needed to be believed and that African Americans' interpretations of their own experiences were of special value.

Wells-Barnett arrived at intersectional analyses about lynching because her activism remained grounded in the concrete experiences of African Americans, and not in abstract theories about lynching advanced by more powerful groups that proclaimed lynching as an appropriate punishment for Black male rapists. Wells-Barnett's experiences of growing up in the South not far removed from slavery showed her the trials of African American poverty and working-class life in ways that differed dramatically from her more affluent counterparts. She may have spent much of her adult life *in* the Black middle class, but she was not *of* the Black middle class, and thus challenged social injustice from this special location. Instead, Wells-Barnett's "outsider within" social location within established African American and/or women's organizations and her newfound middle-class lifestyle often generated friction, compromise, and insight.

Ida Wells-Barnett's voice in these essays grows from lived experience with Black people, and not simply from theorizing about them. The lynching of her friends revealed in unsettling detail how the absence of social justice for African Americans was a collective problem mandating a collective solution. Neither

her own quality of life as an individual African American woman; nor that of her siblings, husband, and four children; nor that of African Americans as a group was ensured as long as any African American individual was denied equal protection under the law. Ida Wells-Barnett has finally gained the recognition she deserves. Yet her ideas and activism reflect similar paths taken by less famous African American women. The purpose of Wells-Barnetts life's work was not knowledge for knowledges sake. Her work models the adage "speak the truth to power."[25]

Patricia Hill Collins
Charles Phelps Taft Professor of Sociology
Professor and Chair,
Department of African American Studies
University of Cincinnati

Notes

1. All biographical information is taken from Wanda Hendricks, "Ida Bell Wells-Barnett," in *Black Women in America: An Historical Encyclopedia,* ed. Darlene Clark Hine (Brooklyn, N.Y.: Carlson Publishing), 2:1242–46.

2. Paula Giddings, "Missing in Action: Ida B. Wells,, the NAACP, and the Historical Record," *Meridians: Feminism, Race, Transnationalism* 1, no. 2 (2001): 1–17.

3. Alfreda M. Duster, ed., *Crusade for Justice: The Autobiography of Ida B. Wells* (Chicago: University of Chicago Press, 1970).

4. Giddings, "Missing in Action."

5. Ibid., p. 2.

6. Duster, *Crusade for Justice.*

7. Patricia Hill Collins, *Black Feminist Thought: Knowledge, Consciousness, and the Politics of Empowerment* (New York: Routledge, 2000), pp. 201–203.

8. Duster, *Crusade for Justice.*

9. Angela Y. Davis, *Women, Race, and Class,* 1st ed. (New York: Random House, 1981).

10. Bettina Aptheker, *Woman's Legacy: Essays on Race, Sex, and Class in American History* (Amherst: University of Massachusetts, 1982).

11. Mildred I. Thompson, *Ida B. Wells-Barnett: An Exploratory Study of an American Black Woman, 1893–1930* (Brooklyn, N.Y.: Carlson Publishing, 1990).

12. Manning Marable, "Introduction: Black Studies and the Racial Mountain," in *Dispatches from the Ebony Tower: Intellectuals Confront the American Experience,* ed. Manning Marable (New York: Columbia University Press, 2000), pp. 1–28.

13. Duster, *Crusade for Justice,* pp. 3–4.

14. Mary Jo Deegan, *Women in Sociology: A Bio-bibliographical Sourcebook* (New York: Greenwood, 1991).

15. Charles Lemert, *Sociology After the Crisis* (Boulder, Colo.: Westview Press, 1995).

16. Vron Ware, *Beyond the Pale: White Women, Racism and History* (New York: Verso, 1992).

17. Davis, *Women, Race, and Class.*

18. Aptheker, *Woman's Legacy.*

19. Joy James, "The Profeminist Politics of W. E. B. Du Bois with Respects to Anna Julia Cooper and Ida B. Wells Barnett," in *W.E.B. Du Bois on Race and Culture,* ed. Bernard W. Bell, Emily R. Grosholz, and James B. Stewart (New York: Routledge, 1996), pp. 141–60.

20. Collins, *Black Feminist Thought.*

21. Ibid., pp. 123–48.

22. Ibid., pp. 227–29.

23. Siobhan B. Somerville, *Queering the Color Line: Race and the Invention of Homosexuality in American Culture* (Durham, N.C.: Duke University Press, 2000).

24. Collins, *Black Feminist Thought,* pp. 251–71.

25. Patricia Hill Collins, *Fighting Words: Black Women and the Search for Justice* (Minneapolis: University of Minnesota), 1998, pp. xi-xv.

THE BLACK AND WHITE OF IT

IDA B. WELLS-BARNETT

The *Cleveland Gazette* of January 16, 1892, publishes a case in point. Mrs. J. S. Underwood, the wife of a minister of Elyria, Ohio, accused an Afro-American of rape. She told her husband that during his absence in 1888, stumping the State for the Prohibition Party, the man came to the kitchen door, forced his way in the house and insulted her. She tried to drive him out with a heavy poker, but he overpowered and chloroformed her, and when she revived her clothing was torn and she was in a horrible condition. She did not know the man but could identify him. She pointed out William Offett, a married man, who was arrested and, being in Ohio, was granted a trial.

The prisoner vehemently denied the charge of rape, but confessed he went to Mrs. Underwood's residence at her invitation and was criminally intimate with her at her request. This availed him nothing against the sworn testimony of a minister's wife, a lady of the highest respectability. He was found guilty, and entered the penitentiary, December 14, 1888, for fifteen years. Some time afterwards the woman's remorse led her to confess to her husband that the man was innocent. These are her words:

> I met Offett at the Post Office. It was raining. He was polite to me, and as I had several bundles in my arms he offered to carry them home for me, which he did.
> He had a strange fascination for me, and I invited him to call on me. He called,

bringing chestnuts and candy for the children. By this means we got them to leave us alone in the room. Then I sat on his lap. He made a proposal to me and I readily consented. Why I did so, I do not know, but that I did is true. He visited me several times after that and each time I was indiscreet. I did not care after the first time. In fact I could not have resisted, and had no desire to resist.

When asked by her husband why she told him she had been outraged, she said: "I had several reasons for telling you. One was the neighbors saw the fellows here, another was, I was afraid I had contracted a loathsome disease, and still another was that I feared I might give birth to a Negro baby. I hoped to save my reputation by telling you a deliberate lie." Her husband horrified by the confession had Offett, who had already served four years, released and secured a divorce.

There are thousands of such cases throughout the South, with the difference that the Southern white men in insatiate fury wreak their vengeance without intervention of law upon the Afro-Americans who consort with their women. A few instances to substantiate the assertion that some white women love the company of the Afro-American will not be out of place. Most of these cases were reported by the daily papers of the South.

In the winter of 1885–86 the wife of a practicing physician in Memphis, in good social standing whose name has escaped me, left home, husband and children, and ran away with her black coachman. She was with him a month before her husband found and brought her home. The coachman could not be found. The doctor moved his family away from Memphis, and is living in another city under an assumed name.

In the same city last year a white girl in the dusk of evening screamed at the approach of some parties that a Negro had assaulted her on the street. He was captured, tried by a white judge and jury, that acquitted him of the charge. It is needless to add if there had been a scrap of evidence on which to convict him of so grave a charge he would have been convicted.

Sarah Clark of Memphis loved a black man and lived openly with him. When she was indicted last spring for miscegenation, she swore in court that she was *not* a white woman. This she did to escape the the penitentiary and continued her illicit relation undisturbed. That she is of the lower class of whites, does not disturb the fact that she is a white woman. "The leading citizens" of Memphis are defending the "honor" of *all* white women, *demi-monde* included.

Since the manager of the *Free Speech* has been run away from Memphis by the guardians of the honor of Southern white women, a young girl living on Poplar St., who was discovered in intimate relations with a handsome mulatto young colored man, Will Morgan by name, stole her father's money to send the young fellow away from that father's wrath. She has since joined him in Chicago.

The *Memphis Ledger* for June 8 has the following:

If Lillie Bailey, a rather pretty white girl seventeen years of age, who is now at the City Hospital, would be somewhat less reserved about her disgrace there would be some very nauseating details in the story of her life. She is the mother of a little coon. The truth might reveal fearful depravity or it might reveal the evidence of a rank outrage. She will not divulge the name of the man who has left such black evidence of her disgrace, and, in fact, says it is a matter in which there can be no interest to the outside world. She came to Memphis nearly three months ago and was taken in at the Woman's Refuge in the southern part of the city. She remained there until a few weeks ago, when the child was born. The ladies in charge of the Refuge were horified. The girl was at once sent to the City Hospital, where she has been since May 30. She is a country girl. She came to Memphis from her father's farm, a short distance from Hernando, Miss. Just when she left there she would not say. In fact she says she came to Memphis from Arkansas, and says her home is in that State. She is rather good looking, has blue eyes, a low forehead and dark red hair. The ladies at the Woman's Refuge do not know anything about the girl further than what they learned when she was an inmate of the institution; and she would not tell much. When the child was born an attempt was made to get the girl to reveal the name of the Negro who had disgraced her, she obstinately refused and it was impossible to elicit any information from her on the subject.

Note the wording. "The truth might reveal fearful depravity or rank outrage." If it had been a white child or Lillie Bailey had told a pitiful story of Negro outrage, it would have been a case of woman's weakness or assault and she could have remained at the Woman's Refuge. But a Negro child and to withhold its father's name and thus prevent the killing of another Negro "rapist." A case of "fearful depravity."

The very week the "leading citizens" of Memphis were making a spectacle of themselves in defense of all white women of every kind, an Afro-American, M. Stricklin, was found in a white woman's room in that city. Although she made no outcry of rape, he was jailed and would have been lynched, but the woman stated she bought curtains of him (he was a furniture dealer) and his business in her room that night was to put them up. A white woman's word was taken as absolutely in this case as when the cry of rape is made, and he was freed.

What is true of Memphis is true of the entire South. The daily papers last year reported a farmer's wife in Alabama had given birth to a Negro child. When the Negro farm hand who was plowing in the field heard it he took the mule from the plow and fled. The dispatches also told of a woman in South Carolina who gave birth to a Negro child and charged three men with being its father, *every one of whom has since disappeared*. In Tuscumbia, Ala., the colored boy who was lynched there last year for assaulting a white girl told her before his accusers that he had met her there in the woods often before.

Frank Weems of Chattanooga who was not lynched in May only because the prominent citizens became his body guard until the doors of the penitentiary closed on him, had letters in his pocket from the white woman in the case, making the appointment with him. Edward Coy who was burned alive in Texarkana, January 1, 1892, died protesting his innocence. Investigation since as given by the Bystander in the *Chicago Inter Ocean*, October 1, proves:

1. The woman who was paraded as a victim of violence was of bad character; her husband was a drunkard and a gambler.
2. She was publicly reported and generally known to have been criminally intimate with Coy for more than a year previous.

3. She was compelled by threats, if not by violence, to make the charge against the victim.
4. When she came to apply the match Coy asked her if she would burn him after they had "been sweethearting" so long.
5. A large majority of the "superior" white men prominent in the affair are the reputed fathers of mulatto children.

These are not pleasant facts, but they are illustrative of the vital phase of the so-called race question, which should properly be designated an earnest inquiry as to the best methods by which religion, science, law and political power may be employed to excuse injustice, barbarity and crime done to a people because of race and color. There can be no possible belief that these people were inspired by any consuming zeal to vindicate God's law against miscegnarionists of the most practical sort. The woman was a willing partner in the victim's guilt, and being of the "superior" race must naturally have been more guilty.

In Natchez, Miss., Mrs. Marshall, one of the *creme de la creme* of the city, created a tremendous sensation several years ago. She has a black coachman who was married, and had been in her employ several years. During this time she gave birth to a child whose color was remarked, but traced to some brunette ancestor, and one of the fashionable dames of the city was its godmother. Mrs. Marshall's social position was unquestioned, and wealth showered every dainty on this child which was idolized with its brothers and sisters by its white papa. In course of time another child appeared on the scene, but it was unmistakably dark. All were alarmed, and "rush of blood, strangulation" were the conjectures, but the doctor, when asked the cause, grimly told them it was a Negro child. There was a family conclave, the coachman heard of it and leaving his own family went West, and has never returned. As soon as Mrs. Marshall was able to travel she was sent away in deep disgrace. Her husband died within the year of a broken heart.

Ebenzer Fowler, the wealthiest colored man in Issaquena County, Miss., was shot down on the street in Mayersville, January 30, 1885, just before dark by an armed body of white men who filled his body with bullets. They charged him with writing a note to a white woman of the place, which they intercepted and which proved there was an intimacy existing between them.

Hundreds of such cases might be cited, but enough have been given to prove the assertion that there are white women in the South who love the Afro-American's company even as there are white men notorious for their preference for Afro-American women.

There is hardly a town in the South which has not an instance of the kind which is well known, and hence the assertion is reiterated that "nobody in the South believes the old thread bare lie that negro men rape white women." Hence there is a growing demand among Afro-Americans that the guilt or innocence of parties accused of rape be fully established. They know the men of the section of the country who refuse this are not so desirous of punishing rapists as they pretend. The utterances of the leading white men show that with them it is not the crime but the *class*. Bishop Fitzgerald has become apologist for lynchers of the rapists of *white* women only. Governor Tillman, of South Carolina, in the month of June, standing under the tree in Barnwell, S.C., on which eight Afro-Americans were hung last year, declared that he would lead a mob to lynch a *negro* who raped a *white* woman. So say the pulpits, officials and newspapers of the South. But when the victim is a colored woman it is different.

Last winter in Baltimore, Md., three white ruffians assaulted a Miss Camphor, a young Afro-American girl, while out walking with a young man of her own race. They held her escort and outraged the girl. It was a deed dastardly enough to arouse Southern blood, which gives its horror of rape as excuse for lawlessness, but she was an Afro-American. The case went to the courts, an Afro-American lawyer defended the men and they were acquitted.

In Nashville, Tenn., there is a white man, Pat Hanifan, who outraged a little Afro-American girl, and, from the physical injuries received, she has been ruined for life. He was jailed for six months, discharged, and is now a detective in that city. In the same city, last May, a white man outraged an Afro-American girl in a drug store. He was arrested, and released on bail at the trial. It was rumored that five hundred Afro-Americans had organized to lynch him. Two hundred and fifty white citizens armed themselves with Winchesters and guarded him. A cannon was placed in front of his home, and the Buchanan Rifles (State Militia) ordered to the scene for his protection. The Afro-American mob did not materialize. Only two weeks before Eph. Grizzard, who had only been *charged* with rape upon a white woman, had been taken from the jail, with Governor Buchanan and the police and militia standing by, dragged through the streets in broad daylight, knives plunged into him at every step, and with every fiendish cruelty a frenzied mob could devise, he was at last swung out on the bridge with hands cut to pieces as he tried to climb up the stanchions. A naked, bloody example of the blood-thirstiness of the nineteenth-century civilization of the Athens of the South! No cannon or military was called out in his defense. He dared to visit a white woman.

At the very moment these civilized whites were announcing their determination "to protect their wives and daughters," by murdering Grizzard, a white man was in the same jail for raping eight-year-old Maggie Reese, an Afro-American girl. He was not harmed. The "honor" of grown women who were glad enough to be supported by the Grizzard boys and Ed Coy, as long as the liaison was not known, needed protection; they were white. The outrage upon helpless childhood needed no avenging in this case; she was black.

A white man in Guthrie, Oklahoma Territory, two months ago inflicted such injuries upon another Afro-American child that she died. He was not punished, but an attempt was made in the same town in the month of June to lynch an Afro-American who visited a white woman.

In Memphis, Tenn., in the month of June, Eilerton L. Dorr, who is the husband of Russell Hancock's widow, was arrested for attempted rape on Mattie Cole, a neighbor's cook; he was only prevented from accomplishing his purpose, by the appearance of Mattie's employer. Dorr's friends say he was drunk and not responsible for his actions. The grand jury refused to indict him and he was discharged.

THE INVASION

JAMES S. HIRSCH

FIVE WHITE MEN in a green Franklin led the charge across the Frisco tracks, but the car had gone no more than a block before it was halted by a cascade of bullets that shattered the windows, chipped the paint, and killed the occupants. Thousands of screaming men, guns in hand, began pouring out from behind the depot, from behind long strings of boxcars and piles of oil well casings. Hundreds more came from behind the nearby Frisco and Santa Fe passenger stations, and they came from behind the Katy depot four blocks north. Rebel yells and "Indian gobblings" were heard above the din of gunshot fire. A machine gun placed on top of a grain elevator opened fired on black Tulsa as cars speeding east on Brady and Cameron provided additional support.

Crowds of people—some just watching, some taking pictures—converged on the southwestern edge of Greenwood. They moved not in one mass but in small groups of four or five, dividing their labor along the way. Reaching an unoccupied home or business, one rioter would put his gun against the lock and blow it off. Once inside, group would confiscate valuables, like jewelry or silver, smash everything breakable, open trunks and bureau drawers, wrench telephones from the walls, and trample it all. Then they piled up all the bedding, furniture, and other inflammables, scattered kerosene, and applied matches.

In one last indignity, the rioters piled the furniture, bedsprings, and other objects in front of the house, literally exposing the inner life of a family. Dr. R. T. Bridgewater, a black assistant county physician, returned to his home at 507 North Detroit to find his piano as well as his elegant furniture on the street. As he described it:

> My safe had been broken open, all of the money stolen, also my silverware, cut glass, all of the family clothing, and everything of value had been removed, even my family Bible. My electric light fixtures were broken, all the window lights and glass in the doors were broken, the dishes that were not stolen were broken, the floors were covered (literally speaking) with glass, even the phone was torn from the wall. In the basement we gathered two tubs of broken glass from the floor. My car was stolen and most of my large rugs were taken.

The fire, moving east along Archer Street, cast a reddish hue in the gray light of early morning. Rows of homes were ignited, and the raiders could be seen in the glow of crackling new fires as the houses burst into flames. Telephone and power lines were toppled, wires whipping about and sparks flying in every direction. On other streets, telephone poles stood like burned matchsticks, lifeless wires dangling in the street. All power was soon shut off in Greenwood.

Dense clouds of smoke began to rise as the torchers moved north on Elgin and Detroit avenues, the latter a western boundary between white and black Tulsa. The arsonists looted and ignited the black homes on the east side of Detroit while carefully avoiding the white homes on the other side. As the warm sun rose, the heat and smoke created a stifling, airless environment. Perspiration soaked men's shirts. Flower gardens wilted. Cats keeled over.

Eighteen-year-old Otis Clark lived on Archer Street with his mother and grandmother as well as his bulldog, Bob. He had seen the blacks shoot out the streetlights in Greenwood to deter whites from invading at night, and he awoke on June 1 assuming the troubles were over. He hoped the ruckus hadn't disturbed his grandmother's vegetable garden, whose tomatoes he sold to the white prostitutes sitting on their porches on First Street, their lace underclothes draped over their knees. He decided to visit a friend who ran Jackson's Funeral Home down the street, but before long he heard more shooting. Jackson's had its own ambulance, and Otis accompanied an attendant to get it from a garage. As the attendant turned the key to open the garage, a rifle blast sounded and a bullet crashed into his hand, spilling blood like water from a fountain. A sniper was on the grain elevator. As Otis and the attendant ran for cover, bullets whistled by their ears, kicking up dust and splitting wood on the building. They made it back to the funeral home, where Otis saw Mr. Jackson tending three or four bodies on tables.

He left the funeral parlor and headed home; but bands of whites blocked his route, so he ducked into an alley and went to his cousin's instead. She and her husband were preparing to flee by car, so Otis joined them to go to Claremore, twenty-nine miles away. Before they got there, white men with guns stopped the vehicle and demanded that they give up their arms.

They returned to Tulsa the following day. Otis found his home destroyed, the vegetable garden covered with ash, his mother and grandmother heartbroken, his bulldog gone. Otis wanted nothing more to do with this city; he decided to go to Milwaukee and live with his father. That night he hopped on a freight train, climbed to the top of a boxcar, and never looked back.

As the morning sun climbed higher, the first buildings burned on West Archer had begun to disintegrate while new fires were running east through Greenwood, then north. At 9 a.m. a white lawyer named Luther Jones stood on top of the Hotel Tulsa and saw thirty or forty separate fires, each with a different dance and shape, the smoke varying in texture and tint. Some blazes produced brownish gray clouds of vapor that turned white as they died out; others unfurled a black haze that settled heavily over the city. A light eastern breeze created an eerie half canopy: west of Cincinnati Avenue was a cerulean southwestern sky, while east was a dark cumulus cover of dust and smoke.

The police appeared more intent on helping the mob than protecting life and property. According to a black deputy sheriff, V. B. Bostic, a white police officer drove him and his wife from their home and then "poured oil on the floor and set a lighted match to it." A white witness said that "a uniformed [white] policeman on East Second Street went home, changed his uniform to plainclothes, and went to the Negro district and led a bunch of whites in Negro houses, some of the bunch pilfering, never offered to protect men, women or children."

A white judge named John Oliphant, testifying after the riot, offered a similar account of the police force. "They were the chief fellows setting the fires," he said. "They were not in uniform, but they had stars on. They had badges on." Henry Pack, the black officer, also testified that he saw about a dozen "special police" knocking down doors and setting fires. Pack subsequently quit the force and moved to Muskogee.

Chief Gustafson, in later court testimony, did not implicate his own officers but suggested that the civilians with special commissions started the fires. "We were unable to limit the commissions to our choice," he said. "I usually talked to the men and those I thought would remain cool-headed I commissioned. But of those who might have lost their heads—they might have applied the torch. But that was positively in contradiction to orders."

The National Guard squared off against blacks in some of the riot's most heated gun battles. Between 8 and 9 a.m., the police urgently requested that two units of the Guard stop black gunmen on the northwestern edge of Greenwood from firing at white homes on Sunset Hill. A force of up to one hundred thirty-five guardsmen, carrying Springfield rifles, .45 Colts, and pistols, advanced in a "skirmish line" to the "military crest" of the hill but were met by blacks firing from the base. The guardsmen, shooting from the prone position, fired back as blacks took cover in "out-buildings;" the battle raged for twenty minutes. Overwhelmed, the blacks began to retreat, using frame buildings to gain better cover, followed by the guardsmen in hot pursuit. The encounter ended badly for the blacks. As Captain John McCuen of Company B wrote in his report of the incident: "Little opposition was met with until about half way through the settlement when some negroes who had barricaded themselves in houses refused to stop firing and had to be killed." He also wrote that in a different battle, "at the north-east corner of the negro settlement," ten or more blacks barricaded themselves in a concrete store, and a "stiff fight ensued between these negroes on one side and guardsmen and civilians on the other." The description suggests that in some cases little difference existed between the Guard and the mob—both were in Greenwood to fight blacks.

The Tulsa Fire Department did not join in the riot, but it was cowered by the mob. The station on North Main Street responded to its first call at 2 a.m., sent a truck to Main and Archer, and had hooked its hose to a water plug when several whites pointed their guns at two firefighters. As the Archer fires roared in the background, the firemen disengaged the hose. "They told us to get away from that hose or someone would get killed," the driver, C. H. Moore, later testified. "We went back to the fire station and we went to sleep."

When the next alarm sounded, the fire truck didn't move. "We had orders not to respond" Moore said.

Even after daybreak, when the department tried to do its job, it was no match for the arsonists' gas-soaked rags. At about 7 a.m. Moore responded to a call that the black district's Frissell Memorial Hospital on East Brady was on fire. With bullets whizzing overhead and the streets packed, Moore laid out the water hose. "I put out [the hospital fire] and by the time I got it out, the house on the corner was afire." As he tended that blaze, the hospital was set on fire again. So he put it out a second time—only to have the mob set the hospital on fire a third time. It too was finally destroyed. At several turns, whites were thwarted from helping blacks. Edward L. Wheeler, who joined the National Guard that day, rode out to Detroit Avenue with a dilapidated machine gun, hoping to frighten the blacks into surrendering. A large group of whites hid behind a boiler, waiting for the blacks to appear. Wheeler, carrying a small pistol in his hip pocket, dismounted from the truck and pleaded with the whites to stop shooting. A man stepped out from behind the crowd, drew his gun, and placed it against Wheeler's abdomen. Declaring that the captain was trying to protect the Negroes, he shot once. The bullet went through Wheeler's right side and broke his arm, but he survived. At forty-five, he was a veteran of the Spanish-American War and the world war who had moved to Tulsa, according to the *Tribune,* "several months ago from the north with the hope of benefiting his health."

As the assault continued, the overwhelmed blacks had few options. Some continued their armed resistance while others tried to hide in abandoned iceboxes or dirty hog pens. One person tried to leave Greenwood through an underground sewer line. Many escaped by foot, walking nine miles or more under the hot sun to Sand Springs and other communities. For those who stayed in Greenwood, saving family heirlooms or assets became unrealistic. Survival was the best most could achieve.

"You could hear shooting everywhere in town, boom, boom, boom," said C. F. Gabe, whose piano was struck by a bullet. "People were saying, 'The white folks are killing all the niggers and burning all their houses.'"

Men and women ran down Greenwood Avenue in their night-clothes and bare feet, carrying their dazed children. One woman had put her stillborn baby in a shoebox, to be buried that morning. But when the riot broke out the woman, running, bumping, tripping down Greenwood Avenue, lost the box. As she desperately searched the ground, shots rang out and her husband yelled for her to get out of the street. "Where's my baby?" she screamed. "Where's my baby?" Watching the futile search was twenty-three-year-old Rosa Davis Skinner, who vividly recalled the incident at the age of ninety-nine.

"They never did find that child," she said softly.

Most blacks peacefully submitted to the guardsmen before their homes were looted and burned, but surrender did not guarantee survival. When A. C. Jackson, one of the most prominent black surgeons in America, walked out of his house on Detroit Avenue with his hands raised, a band of menacing white men approached him. "Here I am," he said. "I want to go with you."

John Oliphant, the white judge, lived a block away and saw trouble coming.

"That's Dr. Jackson," he said. "Don't hurt him."

Two of the whites fired their guns, and Jackson fell with the second shot, a bullet in his chest. The shooters walked away, but not before one of them fired another shot to break the doctor's leg. He died later that day. His house was splashed with gas and coal oil, then torched.

Blacks who resisted arrest or whose homes had firearms—both evidence of being a "bad nigger"—were the most likely to be executed, but the invasion of Greenwood was less about mass killing than about the physical and spiritual destruction of a community. Even acts of mercy were gestures of hate. In one instance, a white man who entered a black home was going to shoot a defenseless resident, but another white stopped him so that the black man could tell others "what happens to niggers who hunt trouble." That same message was delivered by postcards depicting a devastated Greenwood.

With black homes defenseless, whites entered at will—not just men but women and children, who rummaged through drawers and cabinets, stuffed belongings in pillowcases and sheets, and celebrated their good fortune. When the black deputy sheriff, Cleaver, left the courthouse on Wednesday morning and returned to Greenwood, he met two white women carrying a bundle of clothes.

"What have you got there?" he demanded.

"Who wants to know?" one asked.

"Those are my wife's clothes."

"Yonder goes a man on a truck with the rest of the stuff."

In some cases, whites justified the looting on the ground that black wealth was amassed in the underground economy or through some kind of chicanery that would allow an inferior race to prosper. Black success was an intolerable affront to the social order of white supremacy, so taking their possessions not only stripped blacks of their material status but also tipped the social scales back to their proper alignment. This reassertion of authority, expressed through ransacked homes, was a cause for celebration.

"Some [looters] were singing," Judge Oliphant later testified. "Some were playing pianos that were taken out of the building, some were running Victrolas, some dancing a jig, and just having a rollicking easy good time in a business [in] which they thought they were doing what was upright."

The invasion of Greenwood had another chilling dimension—airplanes, flown by whites, swept over Greenwood in the morning hours. Exactly what they did has been debated ever since but numerous black witnesses have said the aircraft were used to assault Greenwood: pilots either dropped incendiary devices like "turpentine balls" and dynamite or used rifles to strafe people from the sky. If true, Tulsa was the first U.S. city to suffer an aerial assault. But police officials said the planes were used only to monitor the fires and to locate refugees. Walter White, the journalist from the NAACP, wrote: "Eight aeroplanes were employed to spy on the movements of the Negroes and according to some were used in bombing the colored section." Even if the planes were not used for offensive purposes, their presence emphasized the total-war atmosphere of the raid and seared another harrowing image into many blacks' memories.

At 9:15 a.m. Adjutant General Charles Barrett arrived on a special train from Oklahoma City with one hundred nine white soldiers and officers under his command. The National Guard's reinforcements had arrived, although much of the destruction was well under way. Barrett later wrote that his train "halted in the midst of fifteen to twenty thousand blood-maddening rioters" (a probable exaggeration) and that "no civil authority could restore order." Barrett then ordered additional troops from Muskogee, Vinita, and Wagoner, and rumors continued to circulate about invasions of blacks from other parts of Oklahoma.

While many black Tulsans widely praised the "state troops," Barrett could not take control of the city without following certain protocols. He needed first to report to the local authorities, which included a fruitless effort to find Sheriff McCullough, and precious minutes passed before martial law could be declared. Later, critics of the National Guard would attach great importance to the apparent decision of the state troops awaiting orders to eat breakfast while homes and businesses were being destroyed. Wherever the fault may lie—with local officials in their delayed request for state help or with the state troops for failing to act with urgency—martial law was not imposed until 11:49 a.m., when the riot was effectively over.

The local guard had a key role in one of the most dramatic moments of the riot.

The new Mount Zion Baptist Church was rumored to be a warehouse for armaments among whites. As the *Daily Oklahoman* reported, the church "was said to have been the rendezvous of the Bolshevik element of the Negroes who are responsible for the outbreak." Word was that twenty caskets had been taken to the church, each filled with high-powered rifles. After the riot, blacks ridiculed this claim—"that church was built to glorify God," said Mabel Little—and assumed that the accusation reflected the resentment toward blacks who built a place of worship as elegant and beautiful as any white church in Tulsa.

With or without ammunition, the sturdy building provided blacks with one of their best fortresses, and any white who charged it or the surrounding houses was repelled by gunmen inside. One firefight lasted an hour. As fire and smoke enveloped nearby streets, Mount Zion stood strong. Seeking greater firepower, the whites called in local guardsmen. They arrived on Elgin Street in a flatbed truck, stopping less than a quarter mile from the church. One soldier jerked back a canvas cover from a machine gun, which was placed on a tripod. Another pulled the lid from a box, withdrawing belts of ammunition. He fit the shells into the grooves of the gun while the gunman adjusted the sights of the barrel. His cap pulled backward, he shifted into a comfortable position, aimed the gun at the church, and pulled the trigger. As bullets flashed from the muzzle, a smoky haze enveloped the men. One witness said the gun started "chattering [in] a stream of bullets" (although the National Guard reported that the gun could only fire one bullet at a time).

Chunks of mortar and brick flew from the belfry, where blacks had been firing through narrow slits. The rioters who had been held at bay swung around the back of the church, taking shelter behind a rim of houses and firing away with their own guns. In five or six minutes, the machine gun had created large jagged holes in the side of the church, and bricks flew wildly about. The gunfire from the church had stopped as windows shattered and the belfry collapsed. The surrounding homes that had been protected by the gunmen in the church were then torched. So too was Mount Zion. Smoke poured out of the top, and fire flashed from every hole "like flaming tongues of dragons." An estimated seven or eight blacks were killed.

The three guardsmen dismounted the machine gun from the tripod, wrapped it in canvas, and laid it on the flatbed. They rolled up the belts with empty shell casings, stored the unused rounds, and drove away not more than ten minutes after they arrived. The battle of Mount Zion was over, leaving nothing left but scorched brick walls and smoldering embers buried beneath piles of rubbish.

Black Tulsa's final humiliation was its exodus from Greenwood.

Removed at gunpoint from their homes throughout the day, the African Americans were lined up on the street, their hands raised above their heads, and slowly marched out of the district. Others were taken in trucks or cars. E. W. Woods, the principal of the high school and perhaps the most respected man in Greenwood, left his home with one arm held high, the other carrying his three-month-old baby. Three whites holding guns urged him forward. Men, women, and children carried bundles of clothing on their heads and backs and pulled wobbly carts with clothes, phonographs, and household goods. Skinny mules lugged wagons carrying ice-filled trunks, huge boxes of food, and tubs of coffee. One aged woman clung to her Bible; young girls held white stuffed dogs and wax dolls. A sickly old man wrapped in quilts and blankets was finally placed in a car and taken to a hospital.

With the city jail full, the blacks were detained at the Convention Hall, a few blocks beyond Greenwood's western boundary. Some whites had already been given the day off—a grocer released his clerk because it was "nigger day"—and the white crowds had to be held back by armed guards as the blacks were brought in. They were ordered through the front door, guarded on both sides by men with bayonets, pistols, and rifles. Before reaching the entrance they were searched, with every knife, pistol, and cartridge taken from them. Inside, the men with families were allowed to try to calm their crying children. The rest went to a balcony, the men on one side and the women on the other. The guards were brusque to the "surly Negroes," especially if they were carrying ammunition. "You're the sort that has caused all of this," said one officer to a black lawyer as he took a handful of pistol cartridges out of his pocket.

Not all blacks went to the hall voluntarily. Officer Leo Irish "captured" six Negroes in the burned district, roped them together in single file, and made them run behind his motorcycle to the detention center. J. W. Hughes, a schoolteacher, was initially taken with his family to the city jail, then forced to march to the Convention Hall. "Many people cheered and clapped their hands as we were marched four abreast with our hands above our head," he said. "A man was shot at the door of the Convention Hall while both hands were above his head. Many men who were shot out in the city were brought in the hall and we heard their cries and groans."

When the Convention Hall was full, blacks were taken through the heart of downtown Tulsa, where spectators were given a further view of the prisoners. The guards shot at the heels of those who couldn't keep pace. Many were taken to McNulty Park, on Tenth and Elgin streets, where the baseball locker rooms were used to separate the men and women, and blacks huddled from one end of the grandstand to another. By Thursday, June 2, 6,000 blacks had been consolidated at the fairgrounds, about one mile northeast of Greenwood, where platforms used to groom cows were transformed into sleeping areas.

Seated on the floor at the fairgrounds was an old woman, a gray handkerchief knotted about her wrinkled face, rocking gently back and forth. In her hand she held a cup of hot vegetable soup. Tears fell from her eyes. "Oh lawdy, me, an old woman that has worked so hard all her life, and now everything is gone. My house burned, my clothes burned, my chickens burned. Nothing have I but the clothes on my back! Oh lawdy, that I should live to see such a day."

Back in Greenwood, a white man surveyed the ruins. Small frame houses had been reduced to charred chimney columns and gateposts. Electric wires and telephone lines hung in tangled loops across pavements and between the shattered walls of brick buildings. Office chairs, sewing machines, trunks, pieces of cars, and piles of clothing and household goods lay in trails of ruin.

"Everything has been destroyed except the earth on which the town was built" he said. "I guess that if there had been any way to set fire to the soil, it would be gone too."

While many white Tulsans acted with depravity, other whites behaved magnanimously, even courageously. They volunteered their services at first-aid stations or tried to douse the raging fires; others stood their ground against armed white vigilantes who went from door to door in search of black cooks, maids, and butlers. White homeowners hid their domestics in basements and attics or smuggled them out of town. When Charles and Amy Arnold refused to release their housekeeper, the marauders yelled "Nigger lovers" and heaved a brick through their front window. A young white stenographer named Mary Jo Erhardt heard the gunshots at night from her room at the YWCA at Fifth and Cheyenne. In the morning, she was heading downstairs when she heard the familiar voice of a black porter who worked there.

"Miss Mary! Oh, Miss Mary!" he said. "Let me in quick." Armed whites, he said, were chasing him.

Erhardt quickly directed him to a walk-in refrigerator and had stashed him behind the beef carcasses when she heard a pounding on the door. She saw three white men with revolvers.

"What do you want?" she asked.

"Where did he go?" one asked.

"Where did who go?"

"That nigger! Did you let him in here?"

"Mister, I'm not letting anybody in here!"

The men left, although ten minutes passed before Erhardt felt the black man could be safely released.

Many blacks sought refuge in Tulsa's white churches, sometimes leaving a trail of blood on their steps. The Holy Family Catholic Church received four hundred refugees on the first day of the riot, twenty-five of them babies. They were bathed and clothed, and the adults were also given clothes and food. The First Presbyterian Church used its basement to shelter mothers with infants, children separated from parents, and terrified women and children. Five dead bodies were also deposited outside the church, perhaps because its pastor, the Reverend Charles Kerr, was known to be sympathetic to African Americans. The First Baptist Church set up cots for the wounded, but many victims had to lie on the floor or on wooden benches. The YWCA opened a Hostess House on Archer Street, which included baths, "disinfection," sewing machines, restrooms, and employment registration.

These acts of kindness could not erase the images of horror for others. Ruth Avery, a white girl in first grade at the time, would often recall two truckloads of dead black bodies riding down the street, their arms and legs protruding through the slats. "I saw a boy on top of the bodies," she told a television interviewer in the 1980s. "He was wearing brown pants and a blue shirt. When the truck hit a pothole, his head flipped over and his mouth was open and his eyes were open. It looked like he was frightened to death. I screamed."

Lucille Kittle, then a white teenager from Sand Springs, recalled in the 1980s how she tried to comfort the destitute Negroes who appeared in her town:

> There must have been two hundred blacks from Tulsa, mostly women and children, who walked that north road out to Sand Springs. I felt so sorry for those people. All I could do was cry, but they were crying too, so that didn't help anyone. But they were terrified, and I was appalled. I'm not sure I even knew what "appalled" meant at age fifteen, but I was appalled at how horrible it was. There was no complaining, no griping, no doing, no nothing. They simply were shocked and stunned into silence. Children, little kids walked those nine miles. It wasn't pleasant, and it's not pleasant to talk about now either.

Some witnesses were less sympathetic. Paul Haggard, who was twelve years old in 1921, was a friend of Don Adkison, the police commissioner's son. The morning after the riot, the commissioner took the two boys with him to inspect Greenwood. "Whoa boy, what I saw," Haggard said in the 1970s. "There was a store whose front had been knocked out, and Don and I found two boxes of Crackerjacks. So we're eating those, and then we came across them colored boys who were down there on the tracks and they'd been shot, and the sun was on them and all that stuff. And that's where we threw the Crack-erjacks." He chuckled at the memory.

The ruins of Greenwood were a grim display of racial hatred, but prejudice alone does not explain the motives of a white community that depended on blacks for so many service jobs. It was also clear, in retrospect, that each side misunderstood the actions of the other and made fateful decisions as a result. The riot was not only an expression of hostility between the two groups but also a reflection of the isolation and mistrust each community felt for the other.

White Tulsa's central miscalculation was that blacks were trying to take over the city, a blunder partly engendered by their own racism. Whites who assumed that blacks were inclined to be violent could believe that a relatively small Negro population would defy all logic and launch a raid against white Tulsans, even though such an attack would be suicidal. Blacks, of course, were not suicidal, but savages were, at least the black savages in the imagination of white America. As blacks in Oklahoma and elsewhere began using force to resist oppression, white Tulsans' anxieties were reinforced by headlines shouting FEARS OF NEGRO UPRISING, which recalled the early slave rebellions.

The armed blacks who drove through white Tulsa and marched to the courthouse were undeniably militant, but the whites assumed that they represented all black Tulsans as well as blacks in Muskogee and the other towns that were supposedly preparing to attack. If such an assault had occurred, then a full-throttle counterattack would have been appropriate. But these assumptions were all wrong. The blacks who left Greenwood hardly formed a monolith of Negro opinion; the whites' bigotry blinded them to the obvious fact that diverse opinions exist among African Americans just as they do among whites.

Most white Tulsans were ignorant of this logic, but the armed blacks were also oblivious of the panic that their actions would create. Segregation imposed an invisible wall between the two communities, making blacks and whites strangers. Even whites who employed black servants often did not know their employees' last names. This isolation and the absence of communication prevented the two sides from comprehending each other's actions in the early evening hours of May 31. The whites did not realize that blacks had legitimate fears that Dick Rowland would be lynched, even after the sheriff reassured them. But the blacks didn't realize that their actions—driving in large groups into white Tulsa, occasionally firing guns in the air—would be interpreted as an attempt to take over the city.

Oddly enough, the safest black man in Tulsa during the riot was Dick Rowland. He stayed in the jail under guard that night, was spirited out of town the next morning, and was never seen again in Tulsa.

CHAPTER 4

BLACK POLITICAL AWAKENING IN AMERICA

THE NEW NEGRO: GARVEYITES AND OTHERS

THEODORE G. VINCENT

WORLD WAR I BROUGHT new hope to black people in many parts of the world. Liberation came to few, but a great number of black people became convinced that, with a concentrated effort, the long era of white domination over blacks could be brought to a close. The new confidence was worldwide, affecting blacks in Africa and Latin America as well as in the United States, and it was part of a larger change that had begun in some places as early as 1910. But for the most part the change came with the war. The Garvey movement was nurtured by, and blossomed in, the climate of hope and the dramatic changes of life-style among black people that followed World War I.

For traditional Western European civilization, World War I was an unmitigated disaster. Militarists, capitalists, despots, benevolent monarchs and liberal democrats joined to direct a grotesque scenario which brought about an unprecedented waste of human lives—and all for that shallowest of motives, the rights of Empire. Blacks and others of the Third World, so long propagandized into thinking of themselves as the "white man's burden," began to question the ability of white colonial rulers who were unable to maintain peaceful relations. This new understanding could not eradicate all vestiges of ingrained inferiority, but it started many in the direction of psychological freedom. Further, blacks fought on battlefields in

Africa, the Near East and Europe, and proved themselves the equals of whites as soldiers; close to one million blacks from Africa, the Caribbean and North America served in World War I (including three hundred seventy thousand from the United States). Even those who did not fight could not fail to notice that the supposedly omnipotent white rulers had been forced to plead for black support in their military efforts.

A heightened political consciousness had been building among black people during the years of World War I in the course of a debate within black society over black involvement in the war. For many it seemed ridiculous for blacks to involve themselves in a war to save democracy in Europe when blacks didn't have democracy at home. One issue of the Richmond *Planet,* a black weekly, was barred from the mails because it contained an article urging blacks not to volunteer for military service. Uzziah Miner of Howard University Law School published—at his own expense—a small book criticizing the hypocrisy of the war and the use of black troops.[1] Meanwhile, a future leading Garveyite, J. C. St. Clair Drake, was telling his friends that he couldn't feel much sympathy for the suffering Belgians after what Belgians had done to blacks in the Congo.[2] Some, however, chose to keep their anti-war sentiments to themselves, since a widespread pro-war chauvinistic hysteria made outspoken opposition dangerous. As in so many wars, the strongest opposition came from the young, and the main support from the old; these stands on the war foreshadowed the coming division in black society between "New Negroes" and "Old Negroes."

The new awareness reached a dramatic height in the United States at the end of World War I as black troops returned from Europe. Writing in the NAACP magazine *Crisis* in 1919, W. E. B. DuBois exemplified the militant mood of the day: "We return. We return from fighting. Make way for Democracy! We saved it in France, and by the Great Jehovah, we will save it in the United States of America, or know the reason why."[3] Men who had seen a comparatively non-racist France wanted to bring some non-racist culture home, and returning blacks refused to accept segregated facilities and protested discriminatory practices. When white America tried to terrorize the Negro back into his "place" by bringing lynch mobs into black communities, the black man fought back. The newly returned black troops took a leading role in defense against the mobs, as the community expected them to. Black soldiers had learned how to fight and, as some three dozen post-war race riots showed, black people pressed together in the compact ghetto could now snipe at invading whites and then escape in the maze of tenements. Participation in community defense was for many a first step toward involvement in a broad political struggle.

The worst of these post-war battles (there were more than twenty in 1919 alone) were fought in Chicago, Omaha, Knoxville, Washington, D.C., Tulsa and Charleston, and in smaller centers such as Elaine, Arkansas; Longview, Texas; and Waukegan, Illinois.[4] Isolated incidents involving blacks and white citizens or white police broke out sporadically in larger cities such as New York and Philadelphia during 1917 and 1918.[5] But the days of the lynching bee were past; white mobs invading black communities now faced well-placed gunfire. In Chicago the death count after two weeks of warfare totaled thirty-five blacks and thirteen whites, and almost every black victim had been killed *outside* the ghetto, usually going to or from work in a white neighborhood. "The colored troops fought nobly. We have something to fight for now," a black defender in Chicago wrote a friend in riot-torn Washington, D.C.[6] In Tulsa, the final toll was one hundred fifty blacks and fifty whites killed, but both sides suffered almost equally for the first two days, with whites unable to cross defensive positions at the railroad tracks which segregated the black community. One Negro weekly headlined its report on Tulsa "Colored Rioters Poorly Armed, But Casualty List Favorable."[7] These strong defenses effectively ended large-scale invasions of black neighborhoods by white mobs. From then on, whites would call upon their trained military, police or National Guard to do the job.

The new militancy was mirrored in Africa and the Caribbean. In the year following the Armistice, strikes and large demonstrations against colonial rule were reported in Sierra Leone, the Gold Coast, South Africa, Trinidad and British Honduras, and blacks in Panama and Costa Rica conducted a series of strikes for better working conditions and an end to racial discrimination.[8] This violent response had been presaged by a revolt of black soldiers of the British West Indian Regiment in December 1918. The uprising at Taranto, Italy, was a protest against racist restrictions promulgated by the British War Office. From fifty to sixty men were arrested, charged with mutiny, and sentenced, and eight battalions—some eight thousand troops—were disarmed. Angered by differential pay for black and white soldiers and by restrictions on advancement, members of the Ninth Battalion of that regiment attacked their officers and severely assaulted their unit commander. The rebellion continued for several days; men refused to work, a shooting and a bombing occurred, and a "generally insubordinate spirit prevailed." One hundred eight sergeants sent a petition to the secretary of state for the colonies protesting military racial discrimination. White troops were finally sent in and the Ninth Battalion was disbanded and its personnel distributed among other units.[9]

(Colonial officials thought the "mutinous spirit of Taranto" was behind the disturbances in Trinidad and British Honduras the following year. They charged that the systematic attack upon colonialists' businesses and residences in Belize, British Honduras, in July 1919, had been planned at Taranto and on the voyage home. However, as no black troops from British Honduras had been present during the Taranto rebellion, it might be more accurate to equate their later action with a desire to "get a piece of the action" they had missed in Italy.)[10]

Within the United States, wartime conscription created a labor shortage in northern industrial centers, and well over a quarter of a million southern blacks, encouraged by the black press and by the advertisements of northern businessmen, deserted their rural cabins for jobs in the northern cities. Within the South itself, a sizable number moved from rural to urban centers. In general, these movements broadened the migrants' outlook and political consciousness.

The war was only one of many factors stimulating migration. In the first twenty years of this century, half a million West Indians moved back and forth across the Caribbean Basin, while close to a hundred thousand others came to live in the United States or Canada. Most of these migrants were displaced when U.S. investors bought out small farmers and developed huge agricultural combines.

In Africa, thousands upon thousands of blacks left rural villages for new urban centers and mining districts. Despite centuries of exploitation through the slave trade, almost all of black Africa had remained free from outright colonial rule until the 1890s. A generation of militants then fell fighting the conquerors from Europe, and the first years of this century—the first years of mining and plantation exploitation—were indeed bleak. But by 1910 a new generation of Africans had emerged, and from it came a group of leaders—skilled workers and the small but increasing number of civil servants—who would define the terms of the struggle which culminated in rebellion and independence forty or fifty years later.

These migrations from farm to city and from nation to nation helped develop race consciousness and camaraderie between black spokesmen throughout the world. The struggle against oppression based on worldwide race unity became a central feature of an emerging black radical movement. Migration also brought expectations of opportunities in skilled jobs and the professions, ambitions common to people on the rise. As the masters of the system thwarted these aspirations, frustration turned many toward militancy. The move from rural settings opened new opportunities to express this militancy: a black farmer who dared attend a protest meeting in Alabama risked eviction or even lynching, but in New York City the black man's landlord and his employer knew (and cared) less about what he did in his free time. A militant would have had great difficulty finding a meeting place in small-town Alabama, but buildings could be rented in New York and, in lieu of a hall, there was always the street corner.

***

With the creation of large urban concentrations of blacks, there emerged new social and political groups which addressed themselves to the new problems of urban life. Life in the ghettoes needed explanation: it was filled with contradictions between the promises of a better scene, and the realities of ghetto conditions. At first there were jobs in heavy industry, but few of these lasted after the white troops returned. Any improvement in living conditions was debatable—in fact, twelve people living in a one-room Alabama shack probably enjoyed some advantages over twelve living in a two-room tenement apartment. The very closeness which was to prove an asset in political action was often detrimental to individual well-being: food in the local store was often moldy, street lighting inadequate, and garbage almost never collected. Those fortunate enough to find work were rarely paid enough to escape to a better neighborhood—if any other area would have allowed a black person in.

Urbanization had a somewhat different impact in the Caribbean and Africa. Kingston, Jamaica, though founded in the mid-1600s, typified the sprawling growth of the Third World. Between 1910 and 1920 huge collages of cardboard and flattened water heaters, with names like Trench Town and Denham Town, mushroomed around the outskirts of central Kingston. Unlike the American migrants, who left the farm willingly, and usually against the wishes of white owners, blacks in the Third World had often been forced to leave their rural setting. Some found jobs in the city, many did not; but, as in the United States, urban existence required initiative and cunning, and there were leaders who directed these energies into political struggle.

Changes in social and economic conditions, then, provided part of the impetus for a new self-confidence. But not all: the "New Negro" who appeared during the war also reflected generational differences.

Most of the new militant leaders were in their twenties or early thirties. Some merely shouted loudly about injustice, but the more thoughtful were seriously considering black nationalism and socialism. Political disagreements among blacks in this period basically reflected varying evaluations of what it meant to be black. These differences were determined not only by socio-economic background but also by national origin, travel, and experience with whites. Some tried to minimize color and to live according to the norms of white society. "New Negroes" rejected this pattern. Black socialists adopted the "un-American" notion of working-class solidarity; nationalists the even more "un-American" notion that black people had a worthwhile culture of their own, distinct from and equal to that of whites.

One cannot distinguish Old Negroes from New by saying the former despaired and the latter had hope. Old Negroes in the academic community had high hopes for substantial social and economic change, but these hopes were grounded in faith in the white-ruled system. The New Negro, in contrast, based his faith on the potential power of black people to change the system. Black socialists hoped to effect such change with the aid of white comrades; the nationalists hoped to do it independently.

Many New Negroes, including some who became high officials in the Garvey movement, entered political struggle through the fight to end white machine politics in the new urban ghettoes. Many who joined the revolt against organized religion and founded new church denominations during the war were attracted to Garveyite and other social protest groups. Garveyites and other New Negro groups also drew many whose first interest had been the protection of immigrants. The New Negroes' interest in peoples from different parts of the world, stimulated by migrations and wartime travel, was sustained by lecturers such as the Jamaican Gabriel Stewart, the Guianese Rudolph Smith and the American Henrietta Vinton Davis—three world travelers who later became able recruiters for the UNIA.

Only one journal which could be described as a New Negro publication appeared until late in the war: the *African Times and Orient Review*. First published in London in 1912 by the Egyptian nationalist Duse Mohammed Ali (who originated the phrase "Africa for the Africans"), the *Review* advocated the study of African cultures, independence for colonial peoples, and the building of international business connections between Africans, Asians, and the colored peoples of the Americas. Marcus Garvey, half a dozen of his leading lieutenants, and numerous other New Negroes contributed articles to the *African Times*. The NAACP journal *Crisis*, founded in 1910, did make important contributions to the development of new ideas, but its editor, Dr. Du Bois, was ostracized by New Negroes because of his endorsement of the war; in the summer of 1918 Dr. Du Bois presented in *Crisis* an article entitled "Close Ranks" in which he urged blacks to support the war effort. However, DuBois's thorough and intelligent critiques of America's racist institutions continued to be admired by many who decried his moderate politics.

In 1917, two socialists, A. Philip Randolph and Chandler Owen, brought out the first issue of the *Messetiger*, a monthly journal of "scientific radicalism." The next year saw the first publication of Garvey's *Negro World*, "the indispensable weekly," which by 1920 had the largest circulation of all black weekly newspapers in the United States. In 1918 Cyril Briggs inaugurated his monthly *Crusader*, advocating black nationalism, Leninism and violent revolution. Two militant magazines emphasizing cultural and literary developments also appeared that year: William Bridges's *Challenge* and Hubert

Harrison's *Negro Voice*. None of these journals could have been published in the South, the Caribbean, or Africa,* and all were cited as seditious in state and federal reports on revolutionary activity. The United States Post Office refused to handle the July 1919 issue of Randolph's *Messenger* because of its militant content—though it was not appreciably different from other issues, this one did carry a drawing depicting a burning lynch victim with the flames forming an inverted American flag, the waving stripes seeming to burn the seared flesh. Printed boldly across the picture was the legend "A Glorious Desecration."[11]

The New Negroes publicly endorsed the militant self-defense of black communities and many participated directly in such actions. Claude McKay, a Jamaican immigrant who wrote for the *Negro World* and many white socialist publications, summed up this new determination in his poem "If We Must Die."

> If we must die, let it not be like hogs
> Hunted and penned in an inglorious spot
> While round us bark the mad and hungry   dogs
> Making their mock at our accursed lot.
> If we must die, O let us nobly die
> So that our precious blood may not be shed
> In vain; then even the monsters we defy
> Shall be constrained to honor us though dead!
> … Like men we'll face the murderous cowardly pack,
> Pressed to the wall, dying, but fighting back.[12]

Printed publications were not the only carriers of new ideas, however. Harlem street corners became free platforms for spokesmen advocating innumerable social and economic alternatives to the status quo. Almost all the prominent New Negro militants built their reputations through street oratory, as Malcolm X did later and as the leather-jacketed Black Panthers and Carlos Cooks and his nationalists (clad in the uniforms of the UNIA's African Legionnaires) do today.†

---

* By 1920 Garvey's Negro World was banned in many parts of colonial Africa and the West Indies.

† The man most responsible for building the tradition was Hubert H. Harrison, "the first professor of Street Corner University." Harrison, a self-educated immigrant from the Virgin Islands, also taught "Contemporary Civilization" at New York University, lectured on such subjects as "Literary Lights of Yesterday and Today" for the New York Board of Education, and served as professor of comparative religion at the Modern School, professor of embryology at the Cosmopolitan College of Chiropractic, and instructor in English and economics at the Harlem School of Social Science. Before the war, he had worked with the socialists around Max Eastman and John Reed, helping to edit the *Masses* magazine.

Marcus Garvey had something of a head start over the others who wanted to build New Negro organizations. He had established the Universal Negro Improvement Association and African Communities League, generally known as the UNIA, in Jamaica in August 1914. (The general offices were transferred to New York in 1917.) The Association's ambitious objectives were set out in a manifesto calling upon "all people of Negro or African parentage" to join in a great crusade to "establish a Universal Confraternity among the race; to promote the spirit of race pride and love; to reclaim the fallen of the race; to administer to and assist the needy; to assist in civilizing the backward tribes of Africa; to strengthen the imperialism of independent African states; to establish Commissionaries or Agencies in the principle countries of the world for the protection of all Negroes, irrespective of nationality; to promote a conscientious Christian worship among the native tribes of Africa; to establish Universities, Colleges and Secondary Schools for the further education and culture of the boys and girls of the race; to conduct a world-wide commercial and industrial intercourse."[13]

Garvey's manifesto shows that he had decided upon the general direction of his movement by the eve of World War I; it also shows that he still had much to learn. In a 1920 version, when Garvey understood the meaning of "imperialism" more clearly, that word was dropped from the part of the manifesto referring to actions of African states. As an attack upon organized Christianity had become a part of Garveyism, he replaced the phrase "Christian worship" with "spiritual worship." The later manifesto also reflected the group's growing political emphasis with a call "to establish a central nation for the race."

It is not surprising that the Garvey of 1914 lacked the political finesse of the Garvey of 1920. For Garvey, as for many other black militants, the war years were a vital period of ideological experimentation, and during these years there was an unusual camaraderie between militants of nationalist and socialist persuasion. Later, when ideological differences were clarified, new ideas were suspect merely on the basis of their source; but until then various black militants often wrote for each other's magazines and shared speaking platforms and insights.

Garvey's first appearance before a large Harlem gathering, in the summer of 1917, illustrates such an exchange. The socialist Hubert Harrison had taken a liking to Garvey, and introduced him at a rally to launch Harrison's anti-war Afro-American Liberty League.[14] Association with the League was no light matter; its call for peace came at the height of patriotic pro-war hysteria. (Nor did Harrison stop at pacifism: in a Boston speech he suggested blacks should rise up against the government—as the Irish were then rising against the British government—if they were not given their rights.)[15] His maiden speech earned Garvey enough notoriety for him to go forward with plans for his own organization, in which Garvey was soon joined by Harrison himself.

With the UNIA and other New Negro organizations based in Harlem, that community emerged as the international center for black liberation struggles, and an entire generation came to think of America as the sanctuary from which to launch the struggle. This helped foster the view that blacks in the United States were significantly more radical than their brethren elsewhere. But while blacks in this country were more literate and enjoyed a higher standard of living than those in the colonial world—and thus read more radical magazines and contributed more money to radical causes—they were not necessarily more radical. Harold Cruse argues that Garvey moved his headquarters to New York because of the "apathy in Jamaica."[16] But people in the West Indies were not apathetic. Urbanization and mass migration within agricultural areas had unleashed hopes of a better world, and Jamaicans flocked to the Garvey movement: by 1920, the Association had branch divisions in every sizable town on the island.

It is somewhat ironic that Harlem should have become the center for this global struggle. In one sense, the United States was the worst of all places for blacks—its lynchings and other barbarities were unequaled anywhere else in the world, with the possible exception of the Belgian Congo, and American blacks suffered the disadvantage of being only ten per cent of the population. On the other hand, black militants in the new urban communities had more freedom than their brothers in the Third World. The United States guaranteed freedom of press and assembly, at least nominally, and blacks could thus hold organizational meetings, set up offices and begin publishing magazines and newspapers. Whites in the United States had failed to make plans for controlling blacks in the new urban setting. Attempts to apply the traditional Southern approach of "pacifying" black communities with lawless citizen mobs only spurred the militants.* But in Third World colonies the government could simply ban public meetings or periodicals.

By 1918—two years after his arrival in America—Garvey had gathered several thousand followers. Most of these were in New York, but through speaking tours and the *Negro World* he had developed a broad base of support, enabling him to build his movement so rapidly after the Armistice that the UNIA could claim two million followers by the end of 1919. (The black left had also made an impact: one out of four Harlem voters chose the Socialist ticket in the 1920 elections.)

During the summer of 1919, numerous rallies were called to denounce the white mob actions and to raise money for the homeless and injured. The mood of the people at these meetings was unmistakably radical. At a rally protesting the white-inspired carnage in Omaha, Nebraska, Marcus Garvey pronounced: "The best thing the Negro of all countries can do is to prepare to match fire with hell-fire. No African is going to allow the Caucasian to trample eternally upon his rights. We have allowed it for five hundred years and we have now struck." Black were told to prepare for a great day, "the day of the war of the races, when Asia will lead out to defeat Europe, and Europe and the white man will again call upon the Negro to save them as we have often done. The New Negro has fought the last battle for the white man, and he "is now getting ready to fight for the redemption of Africa. With mob laws and lynching bees fresh in our memories, we shall turn a deaf ear to the white man. … Let every Negro all over the world prepare for the new emancipation. … (Our commerce, science, art, liberation, and war must be marshaled when Asia or Europe strikes the blow of the Second World War. Black men shall die then and black women shall

---

* That Harlem itself escaped major violence may be attributable to the peculiar cultural character of New York City, where each segregated ethnic community fears every other ethnic community.

succor them, but in the end there shall be a crowning victory for the soldiers of Ethiopia on the African battleground."[17]

Garvey expressed this view again at Madison Square Garden in a speech unnoticed in the American press but reported in the London *Times* for November 1, 1919: "Four hundred million black men are beginning to sharpen their swords for the war of races ... and it will be the bloodiest war the world has ever seen. It will be a terrible day when the blacks draw sword and fight for their liberty. ..."

In 1919 this determination to fight was considered respectable by major Negro newspapers which usually criticized Garveyites and other activists. Both the Chicago *Defender* and the Washington *Bee* quoted a black man in Chicago: "It is the duty of every man here to provide himself with guns and ammunition. I myself have at least one gun and at least enough ammunition to make it useful." And *Bee* editor Calvin Chase added, "We are only fighting for our rights." The Pittsburgh *Courier* commented, "As long as the Negro submits to lynchings, burnings, and oppression—and says nothing, he is a loyal American citizen. But when he decides that lynchings and burnings shall cease, even at the cost of some bloodshed in America, then he is a Bolshevist."[18]

Amid the fervor of 1919, even the meetings of respectable black middle-class organizations were taken over by militants and turned into rallies for revolution. That July the National Equal Rights League, a civil rights organization composed primarily of professionals and academicians, called a meeting in New York to welcome its president, William Monroe Trotter, home from France. In a hall crowded to suffocation, speaker after speaker fought his way to the podium to denounce America, and in the near-hysteria the purpose of the meeting was all but forgotten.[19]

At least until 1919, a major part of the New Negro struggle was simply to become recognized. The uninitiated public did not differentiate nationalists from socialists; rather they distinguished those who wished to upset the status quo from those who did not. For example, A. Philip Randolph was called the "most dangerous Negro in America" in 1918 when he was hauled off a speaker's platform in Cleveland and thrown into jail for talking about racism in America's war involvement.[20] News coverage of this event aided all militants, whose very existence had been largely ignored in the regular press, black or white. When Garvey shared the platform with Randolph at a protest rally in 1919, the audience doubtless included some future Garveyites drawn by Randolph, and vice versa.

In this period, all radicals shared a desire to end discrimination and forced segregation, lynching and disenfranchisement. A well-put phrase of righteous indignation from whatever source carried the message. In the suppressed July 1919 *Messenger,* columnist William N. Colson, a former Army lieutenant, wrote of the fight to be waged by the returning black GI: "Remembering the pleasantness of French life, he will not rest until he has caused to be ushered into the United States a state of complete and uncompromising economic, political and social equality. This program will call for the benefit of every enjoyment, privilege, and immunity which the white race does or will possess in America." Colson himself looked forward to a thoroughly integrated America. Even though the issue between integration and independence remained unresolved, his statement stood as a straightforward call for action.

Garvey's speeches rang with calls to organize and prepare for an imminent rebellion of the oppressed races. In the December 1919 *Messenger* Randolph wrote favorably of current rebellions in Ireland, Bulgaria, Hungary and Germany, and a host of strikes, demonstrations and uprisings in Asia, Africa and America. Of course, Randolph was thinking of a white-led revolution for America, while Garvey had in mind a black one, and both eventually softened their talk of open rebellion. But the white agents of the United States Justice Department who investigated "radicalism and sedition among Negroes" saw little difference between Garvey's *Negro World* and Randolph's *Messenger*.[21]

For a time the two men did cooperate closely. In 1918 Randolph and Garvey joined to form the short-lived International League of Darker Peoples, which was to draw up a list of demands upon the European powers concerning the treatment of colonized peoples. After the war, Garvey announced that the UNIA had chosen Randolph to head a delegation of blacks to the Versailles Peace Conference. Garveyites held a mass meeting to raise passage money for Randolph, but Randolph declined.*[22]

In 1919 the *Messenger* and the monthly *Crusader* exchanged lists of agents, "with mutual profit and fraternity," as Randolph explained.[23] Three years later Randolph and *Crusader* editor Cyril Briggs were bitter enemies. The latter's endorsement of international communism contrasted sharply with Randolph's support for the American Socialist Party. Briggs had discovered Marxism during the war years, and added it to a volatile black nationalism. Early in 1919 he formed the African Blood Brotherhood, which he hoped would become a tightly knit paramilitary cadre within the UNIA. A number of Brotherhood members went to work in the Garvey Association; one, W. A. Domingo, was even the chief editor of the *Negro World* through most of 1919. Briggs's own journal, the *Crusader*, rang with endorsements of the Industrial Workers of the World, the Socialist party and the Russian Bolsheviks. During the war, Briggs lent his support to any and all radicalism, while spewing venom on anything smacking of "American mobocracy," as he called the bourgeois democratic process. The early *Crusader* was an important source of the nationalist ideology Garvey helped foster. One of its first issues carried a "Race Catechism," a classic definition of black nationalism arguing the superiority of the Negro race. The catechism went as follows:

Question: How do you consider yourself in relation to your race?

Answer: I consider myself bound to it by a sentiment which unites us all.

Question: What is it?

Answer: The sentiment that the Negro race is of all the races the most favored by the muses of music, poetry and art and is possessed of those qualities of courage, honor and intelligence necessary to the making of the best manhood and womanhood and the most brilliant development of the human species.

Question: What is one's duty to his race?

Answer: To love one's race above one's self and to further the common interests of all above the private interest of one. To cheerfully sacrifice wealth, ease, luxuries, necessities and, if need be, life itself to attain

---

*   "Needless to say, I never went," commented Randolph sarcastically some years later, during the height of his feud with Garvey.

for the race that greatness in arms, in commerce, in art, the three combined without which there is neither respect, honor, nor security.

Question: How can you further the interest of the race?

Answer: By spreading race patriotism among my fellows; by unfolding the annals of our glorious deeds and the facts of the noble origin, splendid achievements and ancient cultures of the Negro Race to those whom alien education has kept in ignorance of these things; by combatting the insidious, mischievous and false teaching of school histories that exalt the white man and debase the Negro, that tell of the white man's achievements but not of his ignominy, while relating only that part of the Negro's story that refers to his temporary enslavement and partial decadence; by helping race industries in preference to all others; by encouraging race enterprise and business to the ends of an ultimate creation of wealth, employment and financial strength within the race; by so carrying myself as to demand honor and respect for my race.

Question: Why are you proud of your race?

Answer: Because in the veins of no human being does there flow more generous blood than in our own; in the annals of the world, the history of no race is more resplendent with honest, worthy glory than that of the Negro Race, members of which founded the first beginnings of civilization upon the banks of the Nile, developing it and extending it southward to Ethiopia and westward over the smiling Sudan to the distant Atlantic, so that the Greeks who came to learn from our fathers declared that they were "the most just of men, the favorites of the Gods."[24]

In the early 1920s, black militants were divided over the question of whether or not a pro-black bias was legitimate. Through 1919, however, the few blacks who publicly objected to such a bias were the conservative leaders of the middle and upper classes. Black leaders especially showed their willingness to share ideas and programs in their general support of cooperative businesses as a solution to the shortage of capital in the black economy. Briggs and his Brotherhood promoted cooperatives; DuBois founded a Negro Cooperative League in 1919; Randolph supported the idea in the *Messenger;* and even the black bourgeoisie's Robert S. Abbott, editor-publisher of the Chicago *Defender,* endorsed the idea. Garvey himself (though he talked in the jargon of free enterprise) built a network of cooperatively owned and managed businesses.

By the end of 1919, the period of cooperation was drawing to a close. The UNIA had become a distinct branch of black militancy, and—though concerted opposition from other black radicals did not come until 1922—opposition groups were encouraging Garvey supporters to leave the UNIA. The Garvey movement took a separate course during the 1920s, establishing its own social and political context. As distinct factions developed within the UNIA itself, differences over tactics and ideology were confined to the separate world of Garveyism. By the mid-1920s, the term "New Negro" was barely used in a political context, either by Garveyites or others who had once coveted the title. The world of Garveyism is the subject of most of this volume, but what follows now is a brief account of the various approaches to liberation taken by blacks outside the UNIA.

ELIJAH MUHAMMAD AND THE NATION OF ISLAM

WILLIAM L. VAN DEBURG

The territorial nationalist stance of the Nation of Islam has been made clear to adherents since its founding in the midst of the Great Depression. Patriarch Elijah Muhammad taught that all Americans of African descent belonged to an "Asian black nation," more specifically to the tribe of Shabazz. It was the mission of the North American branch of this ancient clan to redeem the Black Nation from centuries of unjust white rule. Short of divine intervention, the best solution to black people's problems was thought to be relocation to a state of their own. Separation—"either on this continent or elsewhere"—would enable African Americans to escape the "mental poisoning" of their "400-year-old enemies." Freed from the "blue-eyed devils'" impositions, they would work to create a vibrant Islamic civilization "beyond the white world."

According to the political economy of the Nation, much could be accomplished even before the achievement of full-blown statehood. Members were to pool their resources, spend money among themselves, and create their own institutions. To encourage such endeavor, Muhammad instituted a communalistic tithing/taxation system known as the "Duty." Other trappings of sovereignty included an Islamic flag, said to be several trillion years old; the University of Islam—primarily an elementary and high school system; a paramilitary self-defense corps, the Fruit of Islam; and a wide-ranging economic infrastructure of businesses, factories, and farms.

Foundational to all group economic and cultural activities was a unique messianic theology that transcended normal religious boundaries. To the devout, Elijah Muhammad was the "last Messenger" of a black creator God. Sometime before the year 2000, Allah would reappear, signaling the beginning of a new and glorious epoch in which black people would inherit power over all of creation. Prior to that day, members of the Nation were duty-bound to help protect and sustain other "so-called Negroes" by promoting territorial separatism and economic nationalism.

In the following excerpts, reprinted by permission from Elijah Muhammad's *Message to the Blackman in America* (Chicago: Muhammad's Temple No. 2, 1965), the Nation of Islam leader speaks of separatism as (1) a reflection of self-love; (2) a way to combat the "white devils'" wiles; and (3) an essential step in the quest for black dignity, unity, and independence.

1965: FROM *THE MAKING OF DEVIL*

ELIJAH MUHAMMAD

You have learned, from the reading of history, that a nation's permanent success depends on its obedience to Allah. We have seen the white race (devils) in heaven, among the righteous, causing trouble (making mischief and causing bloodshed), until they were discovered.

They made trouble for six months, right in heaven, deceiving the ancient original people who were holy. But, when they learned just who was causing the trouble; they, as you have learned, cast the troublemakers out into the worst and poorest part of our planet earth.

They were punished by being deprived of divine guidance, for 2,000 years which brought them almost into the family of wild beasts—going upon all fours; eating raw and unseasoned, uncooked food; living in caves and tree tops, climbing and jumping from one tree to the other.

Even today, they like climbing and jumping. The monkeys are from them. Before their time, there were no such things as monkeys, apes and swine. Read the Holy Qur-an (Chapter 18) entitled: "The Cave." The Holy Qur-an mentions them as being turned into apes and swine as a divine curse, because of their disbelief in Moses.

We do know that both of these animals are loved and befriended by the white race, along with the dog. But, all of the divine curses sent upon the white race in these days are not enough to serve as a warning to that race. They rose up from the caves and hillsides of Europe, went back to Asia, and have ruled nine-tenths of that great continent.

Muhammad set the devils back for 1,000 years. They were released on the coming of Columbus, and his finding of this Western Hemisphere. They have been here now over 400 years. Their worst and most unpardonable sins were the bringing of the so-called Negroes here to do their labor.

The so-called Negroes have not only given free labor, but have given their lives on the soil of their masters and, all over the earth wherever his hateful and murdering slave-master wants them to go. Now, the slave wants better treatment. They are fast learning today, that these are the children of those who made merchandise out of their fathers. The devil is the "devil" regardless of place and time.

They deceived our fathers and are now deceiving the children, under many false disguises, (as though they want to be friends of the black man) such as integration and intermarriage.

The devil said to Allah: "I shall certainly come upon them from before them and from behind them; and from their right and from their left; and Thou wilt not find most of them thankful" (Holy Qur-an 7:17) This is being fulfilled before our very eyes today. The devils are doing both.

They come to the so-called Negroes as friends and as open enemies. They go before them, changing the truth into false; and come behind the Truth-bearer to the so-called Negroes, speaking evil of the truth. They threaten the so-called Negroes with poverty and imprisonment, and make rosy promises to them, only to deceive.

They are telling the so-called Negroes that they realized that they used to mistreat the Negroes, but now they are going to do better and forget the past. "Let us live like brothers for we are all from God."

Along with such smooth lies is an offer of one of the devils' women. The poor so-called Negroes fall victim and the devil men raid the neighborhood of the so-called Negro women, day and night, to make all desirous of hell fire.

This is the way they have planned to beat Allah to the so-called Negroes. What should you do? The answer: Stay away from sweet-hearting with devils. Surely this is the end of their time, on our planet. Allah said to the devil: "Get out of it despised, and driven away. Whoever of them (the Negroes) will follow you, I will certainly fill hell with you all" (7:18). So remember, your seeking friendship with this race of devils means seeking a place in their hell.

MALCOLM X AND THE ORGANIZATION OF AFRO-AMERICAN UNITY

GEORGE BREITMAN

B orn into a Garveyite family in 1925, Malcolm Little was converted to the teachings of Elijah Muhammad during the late 1940s while serving a prison sentence for burglary. The Black Muslim "X" replaced his "slave name" and he became a minister of the Nation of Islam shortly after his release in 1952. Over the next decade, Malcolm X became the best-known evangelist for the separatist Muslim faith, organizing temples from coast to coast and recruiting thousands of new members. Eventually, however, a series of theological, intellectual, stylistic, personal, and political issues created tension between the prophet and his disciple. In March 1964, Malcolm X quit the Nation, converted to orthodox Islam, and denounced his spiritual father as a "religious faker." This increasingly open and bitter conflict led to his assassination while he was addressing a rally at New York's Audubon Ballroom.

At the time of his death, Malcolm X—now also known by his Sunni Muslim name, El-Hajj Malik El-Shabazz—was intimately involved in building support for the Organization of Afro-American Unity (OAAU). Founded shortly after he left Muhammad's fold, the OAAU provided Malcolm with an organizational platform on which he could work out the details of his post-Nation political evolution. Only eight months old when its chief attractive force and major financial contributor was murdered, the OAAU survived, but in attenuated form. Even before the assassination it could claim no more than a few hundred members.

The following document was drafted by an OAAU committee and approved by Malcolm X early in 1965. Designed to "galvanize the black masses of Harlem to become the instruments of their own liberation," the Basic Unity Program was to have been introduced to the membership at a 15 February rally. Unfortunately, the Valentine's Day firebombing of Malcolm's home caused the program's presentation to be postponed a week. It was at this 21 February session that the OAAU leader was killed. As can be seen from the text, the OAAU's vision was expansive.

Its program embraced a variety of what soon would be termed "Black Power" beliefs and initiatives.

1965: ORGANIZATION OF AFRO-AMERICAN UNITY

MALCOLM X

Pledging unity …

Promoting justice …

Transcending compromise …

We, Afro-Americans, people who originated in Africa and now reside in America, speak out against the slavery and oppression inflicted upon us by this racist power structure. We offer to downtrodden Afro-American people courses of action that will conquer oppression, relieve suffering and convert meaningless struggle into meaningful action.

Confident that our purpose will be achieved, we Afro-Americans from all walks of life make the following known:

Establishment

Having stated our determination, confidence and resolve, the Organization of Afro-American Unity is hereby established on the 15th day of February, 1965, in the city of New York.

Upon this establishment, we Afro-American people will launch a cultural revolution which will provide the means for restoring our identity that we might rejoin our brothers and sisters on the African continent, culturally, psychologically, economically and share with them the sweet fruits of freedom from oppression and independence of racist governments.

1. The Organization of Afro-American Unity welcomes all persons of African origin to come together and dedicate their ideas, skills and lives to free our people from oppression.

2. Branches of the Organization of Afro-American Unity may be established by people of African descent wherever they may be and whatever their ideology—as long as they be descendants of Africa and dedicated to our one goal: Freedom from oppression.

3. The basic program of the Organization of Afro-American Unity which is now being presented can and will be modified by the membership, taking into consideration national, regional and local conditions that require flexible treatment.

4. The Organization of Afro-American Unity encourages active participation of each member since we feel that each and every Afro-American has something to contribute to our freedom. Thus each member will be encouraged to participate in the committee of his or her choice.

5. Understanding the differences that have been created amongst us by our oppressors in order to keep us divided, the Organization of Afro-American Unity strives to ignore or submerge these artificial divisions by focusing our activities and our loyalties upon our one goal: Freedom from oppression.

Basic Aims and Objectives

Self-Determination

We assert that we Afro-Americans have the right to direct and control our lives, our history and our future rather than to have our destinies determined by American racists ...

We are determined to rediscover our true African culture which was crushed and hidden for over four hundred years in order to enslave us and keep us enslaved up to today ...

We, Afro-Americans—enslaved, oppressed and denied by a society that proclaims itself the citadel of democracy, are determined to rediscover our history, promote the talents that are suppressed by our racist enslavers, renew the culture that was crushed by a slave government and thereby—to again become a free people.

National Unity

Sincerely believing that the future of Afro-Americans is dependent upon our ability to unite our ideas, skills, organizations and institutions ...

We, the Organization of Afro-American Unity pledge to join hands and hearts with all people of African origin in a grand alliance by forgetting all the differences that the power structure has created to keep us divided and enslaved. We further pledge to strengthen our common bond and strive toward one goal: Freedom from oppression.

The Basic Unity Program

The program of the Organization of Afro-American Unity shall evolve from five strategic points which are deemed basic and fundamental to our grand alliance. Through our committees we shall proceed in the following general areas:

I. Restoration

In order to enslave the African it was necessary for our enslavers to completely sever our communications with the African continent and the Africans that remained there. In order to free ourselves from the oppression of our enslavers then, it is absolutely necessary for the Afro-American to restore communications with Africa.

The Organization of Afro-American Unity will accomplish this goal by means of independent national and international newspapers, publishing ventures, personal contacts and other available communications media.

We, Afro-Americans, must also communicate to one another the truths about American slavery and the terrible effects it has upon our people. We must study the modern system of slavery in order to free ourselves from it. We must search out all the bare and ugly facts without shame for we are still victims, still slaves—still oppressed. Our only shame is believing falsehood and not seeking the truth.

We must learn all that we can about ourselves. We will have to know the whole story of how we were kidnapped from Africa, how our ancestors were brutalized, dehumanized and murdered and how we are continually kept in a state of slavery for the profit of a *system* conceived in slavery, built by slaves and dedicated to keeping us enslaved in order to maintain itself.

We must begin to reeducate ourselves and become alert listeners in order to learn as much as we can about the progress of our Motherland—Africa. We must correct in our minds the distorted image that our enslaver has portrayed to us of Africa that he might discourage us from reestablishing communications with her and thus obtain freedom from oppression.

II. Reorientation

In order to *keep* the Afro-American enslaved, it was necessary to limit our thinking to the shores of America—to prevent us from identifying our problems with the problems of other peoples of African origin. This made us consider ourselves an isolated minority without allies anywhere.

The Organization of Afro-American Unity will develop in the Afro-American people a keen awareness of our relationship with the world at large and clarify our roles, rights and responsibilities as human beings. We can accomplish this goal by becoming well informed concerning world affairs and understanding that our struggle is part of a larger world struggle of oppressed peoples against all forms of oppression. We must change the thinking of the Afro-American by liberating our minds through the study of philosophies and psychologies, cultures and languages that did not come from our racist oppressors. Provisions are being made for the study of languages such as Swahili, Hausa and Arabic. These studies will give our people access to ideas and history of mankind at large and thus increase our mental scope.

We can learn much about Africa by reading informative books and by listening to the experiences of those who have traveled there, but many of us can travel to the land of our choice and experience for ourselves. The Organization of Afro-American Unity will encourage the Afro-American to travel to Africa, the Caribbean and to other places where our culture has not been completely crushed by brutality and ruthlessness.

III. Education

After enslaving us, the slavemasters developed a racist educational system which justified to its posterity the evil deeds that had been committed against the African people and their descendants. Too often the slave himself participates so completely in this system that he justifies having been enslaved and oppressed.

The Organization of Afro-American Unity will devise original educational methods and procedures which will liberate the minds of our children from the vicious lies and distortions that are fed to us from the cradle to keep us mentally enslaved. We encourage Afro-Americans themselves to establish experimental institutes and educational workshops, liberation schools and child-care centers in the Afro-American communities.

We will influence the choice of textbooks and equipment used by our children in the public schools while at the same time encouraging qualified Afro-Americans to write and publish the textbooks needed to liberate our minds. Until we completely control our own educational institutions, we must supplement the formal training of our children by educating them at home.

IV. Economic Security

After the Emancipation Proclamation, when the system of slavery changed from chattel slavery to wage slavery, it was realized that the Afro-American constituted the largest homogeneous ethnic group with a common origin and common group experience in the United States and, if allowed to exercise economic or political freedom, would in a short period of time own this country. Therefore racists in this government developed techniques that would keep the Afro-American people economically dependent upon the slavemasters—economically slaves—twentieth century slaves.

The Organization of Afro-American Unity will take measures to free our people from economic slavery. One way of accomplishing this will be to maintain a Technician Pool: that is, a Bank of Technicians. In the same manner that blood banks have been established to furnish blood to those who need it at the time it is needed, we must establish a Technician Bank. We must do this so that the newly independent nations of Africa can turn to us who are their Afro-American brothers for the technicians they will need now and in the future. Thereby, we will be developing an open market for the many skills we possess and at the same time we will be supplying Africa with the skills she can best use. This project will therefore be one of mutual cooperation and mutual benefit.

V. Self-Defense

In order to enslave a people and keep them subjugated, their right to self-defense must be denied. They must be constantly terrorized, brutalized and murdered. These tactics of suppression have been developed to a new high by vicious racists whom the United States government seems unwilling or incapable of dealing with in terms of the law of this land. Before the Emancipation it was the black man who suffered humiliation, torture, castration, and murder. Recently our women and children, more and more, are becoming the victims of savage racists whose appetite for blood increases daily and whose deeds of depravity seem to be openly encouraged by all law enforcement agencies. Over 5,000 Afro-Americans have been lynched since the Emancipation Proclamation and not one murderer has been brought to justice!

The Organization of Afro-American Unity, being aware of the increased violence being visited upon the Afro-American and of the open sanction of this violence and murder by the police departments throughout this country and the federal agencies—do affirm our right and obligation to defend ourselves in order to survive as a people.

We encourage all Afro-Americans to defend themselves against the wanton attacks of racist aggressors whose sole aim is to deny us the guarantees of the United Nations Charter of Human Rights and of the Constitution of the United States.

The Organization of Afro-American Unity will take those private steps that are necessary to insure the survival of the Afro-American people in the face of racist aggression and the defense of our women and children. We are within our rights to see to it that the Afro-American people who fulfill their obligations to the United States government (we pay taxes and serve in the armed forces of this country like American citizens do) also exact from this government the obligations that it owes us as a people, or exact these obligations ourselves. Needless to say, among this number we include protection of certain inalienable rights such as life, liberty and the pursuit of happiness.

In areas where the United States government has shown itself unable and/or unwilling to bring to justice the racist oppressors, murderers, who kill innocent children and adults, the Organization of

Afro-American Unity advocates that the Afro-American people insure ourselves that justice is done—whatever the price and *by any means necessary.*

National Concerns

General Terminologies

We Afro-Americans feel receptive toward all peoples of goodwill. We are not opposed to multi-ethnic associations in any walk of life. In fact, we have had experiences which enable us to understand how unfortunate it is that human beings have been set apart or aside from each other because of characteristics known as "racial" characteristics.

However, Afro-Americans did not create the prejudiced background and atmosphere in which we live. And we must face the facts. A "racial" society does exist in stark reality, and not with equality for black people; so we who are non-white must meet the problems inherited from centuries of inequalities and deal with the present situations as rationally as we are able.

The exclusive ethnic quality of our unity is necessary for self-preservation. We say this because: Our experiences backed up by history show that African culture and Afro-American culture will not be accurately recognized and reported and cannot be respectably expressed nor be secure in its survival if we remain the divided, and therefore the helpless, victims of an oppressive society.

We appreciate the fact that when the people involved have real equality and justice, ethnic intermingling can be beneficial to all. We must denounce, however, all people who are oppressive through their policies or actions and who are lacking in justice in their dealings with other people, whether the injustices proceed from power, class, or "race." We must be unified in order to be protected from abuse or misuse.

We consider the word "integration" a misleading, false term. It carries with it certain implications to which Afro-Americans cannot subscribe. This terminology has been applied to the current regulation projects which are supposedly "acceptable" to some classes of society. This very "acceptable" implies some inherent superiority or inferiority instead of acknowledging the true source of the inequalities involved.

We have observed that the usage of the term "integration" was designated and promoted by those persons who expect to continue a (nicer) type of ethnic discrimination and who intend to maintain social and economic control of all human contacts by means of imagery, classifications, quotas, and manipulations based on color, national origin, or "racial" background and characteristics.

Careful evaluation of recent experiences shows that "integration" actually describes the process by which a white society is (remains) set in a position to use, whenever it chooses to use and however it chooses to use, the best talents of non-white people. This power-web continues to build a society wherein the best contributions of Afro-Americans, in fact of all non-white people, would continue to be absorbed without note or exploited to benefit a fortunate few while the masses of both white and non-white people would remain unequal and unbenefited.

We are aware that many of us lack sufficient training and are deprived and unprepared as a result of oppression, discrimination, and the resulting discouragement, despair, and resignation. But when we are not qualified, and where we are unprepared, we must help each other and work out plans for bettering our own conditions as Afro-Americans. Then our assertions toward full opportunity can be made on the basis of equality as opposed to the calculated tokens of "integration." Therefore, we must reject this term as one used by all persons who intend to mislead Afro-Americans.

Another term, "negro," is erroneously used and is degrading in the eyes of informed and self-respecting persons of African heritage. It denotes stereotyped and debased traits of character and classifies a whole segment of humanity on the basis of false information. From all intelligent viewpoints, it is a badge of slavery and helps to prolong and perpetuate oppression and discrimination.

Persons who recognize the emotional thrust and plain show of disrespect in the southerner's use of "nigra" and the general use of "nigger" must also realize that all three words are essentially the same. The other two: "nigra" and "nigger" are blunt and undeceptive. The one representing respectability, "negro," is merely the same substance in a polished package and spelled with a capital letter. This refinement is added so that a degrading terminology can be legitimately used in general literature and "polite" conversation without embarrassment.

The term "negro" developed from a word in the Spanish language which is actually an adjective (describing word) meaning "black," that is, the *color* black. In plain English, if someone said or was called *A* "black" or *A* "dark," even a young child would very naturally question: *"A* black what?" or *"A* dark what?" because adjectives do not name, they describe. Please take note that in order to make use of this mechanism, a word was transferred from another language and deceptively changed in function from an adjective to a noun, which is a naming word. Its application in the nominative (naming) sense was intentionally used to portray persons in a position of objects or "things." It stamps the article as being "all alike and all the same." It denotes: a "darkie," a slave, a sub-human, an ex-slave, a *"negro."*

Afro-Americans must re-analyze and particularly question our own use of this term, keeping in mind all the facts. In light of the historical meanings and current implications, all intelligent and informed Afro-Americans and Africans continue to reject its use in the noun form as well as a proper adjective. Its usage shall continue to be considered as unenlightened and objectionable or deliberately offensive whether in speech or writing.

We accept the use of Afro-American, African, and Black Man in reference to persons of African heritage. To every other part of mankind goes this measure of just respect. We do not desire more nor shall we accept less.

CHAPTER 5

HUMAN RIGHTS AND PEOPLES' LIBERATION IN THE U.S.

THE BLACK PANTHERS SPEAK

CLAYBORNE CARSON

How do oppressed people with few resources overcome their oppression? The Black Panther Party's grassroots insurgency and ideological innovation produced suggestive answers to this enduring question. More than any other group of the 1960s, the Black Panther Party (BPP) inspired discontented urban African Americans to liberate themselves from oppressive conditions. They provided distinctive guidance for the black struggles of the late 1960s and 1970s, borrowing eclectically from past liberation movements, testing ideas through intense struggle, and sometimes bravely questioning their own approaches and assumptions. As this definitive anthology demonstrates, the Panthers forged their radical ideas through sustained militancy. *The Black Panthers Speak* provides comprehensive documentation of their fascinating and instructive effort to build an insurgent African-American movement in the face of vicious repression.

The Black Panther Party grew out of the African-American political agitation and grass-roots militancy of the 1960s. While attending Oakland's Merritt Junior College, Huey P. Newton and Bobby G. Seale had become familiar with the period's various currents of Hack political thought, identifying initially with the Donald Warden's Afro-American Association, one of the pioneering black nationalist groups on the West Coast. The Association enlarged their understanding of African-American history, but Newton's and Scale's goal was to

Clayborne Carson, "Foreword," *The Black Panthers Speak*, pp. ix–xviii. Copyright © 1995 by Clayborne Carson. Reprinted with permission.

change history rather than simply to study it. After breaking with Warden, they briefly affiliated with the Revolutionary Action Movement (RAM), inspired by Cuban-based guerilla warfare advocate Robert F. Williams. In 1965, Newton and Seale assumed leading roles in the Soul Students Advisory Council, which campaigned for black history courses at Merritt. Working with these groups expanded the two men's political awareness and contacts in the San Francisco Bay Area, but they remained unsatisfied in their search for a way to transform discontent into militant collective action.

Like other grassroots black activists of the period, Newton and Seale saw the need for an organization that would appeal particularly to young urban blacks from working-class backgrounds. Greatly influenced by Marxist literature and Franz Fanon's revolutionary handbook, *The Wretched of the Earth* (1963), they also identified with Malcolm X's rhetorical attacks against white authority and black middle-class leadership. The two saw Malcolm as a model leader who combined erudition with an ability to communicate with black people of all educational levels: "He knew what the street brothers were like, and he knew what had to be done to reach them," Newton wrote. For Newton and Seale, Malcolm's message went beyond nationalist rhetoric about racial pride. They were drawn to his harsh criticisms of established civil rights leaders who were deemed too cautious, dependent on white support, and unwilling to retaliate against white racist violence. Their responsiveness to Malcolm's call for freedom "by any means necessary" increased during 1964 after he broke away from Elijah Muhammad's apolitical Nation of Islam to form the Organization of Afro-American Unity (OAAU). Newton later described the Panthers as "a living testament" to Malcolm's life work.[*]

Following Malcolm X's assassination in February 1965, Newton and Seale became even more determined to find or create a black militant group that embodied Malcolm's political ideas. The massive rebellion in Los Angeles during August 1965 demonstrated that conditions were ripe for a new direction in African-American politics. "At this point, we knew it was time to stop talking and begin organizing," Newton later recalled.[†] In October 1966, Newton and Seale drafted the Platform and Program of the Black Panther Party at the offices of the North Oakland Service Center, a federal anti-poverty agency. Their list of ten demands combined basic needs—full employment and decent housing—with more radical objectives, such as exemption of black men from military service and freedom for all black men held in federal, state, county, and city prisons and jails. The last item on their list summarized their goals: "We want land, bread, housing, education, clothing, justice, and peace. And as our major political objective, a United Nations-supervised plebiscite to be held throughout the black colony in which only black colonial subjects will be allowed to participate for the purpose of determining the will of black people as to their national destiny."[‡]

---

[*]   Huey P. Newton with the assistance of J. Herman Blake, *Revolutionary Suicide* (New York: Harcourt Brace Jovanovich, 1973), p. 71, 113.

[†]   Newton, *Revolutionary Suicide,* p. 113.

[‡]   "Black Panther Party Platform and Program—What We Want/What We Believe," reprinted in this volume, p. 2.

Assuming the posts of defense minister and chairman, respectively, of the Black Panther Party for Self-Defense, Newton and Seale directed the group's rapid growth during the winter and spring of 1967. Their first recruit was a sixteen-year-old Oakland resident, Bobby Hut-ton, who became the Party's treasurer. Another important early recruit was David Hilliard, a childhood friend of Newton's who became the Party's chief of staff, responsible for coordinating its daily activities. Initially concentrated in the San Francisco Bay Area, the Black Panther Party ("for Self Defense" was dropped from its name) would attract dozens of new members during 1967 and 1968.

The Party's considerable appeal among young African Americans was based less on its program or its leaders' Marxist rhetoric than on its willingness to confront police. The issue of police brutality was of great concern to black urban residents, and the Panthers articulated these widespread anti-police sentiments. The first issue of the Party's newspaper, *The Black Panther*, published in April 1967, called on the black community to protest the police killing of Denzil Dowell, who was shot while allegedly running from a stolen car. During this period the Party's principal activity was to "patrol the pigs"—that is, to monitor police activities to insure that civil rights of black people were respected. When Panther members saw police pull over a black driver, they stopped and observed the incident, usually with weapons in hand. Newton carried law books in his car, and, despite police objections, he would question police conduct, often drawing a crowd as he read aloud the relevant portions of the California legal code. As their numbers increased, the Panthers doubled and tripled their patrols, expanding their operations from Oakland to Richmond, Berkeley, and San Francisco. They patrolled at irregular intervals and in various areas to thwart any attempts by the police to track them. In addition to discouraging police harassment, the Panther patrols educated black residents about their ability to contest violations of their rights.

The Black Panther's most publicized early action came after legislation was proposed in the California State Assembly that would make the Panther armed patrols illegal. Seale led a group of Panthers to Sacramento to protest the bill by parading across the State Capitol lawn with guns in plain view. Among the startled witnesses of the protest was Governor Ronald Reagan, who happened to be talking to a group of students on the Capitol lawn. After reporters gathered, the Panther contingent distributed copies of Executive Mandate #1 and Seale read the document to the media. The mandate called upon "the American people in general and the Black people in particular to take careful note of the racist California Legislature, which is now considering legislation aimed at keeping the Black people disarmed and powerless at the very same time that racist police agencies throughout the country are intensifying the terror, brutality, murder and repression of Black people." Charging that the government was preparing to place African Americans in concentration camps, Seale proclaimed:

> The Black Panther Party for Self-Defense believes that the time has come for Black people to arm themselves against this terror before it is too late. … We believe that the Black communities

of America must rise up as one man to halt the progression of a trend that leads inevitably to their total destruction.*

Thirty BPP members, including Seale, were prosecuted as a result of the incident, but the Party nevertheless gained valuable publicity as the new symbol of black militancy in America. According to Newton, "even those who did not hear the complete message saw the arms, and this conveyed enough to black people."[†] The Panthers were soon overwhelmed with new members and calls from people across the country who wanted to establish new chapters. During the months afterward, the Panthers made the transition from a local group to a national organization.

One of those attracted to the Black Panther Party as it became increasingly visible outside the Bay Area was Eldridge Cleaver, a former convict and author whose autobiographical essays were later collected in the bestseller *Soul on Ice* (1968). The Party first attracted Cleaver's attention in February 1967 when he witnessed a tense standoff between police and an armed contingent of Panthers guarding Betty Shabazz, the widow of Malcolm X. impressed by their brash militancy, he attended the Sacramento protest, and, despite his claim that he was merely an observer, was arrested with other Panthers. Threatened with return to prison for violating his parole, Cleaver began a highly publicized legal battle against California authorities. Determined to maintain his ties with the Panthers, Cleaver quickly became one of the Party's most effective and best-known spokespersons. His position as a writer for the New Left journal *Ramparts* brought the group additional publicity and created a link between the Panthers and white leftist sympathizers. After Cleaver became editor of the Party's Black Community News Service and a public speaker on behalf of the group, his uniquely caustic, bombastic verbal attacks on white authorities became part of the Black Panther Party's public image.[‡]

Cleaver's prominence in the Black Panther Party increased after October 28, 1967, when Newton was arrested after an altercation ending in the death of an Oakland police officer. The Panthers immediately mobilized to free Newton, who faced a possible death sentence if convicted. As part of this support effort, Cleaver and Seale contacted Stokely Carmichael, former chairman of the Student Nonviolent Coordinating Committee (SNCC) and a nationally known Black Power proponent. The Panther leaders recognized that they could benefit from SNCC's extensive support network and learn from SNCC's years of community organizing experience (indeed, the Party's name was derived from the black panther symbol used by Lowndes County Freedom Organization, an Alabama political party organized by Carmichael and other SNCC workers). Cleaver and Seale "drafted" Carmichael to be the Panther's Prime Minister, and offered administrative positions to other SNCC officers, including H. Rap Brown and James Forman. Newton later wrote that "we were in effect voting to give leadership of the Party to SNCC. We even

---

* Newton, "In Defense of Self-Defense: Executive Mandate Number One," *The Black Panther,* June 2, 1967, reprinted in this volume, p. 40.

† Newton, *Revolutionary Suicide,* p. 150.

‡ Cleaver's writings as a member of the Black Panther Party appear in this volume and in Robert Scheer, ed., *Eldridge Cleaver; Post-Prison Writings and Speeches* (New York: Random House, 1969).

considered moving our headquarters to Atlanta, where we would be under SNCC, in their buildings, with access to their duplicating equipment and other sorely needed materials."* Carmichael, Brown, and Forman agreed to join leaders from other black militant groups in "Free Huey" rallies to be held in Los Angeles and Oakland during February 1968. These well-attended events increased the national visibility of the Black Panther Party and broadened support for the effort to free Newton.

Despite the success of the February rallies, Panther leaders experienced considerable difficulties in their efforts to build lasting ties with other black militant groups. The internal and external factors that were responsible for these difficulties were evident in the ill-fated effort to build an alliance between the BPP and SNCC. Although Cleaver presumptuously announced at "Free Huey" rally in Oakland that SNCC had merged with the Panthers, he and Panther leaders wrongly assumed that former SNCC chairman Carmichael and other SNCC officers spoke for the SNCC rank-and-file. At a deeper level, the Panther leaders failed to recognize that the BPP's hierarchical leadership style contrasted sharply with SNCC's decentralized structure. The self-conscious effort of Carmichael and other black activists in SNCC to separate themselves from former white allies also adversely affected their relations with the Panthers, who welcomed white support. Moreover, the Panther's recognition that they were under deadly attack made them distrustful of and impatient with black activists who questioned their ideological orientation. By August 1968 relations between the two groups had soured to the point of open conflict. Afterwards, Carmichael decided to ally himself with the Panthers rather than remain in SNCC. His BPP ties helped the group establish strong chapters in the eastern United States, but his advocacy of racial unity rather than interracial coalitions continued to put him at odds with other Panther leaders.† The ideological and personal tensions between Carmichael and other Panther leaders signaled the beginning of a period of pervasive, vicious infighting within the black militant community.

Constant confrontations with police and covert disruptive activities of the FBI's counterintelligence program (COINTELPRO) exacerbated these conflicts within the black community. As explained in a February 1968 memorandum, the FBI's COINTELPRO operations were intended to "neutralize militant black nationalists" and forestall "a coalition of militant Black nationalist groups" and prevent the emergence of a "Black messiah" "who might unify and electrify these violence-prone elements."‡ Numerous FBI "dirty tricks" directed against the Panthers seriously disrupted its organizing efforts and strengthened

---

* Newton, *Revolutionary Suicide,* p. 113, 154, 155.

† For a fuller discussion of the SNCC-Panther ties, see "Huey Newton Talks to the Movement About the Black Panther Party, Cultural Nationalism, SNCC, Liberals and White Revolutionaries" and Eldridge Cleaver, "An Open Letter to Stokely Carmichael," in this volume (p. 50 and p. 104 respectively); David Hilliard and Lewis Cole, *This Side of Glory: The Autobiography of David Hilliard and the Story of the Black Panther Party* (Boston: Little, Brown and Company, 1993), pp. 161, 171–175, 202–204; Clayborne Carson, *In Struggle: SNCC and the Black Awakening of the 1960s* (Cambridge, Mass.: Harvard University Press, 1981), pp. 278–285.

‡ Memorandum is reprinted in Ward Churchill and Jim Vander Wall, *The COINTELPRO PAPERS: Documents from the FBI's Secret Wars Against Domestic Dissent* (Boston: South End Press, 1990), p. 107.

the tendency of Panthers to suspect the motives of black militants who questioned the group's strategy or tactics. FBI disinformation campaigns—anonymous phone calls or letters and planted newspaper stories—exploited the Black Panther Party's vulnerabilities, especially its tendency toward rhetorical excess and its heavy-handed efforts to intimidate critics.

Even as the Panthers deliberated their future course,* direct and covert external attacks threatened their existence. On April 6, 1968 police attacked a house containing several Panthers, killing Hutton, the seventeen-year-old treasurer of the Party, and wounding Cleaver, who was briefly returned to prison as a parole violator. In September 1968 Newton was convicted of voluntary manslaughter and sentenced to two-to-fifteen years in prison. Soon after finishing his 1968 presidential campaign as candidate of the Peace and Freedom Party, Cleaver left for exile in Cuba and then Algeria to avoid returning to prison for parole violation.

During 1969 continued FBI COINTELPRO plots directed against the Black Panther Party decimated its leadership and disrupted its relations with other militant organizations. In southern California, these covert activities exacerbated conflicts between the Party and followers of black cultural nationalist Maulana Karenga. The FBI's disinformation efforts and the Panther's escalating verbal attacks against Karenga (described in Panther literature as a "pork chop" nationalist) culminated in a gun battle in January 1969 on the UCLA campus that left two Panthers dead. In March 1969 Seale was arrested for conspiracy to incite rioting at the 1968 Democratic convention in Chicago, and in May Connecticut officials charged Seale and seven other Panthers with murder in the slaying of Party member Alex Rackley, who was believed to be a police informant. In New York, 21 Panthers were charged with plotting to assassinate policemen and blow up buildings. Then in December 1969 police killed two Chicago Panther leaders, Fred Hampton and Mark Clark, while they were sleeping at Hampton's apartment. The police raid was planned with the help of a police informer and coordinated with the United States Department of Justice. Other covert operations by the FBI and local police forces further intensified the sometimes vicious factionalism within the Black Panther Party.

This was particularly the case after Cleaver, speaking from exile in Algeria, stepped up his calls for violent revolution while Newton and Seale were seeking to moderate the Party's image. FBI heightened mutual suspicions through anonymous letters and other actions that transformed leadership competition and ideological differences into deadly conflicts. Newton, for example, reacted to a planted story that Los Angeles Panther leader Elmer "Geronimo" Pratt was a police agent by expelling him. The FBI later conspired to have Pratt convicted of robbery and murder. In 1971 Newton expelled the New York 21 shortly before their trial on conspiracy charges after the FBI led him to believe that they were plotting with Cleaver to take over the Party.†

---

* See, for example, Huey Newton's statement, "The Correct Handling of a Revolution," in this volume, p. 41.

† On the repression campaign against the Panthers, see "To Judge Murtagh: From the Panther 21," and Charles R. Garry, "The Old Rules Do Not Apply," in this volume (p. 196 and p. 257 respectively); Huey P. Newton, "The War Against the Panthers: A Study of Repression in America," Ph.D. dissertation, University of California at Santa Cruz,

In 1970, when Newton was released on bail after his conviction on a manslaughter charge was reversed on appeal, he returned to find the Party in disarray. Seale still faced conspiracy charges in the murder of Rackley (they were dropped the following year). Chief of staff David Hilliard awaited trial on charges of verbally threatening the life of President Nixon. Some chapters, particularly those in the eastern United States, resisted direction from the Oakland headquarters. Many chapters were heavily infiltrated by police or FBI informants. One of these informants, Earl Anthony, had been active in disrupting the Party's operations in Los Angeles.[*]

Newton sought to revive the Party and reestablish his control by de-emphasizing police confrontations in favor of survival programs that would meet the everyday needs of black communities while also educating black people. During the late 1960s and early 1970s the Black Panther Party concentrated on developing four main programs: the petition campaign for community control of police, free breakfast for school children, free health clinics, and liberation schools. Such programs attracted new members, allowed Panthers to interact with diverse segments of black communities, and helped to counter the Party's negative image in the media.[†]

Newton's decision to shift course prompted an open break with Cleaver, who continued to argue from exile that the black "lumpenproletariat" were ready for revolution. Newton charged that Cleaver had been unduly influenced by the confrontation he had witnessed between police and Panthers guarding Betty Shabazz and, as a result, placed too much emphasis on armed rebellion. Cleaver's attitude, according to Newton, "was that either the community picked up the gun with the Party or else they were cowards and there was no place for them." Newton asserted that Cleaver's leadership had caused the Black Panther Party to become "a revolutionary cult group" that had lost touch with the black community. The group's emphasis on police confrontations had increased the Black Panther Party's appeal among young blacks, but maintaining a "macho" image lessened the Party's actual ability to effectively organize the black community toward concrete political ends. Cleaver's profane, bombastic rhetoric, according to Newton, made the Panthers vulnerable to external repression and increased the influence of those more concerned with displays of bravado than with community organizing. In addition, Cleaver encouraged the Party to develop close ties with white radicals without influence in their own communities. "The Black Panther Party defected from the community long before Eldridge defected from the Party," Newton concluded.[‡]

1980; Kenneth O'Reilly, *"Racial Matters": The* FBI's *Secret File on Black America, 1960–1972* (New York: The Free Press, 1989), chapter 9; *Search and Destroy: A Report by the Commission of Inquiry into the Black Panthers and the Police* (New York: Metropolitan Applied Research Center, 1973); and Assata Shakur, Assafa: An *Autobiography* (Chicago: Lawrence Hill Books, 1987).

[*]   See Earl Anthony, *Spitting in the Wind: The True Story Behind the Violent Legacy of the Black Panther Party* (Malibu, California: Roundtable, 1990).

[†]   See documents in section on Community Activities in this volume, pp. 167–181.

[‡]   Newton, "On the Defection of Eldridge Cleaver from the Black Panther Party and the Defection of the Black Panther Party from the Black Community," *Black Panther Intercommunal News Service,* April 17, 1971, reprinted in

Newton's efforts to shift the Black Panther Party's emphasis from revolutionary rhetoric and armed confrontations to survival programs did not prevent further external attacks and internal conflicts from plaguing the group. Throughout the late 1960s and early 1970s, efforts to purge members considered disloyal or unreliable were at times counterproductive and disrupted Panther chapters. In addition, the Party's hierarchical, military-style structure exposed the limitations of Newton and other officers. As Elaine Brown later conceded, the Party was "not a democratic organization," and by the early 1970s its principle of "democratic centralism" generally was "reduced to one man, Huey Newton, though the Central Committee still influenced the governance of the Party, since its members held individual fields of sway."[*] After years of external attacks, internal conflicts, and legal prosecutions, Newton and other Panther leaders suffered from battle fatigue, and Newton was further debilitated by his increasing use of cocaine and other drugs. Moreover, the Party's authoritarian male leaders were increasingly out of step with the substantial and growing involvement of female rank-and-file members. In ways that distinguished it from other black militant groups of the period, the Black Panther Party encouraged the participation of women by condemning "male chauvinism" and lessening its reliance on a paramilitary style of organization.[†]

By the mid-1970s, the Panthers had been weakened by years of external attacks, legal problems, and internal schisms. Nevertheless, some chapters maintained their activities during the period. In 1973 Bobby Seale ran an unsuccessful, though formidable, campaign for mayor of Oakland, and following Newton's departure for exile in Cuba, Elaine Brown experienced some success in continuing Newton's emphasis on community service programs. Nevertheless, in a hostile political climate, the group could not reverse its decline as a political force. Most Panther veterans, including Seale and Cleaver, left or were expelled from the group. Popular support for the Party declined further after newspaper reports appeared describing the group's involvement in illicit activities such as drug dealing and extortion schemes directed against Oakland merchants.[‡] After Newton returned from exile in 1977, the Black Panther Party never regained its former prominence.

The rapid rise and decline of the Panthers reflected the general course of black political militancy during the late 1960s and 1970s. One of only a few militant political groups to gain widespread support in urban black communities, the Party's achievements and its failures provided instructive lessons for a generation of activists. The Party demonstrated the ability of urban, grassroots, political activists to offer

---

this volume (p. 272). See also Lee Lockwood, *Conversation with Eldridge Cleaver, Algiers* (New York: McGraw-Hill, 1970).

[*] Brown, A *Taste of Power. A Black Woman's Story* (New York: Pantheon Books, 1992), p. 320.

[†] See section Black Panther Women Speak, and Eldridge Cleaver, "Message to Sister Erica Huggins of the Black Panther Party," in this volume (pp. 145–165 and p. 98 respectively); also Bobby Seale, *Seize the Time: The Story of the Black Panther Party and Huey P. Newton* (New York: Random House, 1970), pp. 393–403.

[‡] See, for example, Kate Coleman with Paul Avery, *New Times,* July 10, 1978. The unsavory aspects of the Party's activities are emphasized in Hugh Pearson's *The Shadow of the Panther: Huey Newton and the Price of Black Power in America* (Reading, Massachusetts: Addison-Wesley, 1994).

intellectual and tactical guidance for the ongoing African-American freedom struggle. Although the group was unable to prevent the deterioration of urban black communities that resulted from poverty, powerlessness, and pessimism, the Black Panther Party at its best offers a historical example of brave activists willing to "die for the people" and thus continues to provide discontented African-American youth an alternative to self-destructive despair.

CLAYBORNE CARSON
Stanford University
November 1994

Clayborne Carson is professor of history at Stanford University and director of the Martin Luther King, Jr., Papers Project. He is the author of In Struggle: SNCC and the Black Awakening of the 1960s and Malcolm X: The FBI File. He is an editor of The Eyes on the Prize Civil Rights Reader and The Papers of Martin Luther King, Jr. (volumes I and II).

PATROLLING

HUEY P. NEWTON

It was the spring of 1966. Still without a definite program, we were at the stage of testing ideas that would capture the imagination of the community. We began, as always, by checking around with the street brothers. We asked them if they would be interested in forming the Black Panther Party for Self-Defense, which would be based upon defending the community against the aggression of the power structure, including the military and the armed might of the police. We informed the brothers of their right to possess weapons; most of them were interested. Then we talked about how the people are constantly intimidated by arrogant, belligerent police officers and exactly what we could do about it. We went to pool halls and bars, all the places where brothers congregate and talk.

I was prepared to give them legal advice. From my law courses at Oakland City College and San Francisco Law School I was familiar with the California penal code and well versed in the laws relating to weapons. I also had something very important at my disposal—the law library of the North Oakland Service Center, a community-center poverty program where Bobby was working. The Center gave legal advice, and there were many lawbooks on the shelves. Unfortunately, most of them dealt with civil law, since the antipoverty program was not supposed to advise poor people about criminal law. However, I made good use of the books they had to run down the full legal situation to the brothers on the street. We were doing what the poverty program claimed to be doing but never had-giving help and counsel to poor people about the things that crucially affected their lives.

All that summer we circulated in the Black communities of Richmond, Berkeley, Oakland, and San Francisco. Wherever brothers gathered, we talked with them about their right to arm. In general, they were interested but skeptical about the weapons idea. They could not see anyone walking around with a gun in full view. To recruit any sizable number of street brothers, we would obviously have to do more than talk. We needed to give practical applications of our theory, show them that we were not afraid of weapons and not afraid of death. The way we finally won the brothers over was by patrolling the police with arms.

Before we began the patrols, however, Bobby and I set down in writing a practical course of action. We could go no further without a program, and we resolved to drop everything else, even though it might take a while to come up with something viable. One day, we went to the North Oakland Service Center to work it out. The Center was an ideal place because of the books and the fact that we could work undisturbed. First, we pulled together all the books we had been reading and dozens we had only heard about. We discussed Mao's program, Cuba's program, and all the others, but concluded that we could not follow any of them. Our unique situation required a unique program. Although the relationship between the oppressor and the oppressed is universal, forms of oppression vary. The ideas that mobilized the people of Cuba and China sprang from their own history and political structures. The practical parts of those programs could be carried out only under a certain kind of oppression. Our program had to deal with America.

I started rapping off the essential points for the survival of Black and oppressed people in the United States. Bobby wrote them down, and then we separated those ideas into two sections, "What We Want" and "What We Believe." We split them up because the ideas fell naturally into two distinct categories. It was necessary to explain why we wanted certain things. At the same time, our goals were based on beliefs, and we set those out, too. In the section on beliefs, we made it clear that all the objective conditions necessary for attaining our goals were already in existence, but that a number of societal factors stood in our way. This was to help the people understand what was working against them.

All in all, our ten-point program took about twenty minutes to write. Thinking it would take days, we were prepared for a long session, but we never got to the small mountain of books piled up around us. We had come to an important realization: books could only point in a general direction; the rest was up to us. This is the program we wrote down:

OCTOBER 1966 BLACK PANTHER PARTY PLATFORM AMD PROGRAM WHAT WE WANT / WHAT WE BELIEVE

1. *We want freedom. We want power to determine the destiny of our Black Community.*
   We believe that Black people will not be free until we are able to determine our destiny.

2. *We want full employment for our people.*

We believe that the federal government is responsible and obligated to give every man employment or a guaranteed income. We believe that if the white American businessmen will not give full employment, then the means of production should be taken from the businessmen and placed in the community so that the people of the community can organize and employ all of its people and give a high standard of living.

3. *We want an end to the robbery by the capitalist of our Black community.*

We believe that this racist government has robbed us and now we are demanding the overdue debt of forty acres and two mules. Forty acres and two mules were promised 100 years ago as restitution for slave labor and mass murder of Black people. We will accept the payment in currency which will be distributed to our many communities. The Germans are now aiding the Jews in Israel for the genocide of the Jewish people. The Germans murdered six million Jews. The American racist has taken part in the slaughter of millions of Black people; therefore, we feel that this is a modest demand that we make.

4. *We want decent housing, fit for shelter of human beings.*

We believe that if the white landlords will not give decent housing to our Black community, then the housing and the land should be made into cooperatives so that our community, with government aid, can build and make decent housing for its people.

5. *We want education for our people that exposes the true nature of this decadent American society. We want education that teaches us our true history and our role in the present-day society.*

We believe in an educational system that will give to our people a knowledge of self. If a man does not have knowledge of himself and his position in society and. the world, then he has little chance to relate to anything else.

6. *We want all Black men to be exempt from military service.*

We believe that Black people should not be forced to fight in the military service to defend a racist government that does not protect us. We will not fight and kill other people of color in the world who, like Black people, are being victimized by the white racist government of America. We will protect ourselves from the force and violence of the racist police and the racist military, by whatever means necessary.

7. *We want an immediate end to POLICE BRUTALITY and MURDER of Black people.*

We believe we can end police brutality in our Black community by organizing Black self-defense groups that are dedicated to defending our Black community from racist police oppression and brutality. The Second Amendment to the Constitution of the United States gives a right to bear arms. We therefore believe that all Black people should arm themselves for self-defense.

8. *We want freedom for all Black men held in federal, state, county, and city prisons and jails.*
    We believe that all Black people should be released from the many jails and prisons because they have not received a fair and impartial trial.

9. *We want all Black people when brought to trial to be tried in court by a jury of their peer group or people from their Black communities, as defined by the Constitution of the United States.*
    We believe that the courts should follow the United States Constitution so that Black people will receive fair trials. The Fourteenth Amendment of the U.S. Constitution gives a man a right to be tried by his peer group. A peer is a person from a similar economic, social, religious, geographical, environmental, historical, and racial background. To do this the court will be forced to select a jury from the Black community from which the Black defendant came. We have been and are being tried by all-white juries that have no understanding of the "average reasoning man" of the Black community.

10. *We want land, bread, housing, education, clothing, justice, and peace. And as our major political objective, a United Nations—supervised plebiscite to be held throughout the Black colony in which only Black colonial subjects will be allowed to participate, for the purpose of determining the will of Black people as to their national destiny.*
    When, in the course of human events, it becomes necessary for one people to dissolve the political bands which have connected them with another, and to assume, among the powers of the earth, the separate and equal station to which the laws of nature and nature's God entitle them, a decent respect to the opinions of mankind requires that they should declare the causes which impel them to the separation.

    We hold these truths to be self-evident, that all men are created equal; that they are endowed by their Creator with certain unalienable rights; that among these are life, liberty, and the pursuit of happiness. *That, to secure these rights, governments are instituted among men, deriving their just powers from the consent of the governed; that, whenever any form of government becomes destructive of these ends, it is the right of the people to alter or to abolish it, and to institute a new government, laying its foundation on such principles, and organizing its powers in such form, as to them shall seem most likely to effect their safety and happiness.* Prudence, indeed, will dictate that governments long established should not be changed for light and transient causes; and, accordingly, all experience hath shown, that mankind are more disposed to suffer, while evils are sufferable, than to right themselves by abolishing the forms to which they are accustomed. *But, when a long train of abuses and usurpations, pursuing invariably the same object, evinces a design to reduce them under absolute despotism, it is their right, it is their duty, to throw off such government, and to provide new guards for their future security.*

With the program on paper, we set up the structure of our organization. Bobby became Chairman, and I chose the position of Minister of Defense. I was very happy with this arrangement; I do not like to lead formally, and the Chairman has to conduct meetings and be involved in administration. We also discussed having an advisory cabinet as an information arm of the Party. We wanted this cabinet to do research on each of the ten points and their relation to the community and to advise the people on how to implement them. It seemed best to weight the political wing of the Party with street brothers and the advisory cabinet with middle-class Blacks who had the necessary knowledge and skills. We were also seeking a functional unity between middle-class Blacks and the street brothers. I asked my brother Melvin to approach a few friends about serving on the advisory cabinet, but when our plan became clear, they all refused, and the cabinet was deferred.

The first member of the Black Panther Party, after Bobby and myself, was Little Bobby Hutton. Little Bobby had met Bobby Seale at the North Oakland Service Center, where both were working, and he imme diately became enthusiastic about the nascent organization. Even though he was only about fifteen years old then, he was a responsible and mature person, determined to help the cause of Black people. He became the Party's first treasurer. Little Bobby was the youngest of seven children; his family had come to Oakland from Arkansas when he was three years old. His parents were good, hard-working people, but Bobby had endured the same hardships and humiliations to which so many young Blacks in poor communities are subjected. Like many of the brothers, he had been kicked out of school. Then he had gotten an apartment and a job at the Service Center. After work he used to come around to Bobby Seale s house to talk and learn to read. At the time of his murder, he was reading Black *Reconstruction in America* by W.E.B. DuBois.

Bobby was a serious revolutionary, but there was nothing grim about him. He had an infectious smile and a disarming quality that made people love him. He died courageously, the first Black Panther to make the supreme sacrifice for the people. We all attempt to carry on the work he began.

We started now to implement our ten-point program. Interested primarily in educating and revolutionizing the community, we needed to get their attention and give them something to identify with. This is why the seventh point—police action—was the first program we emphasized. Point 7 stated: "We want an immediate end to police brutality and murder of Black people." This is a major issue in every Black community. The police have never been our protectors. Instead, they act as the military arm of our oppressors and continually brutalize us. any communities have tried and failed to get civilian review boards to supervise the behavior of the police. In some places, organized citizen patrols have followed the police and observed them in their community dealings. They take pictures and make tape recordings of the encounters and report misbehavior to the authorities. However, the authorities responsible for overseeing the police are policemen themselves and usually side against the citizens. We recognized that it was ridiculous to report the police to the police, but we hoped that by raising encounters to a higher level, by patrolling the police with arms, we would see a change in their behavior. Further, the community would notice this and become interested in the Party. Thus our armed patrols were also a means of recruiting.

At first, the patrols were a total success. Frightened and confused, the police did not know how to respond, because they had never encountered patrols like this before. They were familiar with the community alert patrols in other cities, but never before had guns been an integral part of any patrol program. With weapons *in* our hands, we were no longer their subjects but their equals.

Out on patrol, we stopped whenever we saw the police questioning a brother or a sister. We would walk over with our weapons and observe them from a "safe" distance so that the police could not say we were interfering with the performance of their duty. We would ask the community members if they were being abused. Most of the time, when a policeman saw us coming, he slipped his book back into his pocket, got into his car, and left in a hurry. The citizens who had been stopped were as amazed as the police at our sudden appearance.

I always carried lawbooks in my car. Sometimes, when a policeman was harassing a citizen, I would stand off a little and read the relevant portions of the penal code in a loud voice to all within hearing distance. In doing this, we were helping to educate those who gathered to observe these incidents. If the policeman arrested the citizen and took him to the station, we would follow and immediately post bail. Many community people could not believe at first that we had only their interest at heart. Nobody had ever given them any support or assistance when the police harassed them, but here we were, proud Black men, armed with guns and a knowledge of the law. Many citizens came right out of jail and into the Party, and the statistics of murder and brutality by policemen in our communities fell sharply.

Each day we went out on our watch. Sometimes we got on a policeman's tail and followed him with our weapons in full view. If he darted around the block or made a U-turn trying to follow us, we let him do it until he got tired of that. Then, we would follow him again. Either s way, we took up a good bit of police time that otherwise would have been spent in harassment.

As our forces built up, we doubled the patrols, then tripled them; we began to patrol everywhere— Oakland, Richmond, Berkeley, and San Francisco. Most patrols were a part of our normal movement around the community. We kept them random, however, so that the police could nof set a network to anticipate us. They never knew when or where we were going to show up. It might be late at night or early in the morning; some brothers would go on patrol the same time every day, but never in a specific pattern or in the same geographical area. The chief purpose of the patrols was to teach the community security against the police, and we did not need a regular schedule for that. We knew that no particular area could be totally defended; only the community could effectively defend and eventually liberate itself. Our aim was simply to teach them how to go about it. We passed out our literature and ten-point program to the citizens who gathered, discussed community defense, and educated them about their rights concerning weapons. All along, the number of members grew.

The Black Panthers were and are always required to keep their activities within legal bounds. This was emphasized repeatedly in our political education classes and also when we taught weapons care. If we overstepped legal bounds, the police would easily gain the upper hand and be able to continue their intimidation. We also knew the community was somewhat fearful of the gun and of the policeman who had it. So, we studied the law about weapons and kept within our rights. To be arrested for having weapons would be a. setback to our program of teaching the people their constitutional right to bear arms. As long as we kept everything legal, the police could do nothing, and the people would see that armed defense was a legitimate, constitutional right. In this way, they would lose their doubts and fears and be able to move against their oppressor.

It was not all observation and penal code reading on those patrols. The police, invariably shocked to meet a cadre of disciplined and armed Black men coming to the support of the community, reacted in strange and unpredictable ways. In their fright, some of them became children, cursing and insulting us. We responded in kind, calling them swine and pigs, but never cursing; this could be cause for arrest—and we took care not to be arrested with our weapons. But we demonstrated their cowardice to the community with our "shock-a-buku." It was sometimes hilarious to see their reaction; they had always been cocky and sure of themselves as long as they had weapons to intimidate the unarmed community. When we equalized the situation, their real cowardice was exposed.

Soon they began to retaliate. We expected this—they had to get back at us in some way—and were prepared. The fact that we had conquered our fear of death made it possible to face them under any circumstances. The police began to keep a record of Black Panther vehicles; whenever they spotted one, it would be stopped and investigated for possible violations. This was a childish ploy, but it was the police way. We always made sure our vehicles were clean, without violations, and the police were usually hard-pressed to find any justification for stopping us.

Since we were within the law, they soon resorted to illegal tactics. I was stopped and questioned forty or fifty times by police without being arrested or even getting a ticket in most instances. The few times I did end up on the blotter it merely proved how far they were willing to go. A policeman once stopped me and examined my license and the car for any violation of the Motor Vehicle Code. He spent about half an hour going over the vehicle, checking lights, horn, tires, everything. Finally, he shook the rear license plate, and a bolt dropped off, so he wrote out a ticket for a faulty license plate.

Some encounters with the police were more dramatic. At times they drew their guns and we drew ours, until we reached a sort of standoff. This happened frequently to me. I often felt that someday one of the police would go crazy and pull the trigger. Some of them were so nervous that they looked as if they might shake a bullet out of their pistols. I would rather have a brave man pull a gun on me, since he is less likely to panic; but we were prepared for anything. Sometimes they threatened to shoot, thinking I would lose courage, but I remembered the lessons of solitary confinement and assigned every silly action its proper significance: they were afraid of us. It was as simple as that. Each day we went forth fully aware that we might not come home or see each other ever again. There is no closeness to equal that.

In front of our first Black Panther office, on Fifty-eighth Street in Oakland, a policeman once drew his gun and pointed it at me while I sat in my car. When people gathered to observe, the police told them to clear the area. I ignored the gun, got out of the car, and asked the people to go into the Party office. They had a right to observe the police. Then I called the policeman an ignorant Georgia cracker who had come West to get away from sharecropping. After that, I walked around the car and spoke to the citizens about the police and about every man's right to be armed. I took a chance there, but I figured the policeman would not shoot me with all those eyes on him. He was willing to shoot me without cause, I am sure, but not before so many witnesses.

Another policeman admitted as much during an incident in Richmond. I had stopped to watch a motorcycle cop question a citizen. He was clearly edgy at my presence, but i stood off quietly at a reasonable distance with my shotgun in hand. After writing up the citizen, he rode his motorcycle over to me and asked if I wanted to press charges for police brutality. About a dozen people were standing around watching us. "Are you paranoid?" I replied. "Do you think you're important? Do you think I would waste my time, going down to the police station to make a report on you? No. You're just a coward anyway." With that, i got into my car. When he tried to hold my door open, I slammed it shut and told him to get his hands off. By now people were laughing at the cop, and rather than suffer further humiliation, he drove off, steaming mad. About halfway down the street, he turned around and came back; he wanted to do something, and he was about fifty shades of red. Pulling up beside me, he stuck his head close and said, "If it was night, you wouldn't do this." "You're right," I replied, "I sure wouldn't, but you're threatening me now, aren't you?" He got a little redder and kicked his machine into gear, and took off.

The police wanted me badly, but they needed to do their dirty work out of view of the community. When a citizen was unarmed, they brutalized him anytime, almost casually, but when he was prepared to defend himself, the police became little more than criminals, working at night.

On another occasion I stopped by the Black Panther office after paying some bills for my father. Since I was taking care of family business, I had not carried my shotgun with me—it was at home—but I did have a dagger, fully sheathed, in my belt. In the office were two comrades, Warren Tucker, a captain in the Party, and another member. As we talked, an eleven-year-old boy burst into the office and said, "The police are at my friend's house, and they're tearing up the place." This house was only about three blocks away, so the two Black Panthers and I hurried to the scene. Warren Tucker had a .45 pistol strapped to his hip in full view, but the other two of us had no weapons. We never kept weapons in the office, since we were there only periodically.

When we arrived, we found three policemen in the house, turning over couches and chairs, searching and pushing a little boy around and shouting, "Where's the shotgun?" The boy kept saying, "I don't have a shotgun," but the police went right on looking. I asked the policeman who seemed to be in charge if he had a search warrant, and he answered that he did not need one because he was in "hot pursuit."

Then he told me to leave the house. The little boy asked me to stay, so I continued to question the police, telling them they had no right to be there. The policeman finally turned on me. "You're going to get out of here," he said. "No," I said, "you leave if you don't have a search warrant."

In the middle of this argument the boy's father arrived and also asked the police for a search warrant. When the police admitted they did not have one, he ordered them out. As they started to leave, one of the policemen stopped in the doorway and said to the father, "Why are you telling us to get out? Why don't you get rid of these Panthers? They're the troublemakers." The father replied, "Before this I didn't like the Panthers. I had heard bad things about them, but in the last few minutes I've changed my mind, because they helped my son when you pushed him around."

The police became even more outraged at this. All their hostility now turned toward us. As the whole group went down the steps and out into the yard, more policemen arrived on the scene. The house was directly across the street from Oakland City College, and the dozen or so police cars had attracted a crowd that was milling about. The policeman who had been ordered out of the house took new courage at the sight of reinforcements. Walking over to me in the yard, he came close, saying, "You are always making trouble for us." Coming closer still, he growled at me in a low voice that could not be overheard, "You motherfucker." This was a regular police routine, a transparent strategy. He wanted me to curse him before witnesses; then he could arrest me. But I had learned to be cautious. After he called me a motherfucker, he stood waiting for the explosion, but it did not come in the way he expected. Instead, I called him a swine, a pig, a slimy snake—everything I could think of without using profanity.

By now he was almost apoplectic. "You're talking to me like that and you have a weapon. You're displaying a weapon in a rude and threatening fashion." Then he turned to Warren Tucker—Warren's gun was still in its holster—and said, "And so are you." As if on signal, the fifteen policemen who had been standing around uncertainly stormed the three of us and threw on handcuffs. They did not say they were placing us under arrest. If they had, we would gladly have taken the arrest under the circumstances without any resistance. From the way we went hurtling off in the paddy wagon, with its siren wailing and police cars ahead and behind, you might have thought they had bagged a Mafia capo. After we were booked they searched us and found a penknife in Warren Tucker's pocket, the kind Boy Scouts use. So, they dropped the charge of "displaying a weapon in a rude and threatening manner," and charged him simply with carrying a concealed weapon. Even that charge was eventually dropped.

This was the kind of harassment we went through over and over again, simply because we chose to exercise our constitutional rights to self-defense and stand up for the community. In spite of the fact that we followed the law to the letter, we were arrested and convicted of all sorts of minor trumped-up charges. They sought to frighten us and turn the community against us, but what they did had the opposite effect. For instance, after this encounter, we gained a number of new members from City College students who had watched the incident and had seen how things really were. They had been skeptical about us earlier because of the bad treatment we had received in the press, but seeing is believing.

The policeman who started this particular incident testified against me in 1968 in my trial for killing a policeman. When my attorney, Charles Garry, questioned him under cross-examination, he admitted his fear of the Black Panthers. He is six feet tall and weighs 250 pounds; I am five feet, ten and a half inches, and weigh 150 pounds, yet he said that I "surrounded" him. Straying further from the facts, he testified that he had not said anything to me, that, on the contrary, he was too frightened to open his mouth. The Black Panthers allegedly frightened him by shaking high-powered rifles in his face, calling him a pig, and threatening to kill him. He was fearful, he said, that I would kill him with the dagger, though it was sheathed. He stated that I had come right up to him, that I was "in his face," and, as he put it, "He was all around me." So much for police testimony.

In addition to our patrols and confrontations with the police, I did a lot of recruiting in pool halls and bars, sometimes working twelve to sixteen hours a day. I passed out leaflets with our ten-point program, explaining each point to all who would listen. Going deep into the community like this, I invariably became involved in whatever was happening; this day-to-day contact became an important part of our organizing effort. There is a bar-restaurant in North Oakland known as the Bosn's Locker; I used to call it my office because I would sometimes sit in there for twenty hours straight talking with the people who came in. Most of the time, I had my shotgun with me; if the owners of the establishment did not object. If they did, I left it in my car.

At other times I would go to City College or to the Oakland Skills Center—anywhere people gathered. It was hard work, but not in the sense of working at an ordinary job, with its deadly routine and sense of futility in performing empty labor. It was work that had profound significance for me; the very meaning of my life was in it, and it brought me closer to the people

This recruiting had an interesting ramification in that I tried to transform many of the so-called criminal activities going on in the street into something political, although this had to be done gradually. Instead of trying to eliminate these activities—numbers, hot goods, drugs—I attempted to channel them into significant community actions. Black consciousness had generally reached a point where a man •felt guilty about exploiting the Black community. However, if his daily activities for survival could be integrated with actions that undermined the established order, he felt good about it. It gave him a feeling of justification and strengthened his own sense of personal worth. Many of the brothers who were burglarizing and participating in similar pursuits began to contribute weapons and material to community defense. In order to survive they still had to sell their hot goods, but at the same time they would pass some of the cash on to us. That way, ripping off became more than just an individual thing.

Gradually the Black Panthers came to be accepted in the Bay Area community. We had provided a needed example of strength and dignity by showing people how to defend themselves. More important, we lived among them. They could see every day that with us the people came first.

GLORY DAYS

RANDY SHILTS

June 29, 1980
San Francisco

The sun melted the morning fog to reveal a vista so clear, so crystalline that you worried it might break if you stared too hard. The Transamerica Pyramid towered over the downtown skyline, and the bridges loped toward hills turning soft gold in the early summer heat. Rainbow flags fluttered in the gentle breezes.

Seven men were beginning their day. Bill Kraus, fresh from his latest political triumph in Washington, D.C., was impatient to get to the foot of Market Street to take his place at the head of the largest parade in San Francisco. There was much to celebrate.

In his apartment off Castro Street, in the heart of San Francisco's gay ghetto, Cleve Jones waited anxiously for his lover to get out of bed. This was parade day, Cleve kept repeating. No man, even the delightful muffin lolling lazily in the bed next to him, would make him late for this day of days. Cleve loved the sight of homosexuals, thousands strong. It was he who had led the gay mob that rioted at City Hall just a year ago, although he had now refashioned himself into the utterly respectable aide to one of California's most powerful politicians. He wasn't selling out, Cleve told friends impishly; he was just adding a new chapter to his legend. "Meet me at the parade," he called to his sleepy partner as he finally dashed for the door. "I can't be late."

A few blocks away, Dan William waited to meet David Ostrow. The two doctors were in town for a gathering of gay physicians at San Francisco State University. At home in New York City, gay parades drew only 30,000 or so; Dan William tried to imagine what a parade with hundreds of thousands of gays would look like. From what he had heard, David Ostrow was glad they didn't have parades like San Francisco's in Chicago; it would never play.

On California Street, airline steward Gaetan Dugas examined his face closely in the mirror. The scar, below his ear, was only slightly visible. His face would soon be unblemished again. He had come all the way from Toronto to enjoy this day, and for the moment he would put aside the troubling news the doctors had delivered just a few weeks before.

In the Mission District, the Gay Freedom Day Parade was the event twenty two-year-old Kico Govantes had anticipated the entire five weeks he'd been in San Francisco. The tentative steps Kico had taken in exploring his homosexuality at a small Wisconsin college could now turn to proud strides. Maybe among the thousands who had been streaming into the city all week, Kico would find the lover he sought.

***

Before

It was to be the word that would define the permanent demarcation in the lives of millions of Americans, particularly those citizens of the United States who were gay. There was life after the epidemic. And there were fond recollections of the times before.

Before and after. The epidemic would cleave lives in two, the way a great war or depression presents a commonly understood point of reference around which an entire society defines itself.

Before would encompass thousands of memories laden with nuance and nostalgia. Before meant innocence and excess, idealism and hubris. More than anything, this was the time before death. To be sure, Death was already elbowing its way through the crowds on that sunny morning, like a rude tourist angling for the lead spot in the parade. It was still an invisible presence, though, palpable only to twenty, or perhaps thirty, gay men who were suffering from a vague malaise. This handful ensured that the future and the past met on that single day.

People like Bill Kraus and Cleve Jones, Dan William and David Ostrow had lived through a recent past that had offered triumphs beyond their hopes; the future would present challenges beyond anything they could possibly fear. For them, and millions more, including many who considered themselves quite separate from such lives in San Francisco, this year would provide the last clear memories of the time before. Nothing would ever be the same again.

***

Bill Kraus looked up Market Street toward the Castro District, unable to find an end to the colorful crowd that had converged on downtown San Francisco for the Gay Freedom Day Parade. Bill ran his hands through his thick, curly brown hair and decided again that never was there a better place and time to be homosexual than here in this beautiful city on this splendid day when all gay people, no matter how diverse, became expressions of the same thought: We don't need to hide anymore.

Standing at the front of the parade, behind the banner announcing the gay and lesbian delegates to the 1980 Democratic National Convention, Bill Kraus retraced the steps that had brought him to this day and this parade. Primarily, he recalled the hiding and that nameless fear of being what he was, a homosexual. For years he had hidden the truth from others and, even worse, from himself. It was hard now to fathom the fear and self-hatred of those years without hope. The entire epoch seemed some kind of dream, a memory that had no real part in his waking life today.

At times, he wondered what he had been thinking all those years. Of what had he been so afraid? It wasn't just being Catholic. The edification of thirteen years of Cincinnati parochial schools dissipated within months of his arrival at Ohio State in 1968. There, he grew his hair long and answered the call of the Bob Dylan songs he played incessantly on his beat-up stereo. "The first one now will later be last," Dylan said. The times, they were a-changing. The message never rang true to him, not in the years of anti-Vietnam War marches or social activism, not until Bill had moved to Berkeley just a decade ago and discovered Castro Street and the promise of a new age.

There, with a middle-aged camera shop owner named Harvey Milk, Bill had learned the nuts and bolts of ward politics. He had learned how to walk precincts, study election maps, and forge coalitions. He had seen how everyone had power, how everyone could make a difference if only they believed and acted as if they could. This became the central tenet of his political catechism: "We can make a difference." Bill now repeated it in every speech, and on this Gay Freedom Day he felt it more strongly than ever. Everything in the last three years—Harvey Milk's election as supervisor and the first openly gay elected official in the nation, the political assassinations, and the consolidation of power after that—had conspired to convince Bill that it was true. Castro Street couldn't even get its gutters swept a few years back; today, gays were the most important single voting bloc in the city, comprising at least one in four registered voters. Bill Kraus had become president of the city's most powerful grass-roots organization, the Harvey Milk Gay Democratic Club.

The organizational power that he helped build had kept a gay seat on the board of supervisors after Harvey Milk's assassination in 1978 for a one-time Methodist minister and Milk crony named Harry Britt. Bill Kraus had replaced Britt as president of the Milk Club and now worked as his aide in City Hall. He had also managed Britt's reelection campaign in 1979, securing his reputation as the city's leading gay tactician.

The city's gay community was acquiring a legendary quality in political circles with influence far beyond the 70,000-odd votes it could boast in a city of 650,000. For the past three months, emissaries for presidential candidates had scoured the Castro neighborhood for votes. As other cities followed San Francisco's blueprint for political success, a national political force was coalescing. Bill Kraus and Harry Britt were leaving in two weeks for New York to be Ted Kennedy delegates to the Democratic National Convention. With seventy delegates, the convention's gay caucus was larger than the delegations of twenty states. This year, they would make a difference.

***

The gay parade had grown so mammoth in recent years that a good chunk of downtown San Francisco was needed just to get the scores of floats, contingents, and marching bands in proper order. While the parade assembled, Gwenn Craig smiled as she watched the young men mill near Bill Kraus, all thinking of some excuse to approach the famous young activist. Friends had teased Bill about his thirty-third birthday just days before; he was "l'age du Christ," somebody had joked. Bill was scarcely the scruffy malcontent with whom Gwenn had spent so many leisurely afternoons in Castro Street cafes. His once-shaggy hair was now neatly cut, and his thick glasses were replaced by contacts, eliminating an owlish stare and revealing startling blue eyes. His body was superbly toned. He carried himself with increasing confidence, much like the body politic whose ideals he was articulating.

Bill Kraus was even beginning to cut his own national reputation. Just two weeks earlier, he had delivered an impassioned plea for a gay rights plank to the Democratic Platform Committee, which was hammering together a party agenda to present at the Democratic National Convention in July. Bill had delivered the address as a gay rights manifesto, articulating the goals of the nascent political force. Gay papers across the country had written up the performance for the issues being distributed on the gay pride weekend.

The gay rights plank, Bill Kraus said, "does not ask you to give us special privileges. It does not ask anyone to like us. It does not even ask that the Democratic party give us many of the legal protections which are considered the right of all other Americans.

"Fellow members of the Platform Committee, what this amendment asks in a time when we hear much from prominent members of the Democratic party about human rights is that the Democratic party recognize that we, the gay people of this country, are also human."

***

The San Francisco Gay Freedom Day Marching Band blared the opening notes of "California Here I Come," and the parade started its two-mile trek down Market Street toward City Hall. More than 30,000 people, grouped in 240 contingents, marched in the parade past 200,000 spectators. The parade was the best show in town, revealing the amazing diversity of gay life. Clusters of gay Catholics and Episcopalians, Mormons and atheists, organized for years in the city, marched proudly beneath their banners. Career-designated contingents of gays included lawyers and labor officials, dentists and doctors, accountants and the ubiquitous gay phone-company employees. There were lesbian moms, gay dads, and homosexual teenagers with their heterosexual parents. Gay blacks, Latinos, Asian-Americans, and American Indians marched beneath banners proclaiming their dual pride. The campy Gays Against Brunch formed their own marching unit. A group of drag queens, dressed as nuns and calling themselves the Sisters of Perpetual Indulgence, had picked the day for their debut.

Gay tourists streamed to this homophile mecca from all over the world for the high holy day of homosexual life. Floats came from Phoenix and Denver; gay cowboys from the Reno Gay Rodeo pranced their horses down Market Street, waving the flags of Nevada and California, as well as the rainbow flag that had become the standard of California gays.

Although the parade route was only two miles, it would take four hours for the full parade to pass. Within an hour, the first contingents arrived at the broad Civic Center Plaza, where a stage had been erected in front of the ornate facade of City Hall.

Radical gay liberationists frowned at the carnival rides that had been introduced to the rally site. Parade organizers had decided that the event had grown "too political" in recent years, so the chest-pounding rhetoric that marked most rallies was given a backseat to the festive feeling of a state fair.

"We feel it definitely isn't a time for celebration," complained Alberta Maged to a newspaper reporter. She had marched with a coalition of radical groups including the Lavender Left, the Stonewall Brigade, and the aptly named Commie Queers. "You can't celebrate when you're still being oppressed. We have the illusion of freedom in San Francisco that makes it easy to exist, but the right-wing movement is growing quickly. It's right to be proud to be gay, but it isn't enough if you're still being attacked."

Many hard-line radicals, remembering the days when gay liberation was not nearly as fashionable, agreed. The event, after all, commemorated the riot in which Greenwich Village drag queens attacked police engaged in the routine harassment of a gay bar called the Stonewall Inn. From the Stonewall riot, on the last weekend of June 1969, the gay liberation movement was born, peopled by angry women and men who realized that their fights against war and injustice had a more personal side. This was the gay liberation movement—named after the then-voguish liberation groups sweeping the country—that had taken such delight in frightening staid America in the early 1970s.

By 1980, however, the movement had become a victim of its own success. Particularly in San Francisco, the taboos against homosexuality ebbed easily in the midst of the overall sexual revolution. The promise of freedom had fueled the greatest exodus of immigrants to San Francisco since the Gold Rush. Between 1969 and 1973, at least 9,000 gay men moved to San Francisco, followed by 20,000 between 1974 and 1978. By 1980, about 5,000 homosexual men were moving to the Golden Gate every year. The immigration now made for a city in which two in five adult males were openly gay. To be sure, these gay immigrants composed one of the most solidly liberal voting blocs in America, but this was largely because liberals were the candidates who promised to leave gays alone. It was enough to be left alone. Restructuring an entire society's concept of sex roles could come later; maybe it would happen by itself.

To the veterans of confrontational politics, the 1980 parade was a turning point because it demonstrated how respectable their dream had become. Success was spoiling gay liberation, it seemed. Governor

Edmund G. Brown, Jr., had issued a proclamation honoring Gay Freedom Week throughout the state, and state legislators and city officials crowded the speaker's dais at the gay rally. For their part, gays were eager to show that they were deserving of respectability. The local blood bank, for example, had long ago learned that it was good business to send their mobile collection vans to such events with large gay crowds. These were civic-minded people. In 1980, they gave between 5 and 7 percent of the donated blood in San Francisco, bank officials estimated.

***

The Ferris-wheel gondola rocked gently as it stopped with Cleve Jones at the apex, staring down on the 200,000 milling in front of the majestic City Hall rotunda. This was the gay community Cleve loved. Tens of thousands, together, showing their power. Marches and loud, angry speeches, an occasional upraised fist and drama, such drama. This was what being gay in San Francisco meant to Cleve Jones.

"This is my private party." He grinned. "Just me and a few thousand of my closest friends."

From the time he was a fourteen-year-old sophomore at Scottsdale High School, Cleve Jones knew that this is where he wanted to be, at gay rights marches in San Francisco. He had suffered through adolescent years in which he was the class sissy and the locker room punching bag. But, as soon as he could, he had hitchhiked to San Francisco and marched in the 1973 gay parade. For the rest of his life, he would know that he had arrived at the right place at the right time.

San Francisco in the 1970s represented one of those occasions when the forces of social change collide with a series of dramatic events to produce moments that are later called historic. From the day Cleve walked into Harvey Milk's camera shop to volunteer for campaign work, his life was woven into that history and drama. Political strategists like Bill Kraus recalled the 1970s in terms of votes cast and elections won; Cleve Jones, the romantic, framed the era as a grand story, the movement of a dream through time.

Cleve remembered 1978, when he had walked in the front of the parade dressed all in white, holding the upraised hand of a lesbian, who was also dressed in white, in front of a banner that showed a rainbow arch fashioned from barbed wire. Death-camp motifs had been de rigueur that year because a state senator from Orange County, John Briggs, was campaigning statewide for a ballot measure that would ban gays from teaching in California public schools. The initiative brought an international spotlight both to California, where the anti-gay campaigns started by Anita Bryant in 1977 were culminating, and to the 1978 Gay Freedom Day Parade, where gays made a defiant show of strength. They had come to the parade 375,000 strong, with Harvey Milk defying death threats to ride the long route in an open convertible before mounting the stage to give his "hope speech," prodding the crowd to create the best future by coming out and announcing their homosexuality.

Such public witnessing had always been a central article of faith of the gay liberation movement, Cleve Jones knew. This, after all, would be the only way their political cause could get anywhere because homosexuality was a fundamentally invisible trait. The fact that gays could hide their sexuality presented the gay movement with its greatest weakness and its most profound potential strength. Invisible, gays would always be kicked around, the reasoning went, because they would never assert their power. On that day in 1978, never had the power been so palpable. Months later, when California voters rejected the Briggs Initiative by a ratio of two to one, it appeared to be a wonderful year.

However, three weeks after the election, Supervisor Dan White, San Francisco's only anti-gay politician, had taken his Smith and Wesson revolver to City Hall and shot down Harvey Milk and the liberal mayor, George Moscone. Cleve had helped organize a candlelight march to City Hall that night for Harvey and George. Six months later, when a jury decided that Dan White should go to jail for only six years for killing the two men, Cleve had organized another march to City Hall—the one that turned into a riot, a vivid affirmation that this generation of gay people weren't a bunch of sissies to be kicked around without a fight. This White Night Riot left dozens of policemen injured and the front of City Hall ravaged; gay leaders across the country grimaced at the televised coverage of police cars set aflame by rampaging gay crowds.

By 1980, Cleve had helped fashion the story of Harvey and the 1970s, the Dan White trial, and the White Night Riot into one of the new legends of the fledgling gay movement, a story of assassinations and political intrigue, homophobic zealots and rioting in the streets. From it all, Cleve had emerged as the most prominent street activist in town, the most skillful media manipulator since Harvey Milk. Reporters loved the ever-so-militant pronouncements Cleve Jones was apt to make.

In recent months, Cleve had traded his blue jeans and sneakers for Armani suits to work for the Speaker of the California Assembly. It was a time when the outsiders who once marched angrily on the government were becoming insiders learning how to use the power they had gained. Cleve had spent most of the spring organizing Democratic Assembly campaigns. He split his time between Sacramento and San Francisco, where he was dating a wonderful Mexican-American lawyer named Felix Velarde-Munoz. Both knew the key players in local politics, and both loved to talk politics and liberation movements and make love and dance to the ubiquitous disco music.

That's what the summer of 1980 was to Cleve Jones. The gay community was a burst of creative energy that emanated from San Francisco and spread across America. Gays had staved off challenges that ran from bigots' ballot initiatives to political murder; now they could look forward to greater victories.

Yet like many gay activists, Cleve was troubled by the amusement park rides at Civic Center Plaza. He knew that the gay revolution was, at best, half-completed. Its tenuous gains could be wiped away by some other strongly organized force. He could understand that to a gay refugee from Des Moines, the city represented freedom beyond anything imaginable. He also knew, however, that freedom to go to a gay bar was not real freedom.

What was the right direction? Cleve asked himself. The gay movement had shifted from one of self-exploration, in which people moved through their own fears and self-alienation, to a movement of electoral politics, focused outward. Voter registration tables had replaced consciousness-raising groups as the symbol of liberation. Cleve sometimes wondered whether the new men crowding the Castro had already gone through this personal growth elsewhere or whether they had simply skipped it because being gay in San Francisco was so easy now that you didn't need to plummet to your psychic depths to make a commitment to the life-style.

Too many questions. It was nothing to dwell on today. When Cleve remembered the wonderful 1978 parade, and everything that had happened since, he felt like celebrating too. From his promontory on the Ferris wheel, he once more scanned the thousands stretched for miles around the City Hall rotunda where gay people had once marched and rioted, and where they now exerted so much power. The wheel jerked again, and slowly he began to return to the crowd, turning full circle.

***

A New Disease

It was never a formal topic of discussion, but on that weekend, when gay doctors from across the country gathered in San Francisco, it was discussed occasionally in hallways and over dinners. What would happen if some new disease insinuated itself into the bodies of just a few men in this community? The notion terrified Dr. David Ostrow; it was an idea he tried to put out of his mind as he wandered through the crowded rally site between the whirling amusement park rides with two other doctors from the convention, Manhattan's Dan William and Robert Bolan of San Francisco.

Ostrow grimaced as a Sister of Perpetual Indulgence sashayed by. The sight rankled his midwestern sensibilities. This was all too weird, he thought. The media would play up the open display of sexuality and once again drag queens and half-naked muscle boys would be presented as the emblems of homosexual culture. People like Ostrow, who leaned toward long, steady relationships, would never get the press. The bizarre, it seemed, would always overshadow the positive things going on in the gay community, like the doctors' conference. Doctors weren't flamboyant enough to get in the headlines. They were barely mentioned in the gay newspapers, counting themselves lucky to make it a page ahead of the latest gossip about the hottest leather bar.

While strategists like Bill Kraus read the gay community's future in voter registration rolls, and street activists like Cleve Jones heard it in ringing oratory, the gay doctors had spent that weekend reading the community's prognosis from its medical chart. Like many physicians, Ostrow had been quite troubled when he left the medical conference, which had adjourned in time for the parade.

The fight against venereal diseases was proving a Sisyphean task. Ostrow was director of the Howard Brown Memorial Clinic, which provided a sensitive alternative for gay men who wanted to avoid the sneers of staffers at the Chicago Public Health clinics. The screening in Ostrow's clinic had revealed that one in ten patients had walked in the door with hepatitis B. At least one-half of the gay men tested at the clinic showed evidence of a past episode of hepatitis B. In San Francisco, two-thirds of gay men had suffered the debilitating disease. It was now proven statistically that a gay man had one chance in five of being infected with the hepatitis B virus within twelve months of stepping off the bus into a typical urban gay scene. Within five years, infection was a virtual certainty.

Another problem was enteric diseases, like amebiasis and giardiasis, caused by organisms that lodged themselves in the intestinal tracts of gay men with alarming frequency. At the New York Gay Men's Health Project, where Dan William was medical director, 30 percent of the patients suffered from gastrointestinal parasites. In San Francisco, incidence of the "Gay Bowel Syndrome," as it was called in medical journals, had increased by 8,000 percent after 1973. Infection with these parasites was a likely effect of anal intercourse, which was apt to put a man in contact with his partner's fecal matter, and was virtually a certainty through the then-popular practice of rimming, which medical journals politely called oral-anal intercourse.

What was so troubling was that nobody in the gay community seemed to care about these waves of infection. Ever since he had worked at the New York City Department of Public Health, Dan William had delivered his lecture about the dangers of undiagnosed venereal diseases and, in particular, such practices as rimming. But he had his "regulars" who came in with infection after infection, waiting for the magic bullet that could put them back in the sack again. William began to feel like a parent as he admonished the boys: "I have to tell you that you're being very unhealthy."

Promiscuity, however, was central to the raucous gay movement of the 1970s, and his advice was, as the Texans so charmingly put it, like pissing in the wind. At best, he tried to counsel the Elizabeth Taylor approach to sexuality and suggest serial monogamy, a series of affairs that may not last forever but that at least left you with a vague awareness of which bed you slept in most evenings.

The crowd cheered the parade again when the Bulldog Baths float came rolling into Civic Center. The young musclemen, in black leather harnesses, the best and the most beautiful, jumped from the cages in which they had discoed down Market Street. That night they would be at the huge Cellblock Party at the bathhouse, one of a panoply of celebrations sponsored that day by San Francisco's thriving sex industry.

This commercialization of gay sex was all part of the scene, an aspect of the homosexual life-style in which the epidemics of venereal disease, hepatitis, and enteric disorders thrived. The gay liberation movement of the 1970s had spawned a business of bathhouses and sex clubs. The hundreds of such institutions were a $100-million industry across America and Canada, and bathhouse owners were frequently gay political leaders as well, helping support the usually financially starved gay groups. The businesses serviced men who had long been repressed, gay activists told themselves, and were perhaps now going to the extreme in exploring their new freedom. It would all balance out later, so for now, sex was part and parcel of political liberation. The popular bestseller *The Joy of Gay Sex,* for example, called rimming the "prime taste treat in sex," while a leftist Toronto newspaper published a story on "rimming as a revolutionary act."

It was interesting politics, David Ostrow thought. From a purely medical standpoint, however, the bathhouses were a horrible breeding ground for disease. People who went to bathhouses simply were more likely to be infected with a disease—and infect others—than a typical homosexual on the street. A Seattle study of gay men suffering from shigellosis, for example, discovered that 69 percent culled their sexual partners from bathhouses. A Denver study found that an average bathhouse patron having his typical 2.7

sexual contacts a night risked a 33 percent chance of walking out of the tubs with syphilis or gonorrhea, because about one in eight of those wandering the hallways had asymptomatic cases of these diseases.

Doctors like David Ostrow and Dan William did not consider themselves prudish, even if they were cut from a more staid mold than the people whose pictures were in the newspaper coverage of the Gay Freedom Day Parade. But they were uneasy about the health implication of the commercialization of sex. In a 1980 interview with a New York City gay magazine, *Christopher Street,* William noted, "One effect of gay liberation is that sex has been institutionalized and franchised. Twenty years ago, there may have been a thousand men on any one night having sex in New York baths or parks. Now there are ten or twenty thousand—at the baths, the back-room bars, bookstores, porno theaters, the Rambles, and a wide range of other places as well. The plethora of opportunities poses a public health problem that's growing with every new bath in town."

Such comments were politically incorrect in the extreme, and William suffered criticism as a "monogamist." Self-criticism was not the strong point of a community that was only beginning to define itself affirmatively after centuries of repression.

Altogether, this generation of gay men was blessed by good health. Being a gay doctor was fun, William often told himself. Physical fitness was a community ritual with tens of thousands of gay men crowding Nautilus centers and weight rooms. He rarely had to go to a hospital because none of his patients ever got very sick.

David Ostrow too was haunted by forebodings as he left the parade. Between the bathhouses and the high levels of sexual activity, there would be no stopping a new disease that got into this population. The likelihood was remote, of course. Modern science had congratulated itself on the eradication of infectious disease as a threat to humankind. But the specter sometimes haunted Ostrow because he wondered where all the sexually transmitted disease would end. It couldn't continue indefinitely. He had already noticed that some Chicago gay men were having immune problems. Dan William was seeing strange inflammation of the lymph nodes among his most promiscuous patients. The swelling was curious because it did not seem to be in response to any particular infection but was generalized, all over; maybe it was the effect of overloading the immune system with a variety of venereal diseases.

Years later, Dan William would recall that it was during the days of early 1980 that he saw a man in his mid-forties recovering from a bad bout with hepatitis B. He had strange purplish lesions on his arms and chest. William referred him to Memorial Sloan-Kettering Cancer Center. The man, it turned out, was suffering from a rare skin cancer, Kaposi's sarcoma. William had to look up Kaposi's sarcoma in a medical textbook because he had never heard of the ailment. Fortunately, the book said, the man had a good prognosis. Elderly Jewish or Italian men got Kaposi's sarcoma; twenty years later they usually died of old age. The cancer itself, however, appeared benign.

***

Mervyn Silverman watched the bare-breasted women in leather straps, with rings through their nipples, walk by him, and he definitely had the feeling that he was not in Kansas anymore. In his twenty years in public health, he had traveled around the world and had lived in Bangkok and South America. As he watched the passing parade of humanity at the Gay Freedom Day Parade, he knew he had never lived in a more exciting place than San Francisco, and he sensed that he would not want to live anywhere else.

With his full head of prematurely gray hair, Silverman was easily recognizable to many of the bystanders, who shook his hand and introduced their lovers. Few City Hall officials were more popular than Silverman, the director of the Department of Public Health, and few had gone out of their way to show greater sensitivity to the gay community. Within weeks of his appointment as health director by Mayor George Moscone in 1977, Mervyn Silverman had understood that being public health director in San Francisco was like nowhere else. Every community and interest group had their own advisory board to the health department—there were thirty-four of them in all—and it seemed that no decision went over his desk that was not rife with political overtones. Already, a decision over the closing of a neighborhood health center had prompted a picketing of Silverman's spacious Victorian home on Frederick Street in the Upper Ashbury neighborhood.

Something about the political tension, however, excited Silverman. He enjoyed the challenge, maintained cordial relations with the press, and carved a singularly good reputation in every corner of the city. Silverman was a popular official, and that was the way he liked it. He had avoided hard feelings by making all decisions on the basis of consensus. He had listened to all sides and forged the middle path. All public health policy was basically political, he felt; as someone who relished public approbation, he was a good politician. It was his strength as a public official.

***

"I am the prettiest one."

It had been the standing joke. Gaetan Dugas would walk into a gay bar, scan the crowd, and announce to his friends, "I am the prettiest one." Usually, his friends had to agree, he was right.

Gaetan was the man everyone wanted, the ideal for this community, at this time and in this place. His sandy hair fell boyishly over his forehead. His mouth easily curled into an inviting smile, and his laugh could flood color into a room of black and white. He bought his clothes in the trendiest shops of Paris and London. He vacationed in Mexico and on the Caribbean beaches. Americans tumbled for his soft Quebeçois accent and his sensual magnetism. There was no place that the twenty-eight-year-old airline steward would rather have the boys fall for him than in San Francisco.

Fog streamed over the hills into the Castro, toward the 1980 Civic Center rally. The first cool breezes of evening were thinning the throng downtown, but throughout the city thousands of gay men crowded into giant disco parties that had become a staple of the weekend-long celebration. There was the Heatwave disco party for $25 a head in the Japantown Center, the Muscle Beach party and the trendy Dreamland disco, and Alive, a funkier dance fest a few blocks away.

The hottest and hunkiest, Gaetan knew, would be among the 4,000 streaming to the chic Galleria design center, where the party was just starting when the steward and his friend arrived. Every corner of the lobby and the five-story atrium was crammed with men pulsing to the synthesized rhythms of disco music. Any redundance in the musical patterns was quickly obviated by the cocaine and Quaaludes that were a staple of such parties.

Gaetan easily made his way through the profusion of sweaty bodies with his closest friend, another airline steward from Toronto. They had met in 1977, when they were based in Halifax, Nova Scotia. Together, they had ventured to San Francisco for the 1978 gay parade, and every year they returned for the carnival. They decided that San Francisco would always be their ultimate refuge. The last weekend of every June was now set aside for nonstop partying at bars and baths.

Here, Gaetan could satisfy his voracious sexual appetite with the beautiful California men he liked so much. He returned from every stroll down Castro Street with a pocketful of matchbook covers and napkins that were crowded with addresses and phone numbers. He recorded names of his most passionate admirers in his fabric-covered address book. But lovers were like suntans to him: They would be so wonderful, so sexy for a few days, and then fade. At times, Gaetan would study his address book with genuine curiosity, trying to recall who this or that person was.

As Gaetan neared the crowded dance floor at the Galleria, various men shouted greetings, and he hugged them ebulliently like long-lost brothers. "Who was that?" his friend would ask. "I don't know," Gaetan laughed offhandedly. "Somebody."

Here, swaying and stomping to the music, Gaetan was completely in his element. San Francisco was the hometown he never had. It helped him forget the other, distant life, long ago, when he was the major sissy of his working class neighborhood in Quebec City. Being gay then meant constantly fighting taunts hurled by the other kids and being gripped by guilt, by his own conscience. But that was then and this was San Francisco. On June 29, 1980, Gaetan was the ugly duckling who had become the swan.

At the first opportunity on the dance floor, Gaetan stripped off his T-shirt and fished out a bottle of poppers, nitrite inhalants, from his jeans pocket in one swift, practiced move. Fine blond hair outlined the trim natural proportions of his chest.

He felt strong and vital.

He didn't feel like he had cancer at all.

That was what the doctor had said after cutting that bump from his face. Gaetan had wanted the small purplish spot removed to satisfy his vanity; the doctor had wanted it for a biopsy. Weeks later, the report came back from New York City, and the Toronto specialist told Gaetan that he had Kaposi's sarcoma, a bizarre skin cancer that hardly anybody got. Maybe that explained why his lymph nodes had been swollen for a year. Gaetan hadn't told friends until June, after the biopsy. He was terrified at first, but he consoled himself with the knowledge that you can beat cancer. He had created a life in which he could have everything and everyone he wanted. He'd figure a way around this cancer too.

As he felt the poppers surge through him, Gaetan realized that his high might last longer than this crowd. There were always the baths. He reviewed his choices, as he had so many times before during his regular visits to the city. The Club Baths was guaranteed to be crowded with those Anglo-Saxon men who were so well built, vaguely wholesome, and, well, so American. The fantasy rooms at the Hothouse were intriguing, as was the Bulldog Baths's promise of a Cellblock Party.

The summer was just beginning. The beaches of Fire Island and the pool parties of Los Angeles all lay ahead. Later, when the researchers started referring to Gaetan Dugas simply as Patient Zero, they would retrace the airline steward's travels during that summer, fingering through his fabric-covered address book to try to fathom the bizarre coincidences and the unique role the handsome young steward performed in the coming epidemic.

On that day in 1980, Gaetan danced to forget under the pulsing colored lights. Feeling whole again, he told himself that one day he would like to move to San Francisco.

***

"It looks like that guy has his arm up the other guy's ass."

Kico Govantes thought maybe the man standing between the legs of the guy in the sling was an amputee. Maybe he was just rubbing his stump next to the guy's butt.

"He does have an arm up his ass," Kico's friend said.

Kico was sickened. He had heard a lot about bathhouses since moving to San Francisco five weeks before. The local gay papers were filled with ads and catchy slogans for the businesses. The Handball Express motto was "find your limits;" the Glory Holes pledged to be "the most unusual sex place in the world;" the Jaguar sex club in the Castro hyped "your fantasy, your pleasure;" while the coeducational Sutro Baths had a "Bisexual Boogie" every weekend. The Cornholes's advertising was more pointed, featuring the unclad torso of a man lying on his stomach.

The handsome psychologist Kico had met at the gay parade had promised to take him to the largest gay bathhouse in the world, the Bulldog Baths. Decorated in San Quentin motif, the place was something of a legend in sexual circles. The leather magazine *Drummer* had gushed that the central "two-story prison is so incredibly real (real cells, real bars, real toilets....) that when you see a guard standing on the second tier looking down on you, you're ready to kneel down."

This is insane, thought Kico.

Kico had moved from Wisconsin to San Francisco with a clear sense of what being gay meant. He figured gay people dated and courted; you certainly never went to bed with someone you just met. Kico wouldn't mind if he had to date someone months before they consummated their relationship and settled into some hip approximation of marriage. As the scion of an aristocratic Cuban family that fled Havana when Kico was three, the young man had led a relatively sheltered life. Suddenly, he was very confused.

The Cellblock Party, just a few blocks from a rally where speakers were so loftily discussing the finer points of gay love, was like some scene from a Fellini film, intriguing and inviting to the eye, but altogether repulsive to Kico. The scene was even more alienating because these guys were so attractive, and they obviously found Kico attractive. He could sense that, physically, he fit in with these people. With his trim body and handsome swarthy features, he was what they wanted. Every floor was packed with the firm bodies of men clad in towels. Attendants cheerfully passed out free beer while disco music blared. The air felt thick and steamy, heavy with the acrid smell of nitrite inhalants.

Kico turned to his companion. Certainly, a psychologist would see that this was unhealthy, a corruption of the very gay love that this day was supposed to celebrate. The shrink eyed him curiously, as if he were a naive child. He seemed to enjoy guiding the twenty-two-year-old through the labyrinthine hallways.

"That's fist-fucking," the psychologist said.

"Oh," Kico said.

Knowing the words for the acts didn't help him fathom the meaning of what he was seeing. Where was the affection? he wondered. Where was the interaction of mind and body that creates a meaningful sexual experience? It was as if these people, who had been made so separate from society by virtue of their sexuality, were now making their sexuality utterly separate from themselves. Their bodies were tools through which they could experience physical sensation. The complete focus on the physical aspect of sex meant constantly devising new, more extreme sexual acts because the experience relied on heightened sensory rather than emotional stimulation.

Kico thought it ironic that a community so entirely based on love should create institutions so entirely devoid of intimacy. He left the bathhouse feeling horrified and disillusioned. He walked through the empty Civic Center Plaza where street sweepers were clearing the debris from the rally and muscular carny men were dismantling the amusement park rides. The fog had swept across the city on this day of interregnum. Kico was cold.

LEARNING TO TALK OF RACE

CORNEL WEST

What happened in Los Angeles this past April was neither a race riot nor a class rebellion. Rather, this monumental upheaval was a multiracial, trans-class, and largely male display of justified social rage. For all its ugly, xenophobic resentment, its air of adolescent carnival, and its downright barbaric behavior, it signified the sense of powerlessness in American society. Glib attempts to reduce its meaning to the pathologies of the black underclass, the criminal actions of hoodlums, or the political revolt of the oppressed urban masses miss the mark. Of those arrested, only 36 percent were black, more than a third had full-time jobs and most claimed to shun political affiliation. What we witnessed in Los Angeles was the consequence of a lethal linkage of economic decline, cultural decay, and political lethargy in American life. Race was the visible catalyst, not the underlying cause.

The meaning of the earthshaking events in Los Angeles is difficult to grasp because most of us remain trapped in the narrow framework of the dominant liberal and conservative views of race in America, which with its worn-out vocabulary leaves us intellectually debilitated, morally disempowered, and personally depressed. The astonishing disappearance of the event from public dialogue is testimony to just how painful and distressing a serious engagement with race is.

Our truncated public discussions of race suppress the best of who and what we are as a people because they fail to confront the complexity of the issue in a candid and critical manner. The predictable pitting of liberals against conservatives, Great Society Democrats against self-help Republicans, reinforces intellectual parochialism and political paralysis.

The liberal notion that more government programs can solve the problems is simplistic—precisely because it focuses *solely* on the economic dimension. And the conservative idea that what is needed is a change in the moral behavior of poor black urban dwellers (especially poor black men, who, they say, should stay married, support their children, and stop committing so many crimes) highlights immoral actions while ignoring public responsibility for the immoral circumstances that haunt our fellow citizens.

The common denominator of these views of race is that each still sees black people as a "problem people," in the words of Dorothy I. Height, president of the National Council of Negro Women, rather than as fellow American citizens with problems. Her words echo the poignant "unasked question" of W. E. B. DuBois, who wrote:

> They approach me in a half-hesitant sort of way, eye me curiously or compassionately, and then instead of saying directly, How does it feel to be a problem? they say, I know an excellent colored man in my town. ... Do not these Southern outrages make your blood boil? At these I smile, or am interested, or reduce the boiling to a simmer, as the occasion may require. To the real question, How does it feel to be a problem? I answer seldom a word.

Nearly a century later, we confine discussions about race in America to the "problems" black people pose for whites rather than considering what this way of viewing black people reveals about us as a nation.

This paralyzing framework encourages liberals to relieve their guilty consciences by supporting public funds directed at "the problems;" but at the same time, reluctant to exercise principled criticism of black people, they deny them the freedom to err. Similarly, conservatives blame the "problems" on black people themselves—and thereby render black social misery invisible or unworthy of public attention.

Hence, for liberals, black people are to be "included" and "integrated" into "our" society and culture, while for the conservatives they are to be "well behaved" and "worthy of acceptance" by "our" way of life. Both fail to see that the presence and predicaments of black people are neither additions to nor defections from American life, but rather *constitutive elements of that life.*

To engage in a serious discussion of race in America, we must begin not with the problems of black people but with the flaws of American society—flaws rooted in historic inequalities and longstanding cultural stereotypes. How we set up the terms for discussing racial issues shapes our perception and response to these issues. As long as black people are viewed as a "them," the burden falls on blacks to do all the "cultural" and "moral" work necessary for healthy race relations. The implication is that only certain Americans can define what it means to be American—and the rest must simply "fit in."

The emergence of strong black-nationalist sentiments among blacks, especially young people, is a revolt against this sense of having to "fit in." The variety of black-nationalist ideologies, from the moderate views of Supreme Court Justice Clarence Thomas in his youth to those of Louis Farrakhan today, rest upon a fundamental truth: white America has been historically weak-willed in ensuring racial justice and has continued to resist accepting fully the humanity of blacks. As long as double standards and differential treatment abound—as long as the rap performer Ice-T is harshly condemned while former Los Angeles Police Chief Daryl F. Gates's antiblack comments are received in polite silence, as long as Dr. Leonard Jeffries's anti-Semitic statements are met with vitriolic outrage while presidential candidate Patrick J. Buchanan's are received with a genteel response—black nationalisms will thrive.

Afrocentrism, a contemporary species of black nationalism, is a gallant yet misguided attempt to define an African identity in a white society perceived to be hostile. It is gallant because it puts black doings and sufferings, not white anxieties and fears, at the center of discussion. It is misguided because—out of fear of cultural hybridization, silence on the issue of class, retrograde views on black women, homosexuals, and lesbians, and a reluctance to link race to the common good—it reinforces the narrow discussions about race.

To establish a new framework, we need to begin with a frank acknowledgment of the basic humanness and Americanness of each of us. And we must acknowledge that as a people—*E Pluribus Unum*—we are on a slippery slope toward economic strife, social turmoil, and cultural chaos. If we go down, we go down together. The Los Angeles upheaval forced us to see not only that we are not connected in ways we would like to be but also, in a more profound sense, that this failure to connect binds us even more tightly together. The paradox of race in America is that our common destiny is more pronounced and imperiled precisely when our divisions are deeper. The Civil War and its legacy speak loudly here. Eighty-six percent of white suburban Americans live in neighborhoods that are less than one percent black, meaning that the prospects for the country depend largely on how its cities fare in the hands of a suburban electorate. There is no escape from our interracial interdependence, yet enforced racial hierarchy dooms us as a nation to collective paranoia and hysteria—the unmaking of any democratic order.

The verdict that sparked the incidents in Los Angeles was perceived to be wrong by the vast majority of Americans. But whites have often failed to acknowledge the widespread mistreatment of black people, especially black men, by law-enforcement agencies, which helped ignite the spark. The Rodney King verdict was merely the occasion for deep-seated rage to come to the surface. This rage is fed by the "silent" depression ravaging the country—in which real weekly wages of all American workers since 1973 have declined nearly twenty percent, while at the same time wealth has been upwardly distributed.

The exodus of stable industrial jobs from urban centers to cheaper labor markets here and abroad, housing policies that have crated "chocolate cities and vanilla suburbs" (to use the popular musical artist George Clinton's memorable phrase), white fear of black crime, and the urban influx of poor Spanish-speaking and Asian immigrants—all have helped erode the tax base of American cities just as the federal government has cut its supports and programs. The result is unemployment, hunger, homelessness, and sickness for millions.

Driving that rage is a culture of hedonistic self-indulgence and narcissistic self-regard. This culture of consumption yields coldhearted and meanspirited attitudes and actions that turn poor urban neighborhoods into military combat zones and existential wastelands.

And the pervasive spiritual impoverishment grows. The collapse of meaning in life—the eclipse of hope and absence of love of self and others, the breakdown of family and neighborhood bonds—leads to the social deracination and cultural denudement of urban dwellers, especially children. We have created rootless, dangling people with little link to the supportive networks—family, friends, school—that sustain some sense of purpose in life. We have witnessed the collapse of the spiritual communities that help us face despair, disease, and death and that transmit through the generations dignity and decency, excellence, and elegance.

The result is lives of what we might call "random nows," of fortuitous and fleeting moments preoccupied with "getting over"—with acquiring pleasure, property, and power by any means necessary. (This is not what Malcolm X meant by this famous phrase.) Postmodern culture is more and more a market culture dominated by gangster mentalities and self-destructive wantonness. This culture engulfs all of us—yet its impact on the disadvantaged is devastating, resulting in extreme violence in everyday life. Sexual violence against women and homicidal assaults by young black men on one another are only the most obvious signs of this empty quest for pleasure, property, and power.

Lastly, this rage is fueled by a political atmosphere in which images, not ideas, dominate, where politicians spend more time raising money than issues. The functions of parties have been displaced by public polls, and politicians behave less as thermostats that determine the climate of opinion than as thermometers registering the public mood. American politics has been rocked by an unleashing of greed among opportunistic public officials—following the lead of their counterparts in the private sphere, where, as of 1989, one percent of the population owned thirty-seven percent of the wealth—leading to a profound cynicism and pessimism among the citizenry.

And given the way in which the Republican party since 1968 has appealed to popular xenophobic images—playing the black, female, and homophobic cards and realigning the electorate along race, sex, and sexual-orientation lines—it is no surprise that the notion that we are all part of one garment of destiny is discredited. Appeals to special interests rather than public interests reinforce this polarization. The Los Angeles upheaval was an expression of utter fragmentation by a powerless citizenry that includes not just the poor but all of us.

What is to be done? How do we capture a new spirit and vision to meet the challenges of the postindustrial city, post modern culture, and postparty politics?

First, we must admit that the most valuable sources for help, hope, and power consist of ourselves and our common history. As in the ages of Lincoln, Roosevelt, and King, we must look to new frameworks and languages to understand our multilayered crisis and overcome our deep malaise.

Second, we must focus our attention on the public square—the common good that undergirds our national and global destinies. The vitality of any public square ultimately depends on how much we *care* about the quality of our lives together. The neglect of our public infrastructure, for example—our water and sewage systems, bridges, tunnels, highways, subways, and streets—reflects not only our myopic economic policies, which impede productivity, but also the low priority we place on our common life.

The tragic plight of our children clearly reveals our deep disregard for public well-being. With about one out of five children living in poverty in this country and one out of two black children and two out of five Hispanic children doing so—and with most of our children ill-equipped to live lives of spiritual and cultural quality, neglected by overburdened parents, and bombarded by the market values of profit-hungry corporations—how do we expect ever to constitute a vibrant society?

One essential step is some form of large-scale public intervention to ensure access to basic social goods—housing, food, health care, education, child care, and jobs. We must invigorate the common good with a mixture of government, business, and labor that does not follow any existing blueprint. After a period in which the private sphere has been sacralized and the public square gutted, the temptation is to make a fetish of the public square. We need to resist such dogmatic swings.

Last, the major challenge is the need to generate new leadership. The paucity of courageous leaders—so apparent in the response to the events in Los Angeles—requires that we look beyond the same elites and voices that recycle the older frameworks. We need leaders—neither saints nor sparkling television personalities—who can situate themselves within a larger historical narrative of this country and world, who can grasp the complex dynamics of our peoplehood and imagine a future grounded in the best of our past, yet attuned to the frightening obstacles that now perplex us. Our ideals of freedom, democracy, and equality must be invoked to invigorate all of us, especially the landless, propertyless, and luckless. Only a visionary leadership that can motivate "the better angels of our nature," as Lincoln said, and activate possibilities for a freer, more efficient, and stable America—only that leadership deserves cultivation and support.

This new leadership must be grounded in grass-roots organizing that highlights democratic accountability. Regardless of whether Bill Clinton's cautious neoliberal programs or George Bush's callous conservative policies prevail in November, the challenge to America will be determining whether a genuine multiracial democracy can be created and sustained in an era of global economies and a moment of xenophobic frenzy.

Let us hope and pray that the vast intelligence, imagination, humor, and courage in this country will not fail us. Either we learn a new language of empathy and compassion, or the fire this time will consume us all.

CPSIA information can be obtained
at www.ICGtesting.com
Printed in the USA
FSHW021737081220
76723FS